# BLOOD IN THE BANK

# Advances in Criminology

*Series Editor: David Nelken*

**Titles in the Series**

# Blood in the Bank

Social and legal aspects of death at work

GARY SLAPPER
*The Open University*

*with an Introduction by*
NOAM CHOMSKY

## Ashgate

DARTMOUTH

Aldershot • Brookfield USA • Singapore • Sydney

Published by
Dartmouth Publishing Company Limited
Ashgate Publishing Limited
Gower House
Croft Road
Aldershot
Hants GU11 3HR
England

Ashgate Publishing Company
Old Post Road
Brookfield
Vermont 05036
USA

Ashgate website: http://www.ashgate.com

**British Library Cataloguing in Publication Data**
Slapper, Gary
  Blood in the bank : social and legal aspects of death at
  work. - (Advances in criminology)
  1.Employees - Death - Law and legislation - Great Britain
  2.Industrial safety - Law and legislation - Great Britain
  3. Employers' liability - Moral and ethical aspects - Great
  Britain  4.Criminal liability of juristic persons - Great Britain
  I.Title
  344.4'1'0465

**Library of Congress Cataloging-in-Publication Data**
Slapper, Gary.
    Blood in the bank : social and legal aspects of death at work /
Gary Slapper with an introduction by Noam Chomsky.
        p.   cm.
    Includes bibliographical references.
    ISBN 1-84014-079-8
    1. Murder–Great Britain. 2. Violence in the workplace–Great Britain.
    I. Title.
    KD7964.S59    2000
    658.4'08 21–dc21                                           99-46216


ISBN 1 84014 079 8

Printed and bound in Great Britain by MPG Books Ltd, Bodmin, Cornwall

# Acknowledgements

This book is primarily dedicated to the lives of those people whose cases I discuss in the text.

I owe a deep debt to Suzanne, Hannah, Emily, and Charlotte for their forbearance and patience while I was researching and writing this book. Among the great many for whose assistance I am also very indebted are Professor Robert Reiner at the Law Department of The London School of Economics, for his supervision of my research; Elaine Genders at the Faculty of Laws, University College, London for her supervision on an earlier and similar project; Marilyn Lannigan for her excellent research assistance in helping me update and refine this text; Hugh McLaughlan, Doreen and Ivor Slapper, Raie Schwartz, Julie and David Whight, Professor Steve Tombs, Professor David Nelken, and Frances Gibb. I would like to thank the OUBS Research Committee for supporting this project. I am also very grateful to John Irwin at Ashgate for his support and encouragement, Pat FitzGerald for her fastidious copy-editing, and Professor Noam Chomsky of the Massachusetts Institute of Technology for his inspiring introduction.

# Contents

# List of Cases

# Introduction

NOAM CHOMSKY

In January 1999, the US Supreme Court rejected the appeal of a defendant who had been sentenced to 25 years to life for stealing a bottle of vitamins from a supermarket. It was 'a petty theft motivated by homelessness and hunger', the California Court of Appeals concluded, rejecting the defendant's earlier appeal while ruling that the 'defendant has proven that he cannot conform to society's rules'. Accordingly, the sentence must stand.

The Court rulings broke no new ground. For example, in 1980 the Supreme Court upheld the life sentence of a Texas man convicted for minor fraud amounting to $228 (credit cards, cheques, falsely obtaining money). These are the kinds of decisions that led a distinguished jurist, former Chief Judge Bazelon, to observe that Congress 'envisions the criminal process as a vast engine of social control'.

Judge Bazelon's conclusion gains support from the extraordinary growth of incarceration in the United States of America during and since the Reagan years, increasingly for victimless crimes (drug possession), and a natural component of social policy that greatly enriches a tiny fraction of the population while leaving the majority with stagnating or declining incomes and increasing working hours, and that consigns others to the category of 'disposable people', in the terminology of US dependencies. It is worth bearing in mind that the consequences of policy were predictable from the most casual look at social statistics. By declaring the 'drug war' at a time when use of 'substances' (drugs, tobacco, red meat, etc.) was declining among educated and privileged sectors, 'we are choosing to have an intense crime problem concentrated among minorities', Senator Daniel Patrick Moynihan observed. Exactly what ensued – as intended, at least if we adopt the legal principle that predictable consequences are evidence of intent. 'The war's planners knew exactly what they were doing', criminologist Michael Tonry comments, spelling out the details.

In 1996, after seven years of delay, three coal executives drew sentences of five to 18 months in prison, and fines of $375 to $3,000, for causing the death of ten workers in a mine explosion, having lied to federal inspectors about hazardous conditions. The conviction was unusual. The *Wall Street*

*Journal* reported that 'Most criminal complaints filed on behalf of the federal Mine Safety and Health Administration result in no prison time', and sentences are so light that it is hardly cost-effective to observe safety regulations. Only some forms of 'social control' fall within 'the criminal justice system', in practice, and 'conformity to social rules' is a carefully structured concept.

The same is true of other regulations. The *Journal* reported a study of an employer-supported think tank concluding that workers would receive an additional $19 billion a year if rules for overtime were obeyed. A review of Reaganite labour policies in *Business Week* reported that Administration signals to corporations led to tripling of illegal firings for organizing efforts, while 'even more significant than the numbers is the perception of risk among workers, who think they'll be fired in an organizing campaign', according to a Harvard law professor quoted by the journal. The policies continue under Reagan's successors. One device is illegal threat of plant closing, used very effectively to undermine union organizing efforts after the passage of NAFTA, as revealed by academic studies carried out under NAFTA regulations. By 1994, four-fifths of workers felt that attempts to organize might cost them their jobs. There are laws, but they are rendered ineffective by the combination of private power and government complicity. It is understandable that Federal Reserve chair Alan Greenspan should have informed Congress in 1997 that 'greater worker insecurity' is a leading factor in the 'fairy tale economy' over which he had been presiding, keeping wages and benefits low and thus improving 'the health of the economy', in the technical sense of the phrase.

The same *Business Week* study reports Administration failure to enforce safety regulations. 'The Occupational Safety & Health Administration under Reagan and Bush was a hands-off agency', encouraging lawlessness, and an increase in days lost to injury 'from 58 per 100 workers in 1983 to 86 in 1991'. Another factor facilitating corporate crime is state-supported demolition of unions, removing the barrier they pose to violation of legally-mandated responsibilities to maintain health and safety standards.

Commonly, corporate criminals have more than sufficiently 'proven that they cannot conform to society's rules' – but then, they need not, given the way the rules are enforced. 'Giant corporations like Unocal are repeat offenders of our environmental, labor, business and human rights laws year after year', Loyola Law School Professor Robert Benson writes. Discussing a Petition to the Attorney General of California to revoke Unocal's Corporate Charter, he points out that 'under a familiar but ignored California law, the Attorney General has a legal duty to go to court to revoke a corporation's charter whenever a private party gives him "reason to believe" the company is breaking the law'. The Petition reviews a record of corporate complicity in major crimes abroad (Burma, Afghanistan, etc.), and a long list of serious violations of law in California, involving 'many thousands of victims – 18,000 alone in one incident in the San Francisco Bay area'. The Petition notes that corporations have been granted the legal rights of persons (by radical judicial activism early in this century), but demand immunity from the legal obligations of persons of flesh and blood. There is surely no thought of subjecting them to the 'three strikes' legislation that sent a hungry homeless man to prison for 25 years to life for stealing a bottle of vitamins.

For fairness, it should be added that corporate crime is sometimes punished. An example that should be famous is the illegal conspiracy by General Motors, Firestone Rubber, and Standard Oil of California to purchase electric public transportation systems in Los Angeles and dozens of other cities, then dismantling them to be replaced by buses and private automobiles. This was the opening step in what may be the most remarkable social engineering project in history: the suburbanization of America, and the shift of transportation from electricity and rail to private cars, trucks, and aeroplanes.

After the initial conspiracy, the programme was taken over by the federal government, adopting the pretext of 'national defence' that is reflexively invoked to justify the enormous state sector of the economy, the source of much of its dynamism in the past half century. Huge federal expenditures were supplemented by spending by states and accompanying legislation to accelerate the process. The country and its culture were radically changed, in every dimension. The social policies impose severe costs on much of the population, primarily those consigned to rotting urban slums, not to speak of the costs transferred to future generations as inestimable 'externalities'.

The three initial conspirators reaped enormous profits, as did other sectors of private power. But GM, Firestone, and Standard Oil did not escape the reach of the law: they were convicted of criminal conspiracy and fined $5,000.

One can find other examples of punishment of corporate crime. In 1988, two major US pharmaceutical companies, Lilly and Smithkline, pleaded guilty to criminal charges for withholding information from the Food and Drug Administration about dangerous effects of their products. The corporations and their executives were fined $80,000, almost $1,000 for each death they caused.

Another relevant example is the Ethyl Corporation, formed in a joint venture by GM-DuPont and Standard Oil of New Jersey (Exxon) in 1922 to market tetraethyl lead as a gasoline additive. Its official history observed that the company 'started its corporate life under bleak circumstances', with warnings by scientists that leaded gasoline was 'a serious menace to the public health', followed by revelations two years later that 80 per cent of workers producing the additive had been killed or were suffering acute poisoning. But GM-Dupont and Exxon succeeded in deflecting the matter for 50 years with public relations and lobbying campaigns. The additive was finally banned in 1972; the level of lead in Americans' blood fell on average by 75 per cent.

The official history explains that 'to compensate for the decline in the domestic consumption of tetraethyl lead, Ethyl looked with hope ... to the foreign sale of antinox', now estimated to be responsible for some 90 per cent of airborne lead pollution in Third World cities. The tobacco industry has followed a similar path, in this case relying on state power (threat of severe trade sanctions) to force open the doors for its murderous poisons, and for advertising that targets vulnerable populations, particularly women and young people. Much as in the case of Ethyl, foreign sales became necessary as juries began to impose substantial costs on the companies for massive killing at home. That tobacco would be effectively criminalized within the USA was predicted some time ago by one of the leading historians of drug laws, Professor Charles Whitebread of the UCLA Law School, who noted that its use was becoming class-related, historically a good indicator of criminalization of substances to punish and control 'the dangerous classes'.

Steelworkers who had been locked out of the Ravenswood Aluminum Plant in West Virginia held a 'Workers Memorial Day rally' on 28 April 1991, a national day of mourning established several years earlier by the AFL-CIO to memorialize American workers who lost their lives or were severely injured on the job. The Ravenswood lockout was a company effort to destroy the union after complaints over safety violations. These peaked when five workers died in a 1990 heat wave, working (sometimes on forced double shifts) in the hellish conditions of 'pot rooms' where ore is heated to 1800 degrees Fahrenheit to make molten aluminum. The company refused to discuss the safety and health issues. The Memorial Day rally was attended by thousands of supporters from Massachusetts to Missouri and Illinois. Other rallies were held elsewhere in the country. Among the victims commemorated at the Ravenswood rally were 25 who had died in West Virginia in the preceding year.

Speaking at the memorial rally, West Virginia Governor Caperton opened with a quote from the great American labour activist Mother Jones: 'Let us pray for the dead and fight like hell for the living'. He and the father of Jimmie Rider, the first worker to die in the Ravenswood pot hole in June 1990, joined in signing a proclamation in honour of families 'who know the heartache of losing a loved one' in a workplace fatality.

The Ravenswood (RAC) company finally capitulated after an intense and dramatic struggle, with significant solidarity efforts in the US and abroad. But 'victory, no matter how great, is never simple', labour historians Tom Juravich and Kate Bronfenbrenner comment in their study of this important victory. An indication was the death of Jerry Butcher in 1994. One of the leading figures in the steelworkers campaign, he was crushed by a device used to pour molten aluminum that had been improperly welded by poorly-trained scabs during the lockout. The company was fined $1.175 million for that killing. For Jimmie Rider's death in June 1990, RAC had received the maximum fine of $10,000; a $28,000 fine for the death of another steelworker a month later.

In his pathbreaking study of routine corporate manslaughter, Gary Slapper points out that few work fatalities lead to prosecution in England. He records two convictions for corporate manslaughter from 1965 to 1995; during the same years, 20,000 people were killed in work-related incidents that are 'classifiable, at least *prima facie*, as instances of reckless or gross negligence manslaughter', not including the 10,000 or more who die every year from work-related medical conditions. The first conviction in English legal history was in 1994, six months after RAC was fined for Jerry Butcher's death.

Slapper quotes Blackstone's crucial distinction between private wrongs (civil injuries) and crimes, which 'besides the injury done to individuals ... strike at the very being of society'. It is, accordingly, our social responsibility to determine just who 'has proven that he cannot conform to society's rules', and to react appropriately to wrongs that surely reach Blackstone's standard of crime.

# Series Preface

The new series *Advances in Criminology* builds on the success of the *International Library of Criminology, Criminal Justice and Penology*. But rather than being dedicated to anthologising the best of existing work this venture seeks to publish original cutting-edge contributions to these fields. Volumes so far in press include discussions of Foucault and *governmentality*; critical criminology; victims and criminal justice; corporate crime; postmodern policing; and women's prisons.

This study by Gary Slapper offers an important contribution to the debate over what is being done and what should be done about the high level of avoidable injuries and deaths at work. His original empirical research, based on attending coroner's hearings and interviewing those involved in enforcing safety laws, shows how and why potentially criminal behaviour at work is constructed as merely regulatory misbehaviour or even as no more than unavoidable 'accident'.

DAVID NELKEN
*Series Editor*

# Preface

The immediate trigger of interest for a research project that I eventually pursued for several years arose from two sentences in a *Times* newspaper report, concerning the failure of the prosecution in the Herald of Free Enterprise case on 19 October 1990. Those sentences read:

> The only other case this century, brought against a company at Glamorgan Assizes in 1965, was also unsuccessful. A construction company charged with manslaughter after the collapse of a bridge was acquitted (*The Times*, 20 October 1990 p. 2).

I wanted to know the facts of the earlier case, and why 25 years had passed since that case without any company having been prosecuted for the crime of corporate manslaughter. I do not recall believing that the answers to my curiosity would be difficult to acquire or especially consequential.

As the minutes turned into hours in my search for the information, the questions I had were multiplying. The leading academic criminal text (then Smith and Hogan, the 1988 edition) contained scarcely any more information than was in the news report. The case was not legally reported. I could not trace anything else about the case in legal literature. I telephoned *The Times* legal affairs correspondent who wrote the newspaper report, Frances Gibb, and asked her about the earlier case. She said her information had come from a piece written by a professor at the LSE. I telephoned the professor, who was very helpful about some of the legal background to the P&O prosecution but admitted no special knowledge about the earlier case other than what was in Smith and Hogan.

The following day I returned to the problem. I traced the case file via Cardiff crown court (the main court inheriting the jurisdiction of the Glamorgan Assizes) to the Public Records Office (PRO) in London. I arranged for the file to be sent to Stoke crown court where I could study it. The day before it was due to arrive I was telephoned by someone at the PRO to say that there was nothing in the file, so it would not be sent.

The more elusive the facts of the case became, the more I was intrigued to discover what had happened. I knew the month and year of the case (February

1965), and so by going through national and local newspapers for this period I managed to discover a number of reports and piece together the facts and the arguments of the case. I had also by this time made a rough calculation, using old Health and Safety Executive (HSE) reports and factory inspector reports, that the number of people killed in work-related incidents since the 1965 case was probably over 15,000. Why were none of these cases prosecuted as manslaughter? Were the reasons simply legal or evidential? To what extent had public policy influenced this curious state of affairs? Had cases often been considered by the police and latterly the Crown Prosecution Service, or were they simply not practically classified in such a way?

In seeking to explain prosecutorial policy in respect of commercially caused deaths it is helpful to examine the matter from three retreating points of vision. First, close up, we can examine the operation of the *mechanics* of the criminal justice system in this area, looking at what part the procedures of the police, the HSE inspectors, the Coroners' Courts and the Crown Prosecution Service (CPS) play in precluding the prosecution of companies for manslaughter. Second, stepping back, the role of *public perception* in influencing the judgements of the actors in the criminal justice system is evaluated. What tacit assumptions, if any, inform the personnel whose decisions have resulted in the current prosecutorial policy? Finally, from a distance, we can examine the broader context of the *political economy* to discover what factors may help to explain the development of the axioms which produce the public perception which in turn influences the way that decision-makers in the criminal justice system choose to act.

One perhaps widely accepted charge (Kinsey et al., 1986; J. Young, 1994) against the assumed Marxism of the new criminology (e.g. Taylor et al., 1973; Carlen and Collison, 1980) was its failure to properly articulate the relationship between the structural economic dictates of capital and the personal actions of social actors. A recent criticism from this perspective is made by Young (1995, p. 17 – draft cited in Box, 1987):

> What is striking about left idealist theorising about the state is its almost unwitting functionalist mode of explanation coupled with a strong instrumentalist notion that the operation of every agency or action of powerful individuals is linked in some one-to-one fashion to the needs of the ruling class and capital and that all of the state agencies gear frictionlessly together to promote capitalism.

This text, however, takes it as possible to use the analytic process of historical materialism without falling for the idealism of the left expressed by

Young, or the crude mechanical explanations so often associated with materialist analysis. Materialism never needed to be as mechanical and determinative as the form adopted by many so-called radical criminologists. In answering a similar criticism, Engels, in a letter wrote:

> According to the materialist conception of history, the *ultimately* determining factor history is the production and reproduction of real life. Neither Marx nor I have ever asserted more than this. Hence if somebody twists this into saying that the economic factor is the *only* determining one, he transforms that proposition into a meaningless, abstract, absurd phrase. The economic situation is the basis, but the various elements of superstructure – ... juridical forms, and especially the reflections of all these real struggles in the brains of the participants, political, legal, philosophical theories, religious views, and their further development into systems of dogmas – also exercise their influence upon the course of the historical struggles and in many cases determine their *form* in particular. There is an interaction of all these elements in which, amid all the endless host of accidents (that is, of things and events whose inner interconnection is so remote or so impossible of proof that we can regard it as non-existent and neglect it), the economic movement is finally bound to assert itself. Otherwise the application of the theory to any period of history would be easier than the solution of a simple equation of the first degree. We make our history ourselves, but, in the first place, under very definite antecedents and conditioned. Among these the economic ones are ultimately decisive.[1]

The economic environment gives general shape to most people's fundamental ideas  a slave society produces one set of social axioms, wage-slavery another, in the same way that 'the hand-mill gives you society with the feudal lord; the steam mill, society with the industrial capitalist' (Marx, 1955, p. 122) but ideas react with the environment and can, in turn, change it. Uniquely equipped with self-consciousness and historical awareness, human beings can alter the economy which has shaped them. The reshaped economy will then engender further reactions from people and so the dynamic process of dialectical materialism continues. Critically, there is no reason to suppose that people, individually or organised on the bases of economic classes, will always act perspicaciously in accordance with their real interests, or that the idiosyncratic characteristic of particular influential people will not affect history, albeit in a broadly constrained way. In his study of the history and politics of the police, Reiner argues (1985, p. 33) that the ideas and arguments of individuals assume a significance as independent sources of influence, not just 'more or less wise or misguided epiphenomena hastening or hindering, but not diverting, the course of history'. Furthermore, he notes, while these are shaped by economic dictates, they are subject to being jostled and jolted by morally, ideologically originating imperatives. Sometimes concessions made by capitalist concerns to moral pressure are not without profit. Petroleum companies with 'environmentally friendly' policies, 'ethical investment' organisations, and producers of cosmetic products that do not rely on animal testing are cases in point. Following a recent outrage among certain air and ferry passengers who objected to being carried in aircraft and vessels which transported live animals to countries where they would be slaughtered, the operators decided to stop the practice and end all livestock transportation.[3] These decisions seem to have been made on a financial basis rather than a moral one. Arguably, it made more economic sense to the companies to keep the passenger market happy and shed the livestock carriage market, than to keep taking the livestock and thus lose passengers. In general, moral virtue (in any of its many cultural varieties) is not the operating principle of industry. If the airlines and ferry companies could charge more for shipping sheep than people they would, no doubt, cater to the needs of the livestock trade in preference to humans.

Between 1965 and 1995, 20,000 people were killed in incidents at work or in disasters. In most of these cases companies have been to blame for allowing unnecessary danger, yet there have only been five prosecutions for corporate manslaughter and two convictions (Slapper, 1997). During the same period there were about 5,200 prosecutions against individuals for manslaughter by gross negligence or recklessness.[4]

It may be that the criminal statistics reflect the actual state of criminality: that while individuals have been *prima facie* criminally responsible for so many deaths in personal incidents (the figures are for reported crimes not convictions), companies have simply been well-behaved, i.e. they have not been prosecuted because there has been insufficient evidence that their conduct has been in violation of the ordinary criminal law. The social evidence casts doubt on such an assumption.

Prosecutions against culpable employers have mainly been for regulatory offences under legislation like the Health and Safety at Work Etc. Act 1974. The sanctions are almost invariably low fines which carry no stigma and are, in proportion to the wealth of many companies, the equivalent financial penalty of a parking fine for an individual (Carson, 1970a, 1970b; Ermann and Lundman, 1992; Slapper, 1992d). The result of this is that neither social consciousness nor the annual criminal statistics register any serious homicide committed by companies although there is much *prima facie* evidence to suggest that many people are killed each year as the result of the criminal recklessness of corporations.

In 1989, 627 offences were initially recorded as personal homicides (although 51 were reclassified by 1 June 1990, so the final figure is 576).[5] Fewer than 30 per cent of these were classified as homicides by gross negligence or recklessness.[6] The number of people killed at work during the same period was 514 (Health and Safety Executive, 1989). Most of these deaths were avoidable and unnecessary but none resulted in a prosecution for corporate manslaughter. Indeed, in a report on the construction industry the HSE revealed that of 739 deaths investigated over four years, 70 per cent could have been prevented if managers had taken reasonably basic precautions (Health and Safety Executive, 1988a).

Apart from these *routine* deaths, companies have also been implicated in causing death in 'disaster' scenarios like that of Zeebrugge where 192 died in March 1987. A catalogue of some other recent incidents culminating in the Southall rail crash in September 1997 clarifies the scale of the problem. In all the following cases the relevant company has been implicated by the evidence (and with some an official enquiry report) of contributing in some significant way to the cause of death: the Kings Cross fire, 31 deaths in November 1987; the Piper Alpha oil rig fire, 167 deaths in July 1988; the Clapham train crash, 35 deaths in December 1988; the Purley train crash, five deaths in March 1989; the sinking of the Marchioness, 64 deaths in August 1989. Six disasters, 494 people dead, yet no successful prosecutions.

Why then, are there so few prosecutions for corporate manslaughter since the clear establishment of the charge in 1965? A number of explanations immediately present themselves but none is entirely convincing. The idea that companies simply do not come within the *actus reus* (requirement of conduct) and *mens rea* (culpable frame of mind) of this crime is implausible considering the very high number of deaths and the great diversity of situations from which they result. Alternatively it could be submitted that the reason for the absence of prosecutions for manslaughter is that the HSE has prosecuted for other regulatory crimes. This explanation, however, seems only partly to demystify the issue because it leaves unanswered the question as to why it was thought appropriate for these incidents to result in regulatory offences, yet for only five of them to involve the police and prosecution for manslaughter.

The field work for this research was conducted over a three year period (most of the attendance at cases were in 1992 and 1993, but some of the interviewing ran into 1994). I made a detailed study of 40 cases of death at work, attending inquests at 18 locations: towns and cities throughout the country. Geographically the courts were selected from all major regions, north, south, east and west (with the exception of the outlying west). The jurisdictions of these courts represent a typical demographic mixture of Britain and present a variety of occupation and employment patterns. If local custom, the typical local nature of occupationally-related deaths, assumptions or evolved bureaucratic *modus operandi* had any appreciable effect upon the way cases were processed, or their outcomes, I wanted to be able to identify and control for this. Hence the choice to travel to and witness the proceedings in person and to interview those personnel (coroners, coroners' officers, HSE personnel, lawyers, pathologists and police officers) involved in the process which is the official response to death at work.

Throughout the text the names of the courts, locations, officers and people involved in the proceedings have been altered.

In chapters 3, 4, 5 and 6, I make many judgements about the cases studied. These are necessarily *my* judgements because it was I alone who sat through the inquests, studied the papers and case files, and interviewed those concerned with the cases. On a great number of matters, however, I discussed detailed points with a variety of practitioners, coroners, police officers and HSE inspectors to test the strength of my provisional conclusion. Such assistance is cited and attributed in the text or its endnotes.

## Notes

1   Letter to J. Bloch in Königsberg, 21 September 1890, reproduced in Marx and Engels, 1975, p. 394.
2   Peter Berger draws an analogy between social life and a puppet theatre whilst pointing out the important difference between humans and puppets (1963, 199):

> We locate ourselves in society and thus recognise our own position as we hang from its subtle strings. For a moment we see ourselves as puppets indeed. But then we grasp a decisive difference between the puppet theatre and our own drama. Unlike the puppets we have the possibility of stopping in our movements, looking up and perceiving the machinery by which we have been moved. In this act lies the first step towards freedom.

3   *The Guardian, The Independent,* 5 November, 1994.
4   Criminal Statistics 1965–93, HMSO; Home Office personal communication, 15 January 1991.
5   Criminal Statistics for England and Wales 1989; Home Office News Release, 16 November 1990.
6   Home Office personal communication, 16 November 1990.

# 1 The Theoretical Framework: Criminal Law, Manslaughter, the CPS, the Police, the HSE, and the Coronial Inquest

Before exploring the legal system's *de facto* response to deaths at work it is appropriate to consider the possible *de jure* responses; to examine the relevant law and its putative purpose, the regulatory framework in which the various agencies operate and how the different components are supposed, in theory, to gear together. This chapter begins by exploring the nature and purpose(s) of the criminal law. Next, the chapter examines the law of manslaughter and the official prosecutorial code and practice of the Crown Prosecution Service. The chapter then considers what role in the official response to death at work is supposed to be played by the HSE, the police, and by the coronial inquest. There is a plethora of rules and regulations governing many parts of the systems described below. The aim here is to provide a general context and explanation of official functions, not to detail exhaustively all the law.

## The Criminal Law

The aim of this excursus into criminal jurisprudence is to establish what are the popularly acknowledged purposes of the criminal justice system. There is a rich literature which looks critically at penology and the purposes of the criminal law for example, Thompson (1975); Hay (1977); Foucault (1977); Garland (1990); Cohen (1985); Lacey (1988); Lacey and Wells (1990); Lacey, Wells and Meure (1990); Rutherford (1993); Norrie (1993). Some of the critical approaches become relevant in later chapters. This chapter, however, is principally concerned with setting out the orthodoxies of the criminal justice system. This will be the doctrine against which the success of the system can be judged on its own terms and against which it will be argued in subsequent chapters, that some (if not many) incidents of death in the workplace are suitable for response from the machinery of the ordinary criminal justice system as opposed to adjuncts of it such as health and safety legislation and its inspectorate. The criteria for suggesting that such a response is appropriate are the existing standards, rules, precedents and legislation of the criminal law. It is not argued that the injurious conduct should be treated as criminal simply on the basis of outcome (death) or moral equivalence to that which is already treated as criminal. The argument is accepted, therefore (Tappan, 1947; Tombs, 1995), that to use moral criteria alone to incorporate detrimental conduct within the definition of 'crime' is to present a highly vulnerable case; the limits of the corporate crime thus argued for could extend past ordinary crimes, through administrative offences to civil wrongs and beyond. They could extend to any arbitrary boundary drawn by the critic.

The point at issue, however, is how the nature of legal responses to death at work is affected by the political economy. So, having set out what can be taken as the orthodoxies of the criminal justice system, the chapter will adumbrate a paradigmatic economic analysis, a historical materialist analysis of the *origins* of criminal law and highlight its main points of distinction from legalistic histories. The term 'historical materialism' (and its grammatical variants) is used in a descriptive rather than doctrinaire sense because, following Marx, Engels, Reiner, Nelken, Hay, and others, it is accepted that the influence of personalities, influential individuals and hermeneutical factors cannot be ignored or marginalised in any serious historical analysis. Beck's contention (1992) is also accepted, that risk is a political issue which in some respects can be seen to transcend economic class. Legalistic histories are contrasted with materialist histories by way of introducing, at the outset, the nature of the tension between these epistemologies in the context of explaining the legal response to deaths at work.

## The Nature of Criminal Law

There is a view that it is impossible to be definitive about the nature of a crime because the essence of criminality changes with historical context. As Glanville Williams has observed (1983, p. 27), '... a crime (or offence) is a legal wrong that can be followed by criminal proceedings which may result in punishment'.

A crime is anything that the state has chosen to criminalise. This analysis was also taken by Lord Atkin:

The domain of criminal jurisprudence can only be ascertained by examining what acts at any particular period are declared by the State to be crimes, and the only common nature they will be found to possess is that they are prohibited by the State and that those who commit them are punished.[1]

In an attempt to escape from the circularity of these definitions of crime, some writers have sought to explain its nature in terms of the seriousness of the conduct it prohibits.

Thus Williams eventually concedes (1983, p. 29) that:

... a crime is an act that is condemned sufficiently strongly to have induced the authorities (legislature or judges) to declare it to be punishable before the ordinary courts.

This is a little more helpful but it still leaves unanswered the question – 'condemned sufficiently strongly' by who? The principle appears to owe much to the thinking of Durkheim, who remarked on the way that collective social consciousness can be enhanced by the condemnation and punishment of deviance. Criminal law therefore arguably both arises from and then bolsters social solidarity.

It is this solidarity that repressive law expresses, at least in regard to what is vital to it. Indeed, the acts which such law forbids and stigmatises as crimes are of two kinds: either they manifest directly a too violent dissimilarity between the one who commits them and the collective type; or they offend the organ of the common consciousness. In both cases the force shocked by the crime and that which rejects it is thus the same. It is a result of the most vital social similarities, and thus its effect is to maintain the social cohesion that arises from these similarities (Durkheim, 1984, 1893, p. 61).

The significant point about this view of the criminal law is that it is so widely shared by those who write about and operate the criminal justice system (Lacey, 1988; Taylor (Lord), 1993), even if some of them are unaware of the subtler point made by Durkheim that the solidarity of modern societies no longer can or should be based on the repressive sanctioning of threats to common values (Nelken, 1990, p. 831). There are many variants on this outlook – some writers, for instance, do not share Durkheim's analysis of the criminal law as necessarily enhancing social solidarity – but the perception of this law as concerning serious wrongs whose commission has a deleterious effect on society is ubiquitous.

In one leading theoretical text *Criminal Law*, Smith and Hogan (1992, p. 16) acknowledge the view of Sir Carleton Allen, who writes:

> Crime is crime because it consists in wrongdoing which directly and in serious degree threatens the security or well-being of society, and because it is not safe to leave it redressable only by compensation of the party injured.[2]

The public nature of crimes is evidenced by the fact that technically, any citizen is permitted to bring a prosecution after a crime; he or she does not have to establish a personal interest or *locus standi* as in civil proceedings.[3] If a citizen begins a prosecution, he or she may not discontinue it at will because it is not only his concern but that of all citizens.[4] If a prosecution succeeds and sentence is passed, a pardon cannot be granted by the instigator of the prosecution, it can only be granted by the crown.

In an earlier edition of their text, Smith and Hogan reported (1988, p. 12) with approval the view of Edmund Davies J as he then was, in 1963, speaking about the 'prime object of the criminal law' as being the 'protection of the public and the maintenance of law and order'. Addressing the Magistrates' Association he said: 'It seems to me that … every court sentence should primarily be surveyed in the light of one test: is that the best thing to do in the interest of the community?'

A similar outlook can be found in the writings of early and modern jurisprudence and in many historical accounts. The *raison d'être* of criminal law is seen as the provision of basic protection of social interests. In his *Commentaries on the The Laws of England*, William Blackstone contended (1979,1769, p. 5) that the distinction between private wrongs and crimes was:

> that private wrongs, or civil injuries, are an infringement or privation of the civil rights which belong to individuals, considered merely as individuals; public wrongs or crimes and misdemeanours are a breach and violation of the public rights and duties, *due to the whole community, in its social aggregate capacity.* As if I detain a field from another man, to which the law has given him a right, this is a civil injury, and not a crime; for here only the right of an individual is concerned, and it is immaterial to the public, which of us is in possession of the land: but treason, murder and robbery are properly marked among crimes; since besides the injury done to individuals, they strike at the very being of society … [emphasis added].

Bentham presents a very similar view. Under the heading 'Reasons for Erecting Certain Acts into Offences', he writes in *The Theory of Legislation* that the criterion of whether conduct should be made a criminal offence should be 'utility' rather than the inherited prejudices of custom. Conduct is to be weighed, he suggests, so as to determine whether the good that results from it is outweighed by the bad; a task facilitated by the distinction between evils of the first, second, and third orders (1975, p. 33):

> Am I to examine an act which attacks the security of an individual? I compare all the pleasure, or, in other words, all the profit, which results to the author of the act, with all the evil, or all the loss, which results to the party injured. I see at once that the evil of the first order surpasses the good of the first order. But I do not stop there. The action under consideration produces throughout society danger and alarm. The evil which at first was only individual spreads everywhere, under the form of fear. The pleasure resulting from the action belongs solely to the actor; the pain reaches a thousand – ten thousand – all. This disproportion, already prodigious, appears infinite upon passing to the evil of the third order, and considering that, if the act in question is not suppressed, there will result from it ... the dissolution of society.

The jurisprudence of H.L.A Hart is distinguishable from that of Blackstone in several important areas, but they share a very similar premise relating to the nature of the criminal law. Hart has argued that a legal system arises from a combination of primary and secondary rules. Primary rules concern rudimentary social obligations and impose duties; the rules here relate to the basic needs of society and their aim is to ensure survival: '... for our concern is with social arrangements for continued existence not with those of a suicide club' (Hart, 1961, p. 188).

The secondary rules confer public and private powers regulating the application of primary rules. Criminal law occupies an important place within the province of primary rules. Writing about the 'minimum content of natural law', Hart suggests that, given survival as an aim, law and morals must include a minimum specific content. He bases this contention on 'five simple truisms' (1961, pp. 189–95). Calling a proposition a 'truism' discounts any need to adduce argument or evidence to corroborate or verify it and consequently, Hart's propositions are left unsupported by any appropriate anthropological, economic or historical evidence, and, it is respectfully suggested are highly contentious and questionable. Such argument, though, is outside the purview of this discussion. It is in these 'truisms', however, that we find Hart's justification of criminal law. Hart's first point is that because of our 'human vulnerability' we need rules to restrict the use of violence. We are 'both occasionally prone to, and normally vulnerable to, bodily attack'. Second, we have 'approximate equality' so we need a system of mutual forbearance and compromise. This makes life 'less nasty, less brutish and less short than unrestrained aggression for beings thus approximately equal'. Third, we are all beings of 'limited altruism', neither devils nor angels; this, it is contended, makes a system of mutual forbearance both possible and necessary. Fourth, we suffer scarce and 'limited resources', so property law, it is argued, is necessary to lend order to the process. This essentially political judgement is presented as axiomatic. Fifth, as we have 'limited understanding and strength of will' we need law to deal with those who do not recognise the value of the rules of forbearance:

> All are tempted at times to prefer their own immediate interests and, in the absence of special organisation for their detection and punishment, many would succumb to the temptation (Hart, 1961, p. 193).

Although, as Field and Jörg have commented (1991, p. 159), Hart's notion of moral responsibility is founded upon capacities to differentiate right from wrong and to act accordingly, his ultimate justification for criminal law rests on the less metaphysical dictates of social survival and welfare.

Again, this approach is reflected in many legal-historical accounts. Kiralfy (1958, p. 153) states that the essential object of criminal law is 'the preservation of order in the community, and only indirectly the punishment of any injury that may be done to any individual'.

If there is such clear consensus among those who have influenced the operation of the criminal justice system then it is reasonable to judge the success of the system's functioning (i) by the extent to which it achieves the aims expressed by the consensus view of theoreticians and practitioners and (ii) by whether its policies have been formulated in accordance with its generally accepted purposes. It will be argued in succeeding chapters that the failure to prosecute the crime of corporate manslaughter is inconsistent with the oft-quoted aims of the criminal justice system. Manslaughter is one of the most serious offences in the criminal calendar. It is an offence which, in the words of a leading judgement, goes 'beyond a mere matter of compensation between subjects'.[5] The evidence indicates that the scale of the crime committed by corporations is much larger than that committed by individuals, but the former goes unprosecuted or, camouflaged as a relatively minor infraction of the criminal code, is prosecuted in the Magistrates' Court by the HSE. That constitutes a serious deficiency under criterion (i) above. It will also be argued that the policies of the HSE, the police, the Crown Prosecution

Service (CPS) and the Director of Public Prosecutions amount to a composite policy which is not successful under criterion (ii) above.

## The Origins of Criminal Law

There can be little doubt about the importance of the criminal law as a social institution. The Criminal Law Commissioners noted in 1843:

> The high and paramount importance of the Criminal Law consists in this consideration, that upon its due operation the enforcement of every other branch of the law ... depends. [And] there is [no branch] which is so capable of being made intelligible to all classes of persons, or which, in its relations and bearings, is calculated to excite greater attention and interest – none, the knowledge of which can tend more effectually to convince all ranks of Your Majesty's subjects that the laws are founded on just principles, having regard to the protection of all, and equally binding on all, and consequently to impress the duty and induce the habit of prompt obedience (Seventh Report, p. 4, quoted in Norrie, 1993, p. 17).

This aspect of the criminal law's importance has not diminished over the last 150 years. As Nelken notes (1987b, p. 112), it retains a crucial ideological significance as being *the* form of law in closest touch with the public, and something which reinforces their belief in the need for 'law'.

There are differing explanations accounting for the rise of criminal law as a distinct entity. Some writers have regarded the process as being a rather anarchic development. Harding, for example, looking at nineteenth century changes state (1966, p. 361) that it was manufactured piecemeal by statutes 'listing offence with minute particularity which had long ago obscured any general principles'.

The legal histories are generally chronologies which chart legal developments almost entirely without reference to any social or historical factors precipitating the technical changes. The reasoning is often starkly teleological. Holdsworth, for example, notes that (1936, p. 43):

> as soon as society begins to become more settled some method must be found of stopping the interminable feuds to which an unrestrained recourse to physical force obviously leads ....

This passage in Holdsworth is supposed to bridge the gap between the account of the rules relating to blood feud, and the author's discussion of *bot* and *wer* and the systems of compensation[6] from which primitive criminal law emerged. Why these changes took place are left out of account except for the extraordinary dismissive explanation that the important changes occurred 'as soon as society became more settled'.

Similarly, Milsom locates the point of significant historical change – the genesis of a prototype criminal law recognisable as such to a modern observer – in a procedural issue which he treats as independent of its political and economic context. Thus (Milsom, 1981, p. 403):

> When Glanville distinguished criminal pleas from civil, his civil pleas were the real and the old personal actions; and criminal pleas were those concerning wrongs. Wrongs were not divided into two conceptual categories, offences against society to be punished, and injuries to victims who must be compensated. But they might be brought to justice at the insistence of either authority or the victim, *and it is from these different procedures that the conceptual distinction grew* [emphasis added].

Again, this is historiographically problematic. A diligent and credulous reader of this sort of account would be left with the impression that criminal law arose almost as the result of procedural fortuity. Milson moves on (ibid.) to suggest that the ancestor of the modern criminal law is found in those wrongs which were matters for royal justice, in pleas of the crown; that is 'the mechanism by which pleas of the crown were brought to justice at the instance of the crown'.

History such as this which seeks to explain legal, governmental changes of enormous import by reference to the unfolding logic of existing legal mechanism is of very limited value. It may be helpful for lawyers to be aware of these developments[7] but it is of little use beyond that. A knowledge, botanically, of how a flower blossoms, i.e. what physically in the plant causes its petals to open, will not be very useful to an enthusiast who knows nothing about flower beds, earth, seasonal weather changes or climate.

Marx and Engels, by contrast, regarded the criminal law as a code which generally sought to maintain the social and economic structure and thus could be seen as protecting the long-term economic interests of the ruling class. Unlike Hart's conception of humanity (1961, pp. 189–95), which presupposes that there must always be scarcity and limited understanding, thus warranting the protection of the criminal law, the materialist view accounts historically for the emergence of ordered criminal law, and regards the 'antisocial' element in some people as a product of their historical environment. Thus Marx and Engels argue (1970,1845/6, p. 32) that:

The history of right shows that in the earliest, most primitive epochs these individual, factual relations in their crudest form directly constituted right. With the development of civil society, hence with the development of private interests into class interests, the relations of right underwent changes and acquired a civilised form. They were no longer regarded as individual but as universal relations. At the same time, division of labour placed the protection of the conflicting interests of separate individuals into the hands of a few persons, whereby the barbaric enforcement of right also disappeared.

Moving to the extension of the criminal law, Engels (1969,1845, p. 159) contended that, under pressure in the political economy, people become offenders 'as certainly as water abandons the fluid for the vaporous state at 80 degrees, Reaumur'.

Some modern writers have taken up this analysis and used it to interpret particular legal developments. Hall (1952), for example, has argued that legal principles of theft were evolved and refined to cater for the needs of the ascendant mercantile class, led by Edward IV, who himself had a vested interest in such developments.

There was little, though, by way of an attempt to theorise within the school of historical materialism about the origins of criminal law until Pashukanis developed the application of the materialist conception of history to criminal law (1983,1924). He argued that whereas the form of law in general emerged in line with the requirements of commodity exchange, so that contract law could be seen as the 'reflex' of economic relations, criminal law is an extension of forms generated by relationships between commodity owners. The origin of criminal law is associated with blood vengeance. At first these were not simply based on the principle of equivalent requital, *jus talionis,* but were part of an unending inter-clan fight. Vengeance first begins to be regulated by custom and becomes transformed into equivalent retribution at the time when, apart from revenge, the system of compositions or of expiatory payment is adopted; thus Pashukanis argues that the idea of the equivalent itself originates in the commodity form: felony can be seen as a particular variant of circulation, in which the exchange relation, that is the contractual relation, is determined retrospectively, after an arbitrary action by one of the parties (Pashukanis, 1983, 1924, pp. 168–9).

Public penalties were advantageous to the state in two respects. First, fiscally, and Pashukanis (p. 171) quotes Henry Maine: "The State did not take from the defendant a composition for any wrong supposed to be done to itself, but claimed a share in the compensation awarded to the plaintiff, simply as the fair price of its time and trouble'.[8]

Second, organised punishment was a means of maintaining discipline and protecting the authority of sacerdotal and military power. Diamond notes (1971, pp. 243–4) that in such changing society was to be found 'the great historical watershed'. As:

> it is here that Sir Henry Maine and Paul Vinogradoff located the passage from status to contract, from kinship to the territorial principle, from extended familial controls to public law. One need not be concerned with the important distinctions among archaic societies ... for our understanding of the law. The significant point is that they are transitional. Particularly in their early phase they are the agencies that transmute customary forms of order into legal sanction.

The church's influence over early criminal law is illustrated by the fact that although sentences still retained the character of retribution or an equivalent, the retribution ceased to be directly linked to the loss of the victim based on his claim but acquired a higher abstract significance as a divine punishment. In this way the church attempted to associate the ideological motive of atonement (*expiatio*) with the material aspect of compensation for the injury, and thus to construct, from penal law based on the principle of private revenge, a more effective means of maintaining public discipline (Pashukanis, 1983,1924, p. 172).

Examining the development mindful of who stood to gain (or lose) what from particular changes can assist in understanding those changes. The notion of crime as a type of wrong associated with 'wickedness' or 'evil' was fostered by the early church and its doctrine of atonement by penance. It was under the Norman rule that the judgement of transgressors against the king's peace belonged to royal justice. The degree of royal control, however, was very limited because the initiative for bringing criminals to justice still lay with the victim and his/her kin. The suit against the felon, the 'appeal of felony' was expensive and deterred many victims from taking action. Also, its principal object was retribution – the felon's property was forfeited, his chattels to the king and his lands to his feudal lord so there was no gain for the victim. As an indication of how jealously guarded were these royal bonuses, appeals could be compounded by the victim for money but it was an offence to do so without royal permission. It was also made an offence to settle privately before bringing an appeal – 'compounding a felony'. It was the imperfections of the appeal procedure and the consequent loss to the revenue when claimants started to disregard the felony and sue in trespass, that brought about the introduction, in the twelfth century (Radzinowicz, 1948), of a criminal process at the suit of the Crown.

Although similar in some respects to that of Pashukanis, a subtler and more historically sensitive approach has been advanced by Norrie.[9] He has contended that 'the criminal law is neither rational nor principled', and criticised traditional legal scholarship, according to which (1993, p. 9) the principles upon which the criminal law is founded are natural and unhistoric in the sense that they are never seen as the product of a particular kind of society generating particular forms of social control peculiar to itself.

Norrie contends that in order properly to understand the origins and development of criminal law, its contradictions and anomalies, we must appreciate that its principles are 'historic and relative' rather than natural and general; that these principles were established in 'the crucible of social and political conflict' and bear the stamp of history in the contradictory ways in which they are formulated.

## Manslaughter

The earliest history of the wrong of homicide shows that the offence occupies an indistinct place between, in modern terms, tort and crime. Any killing, even by accident, had been enough to warrant a feud, and the appeal of murder could be brought whenever the appellee's conduct had brought the victim nearer to death. Even accidental or justifiable killings attracted the death penalty and the only remedy lay in a royal pardon. The issue of pardons for such accidents was made virtually automatic by the Statute of Gloucester in 1278.

The kinds of homicide which in reality attracted the death penalty were those which involved a deliberate killing with *malitia excognitata* or 'malice prepense' (Plunckett, 1956, p. 444).

The word 'murder' (from *murdrum*, a fine paid by 100 when a Norman was found dead and the slayer was not caught) originally related to killings by stealth but eventually became linked to the nation of malice aforethought (ibid., p. 445). The residuary category of killing without previous malice, but in circumstances amounting to a felony, was then distinguished as simple 'manslaughter'. This distinction became very material during the reign of Henry VIII when benefit of clergy was removed only from cases of murder (4 Hen. VIII c.2). So, if the killing resulted from malice it was punishable by death and forfeiture, whereas if there was no malice then it was 'clergiable'[10] and punished only by forfeiture of chattels (Baker, 1971, p. 285). A number of statutes were passed addressing this theme and one of them, in 1532, uses the term 'wilful murder', probably for the first time. (23 Hen.VIII 1532). From this time it is clear that the law recognises two types of homicide.

Today, there are several forms of the offence of manslaughter, although only one is generally applicable to the offence of homicide committed by a corporation. 'Voluntary manslaughter' is not relevant to us in this discussion as it concerns voluntary killings that would amount to murder but for the mitigating circumstances of provocation, diminished responsibility or a killing in pursuance of a suicide pact.

'Involuntary manslaughter' occurs when the defendant kills without malice aforethought. Beyond this, it is very difficult to be precise about the definition. As Lord Atkin said:

> ... of all crimes manslaughter appears to afford most difficulties of definition, for it concerns homicide in so many and so varying conditions ... the law ... recognises murder on the one hand based mainly, though not exclusively, on an intention to kill, and manslaughter on the other hand, based mainly though not exclusively, on the absence of an intent to kill, but with the presence of an element of 'unlawfulness' which is the elusive factor.[11]

Nevertheless, two broad categories of involuntary manslaughter can be identified (Smith and Hogan, 1992, p. 365):

(i)  manslaughter by an unlawful and dangerous act;
(ii) manslaughter by gross negligence.

This area of law is in a state of flux. The finer definitional points of what is now commonly labelled as 'gross negligence' (formerly 'reckless') manslaughter have been modified by several House of Lords decisions since the early 1980s. The Court of Appeal decision in *R v Prentice and others* (20 May 1993) changed the law on what had been thereto called 'reckless manslaughter'; a decision upheld by the House of Lords (30 June 1994). Each change has generated a wave of difficulties for Crown Prosecutors, Crown Court judges in summing up the law to jurors, and academic commentators. The law has now been thoroughly reviewed by the Law Commission (1996) and may undergo legislative overhaul in the foreseeable future.

One other difficulty in attempting to use this type of manslaughter against corporations (not evidently canvassed anywhere in the literature) is that the formula is expressed in terms of an 'unlawful act' whereas most company failings which result in work deaths are errors of omission. In *R v Lowe* [1973][12] the Court of Appeal held that a defendant is not guilty of manslaughter simply on the ground that he has committed an offence under s.1(1) of the Children and Young Persons Act 1933 of neglecting his child so as to cause unnecessary suffering or injury to its health, and that neglect has caused death. Smith and Hogan take the view (1992, pp. 369–70) that unlawful act manslaughter should not apply to an omission except where that omission is 'wilful'; something, it seems, that would only apply to possible cases of corporate homicide in the most exceptional circumstances. If the facts would sustain such a case, I think that they would also, possibly sustain a charge of murder: death resulting from the defendant's omission (*R v Gibbons and Proctor* [1918]), which omission was 'virtually certain' to result in death or serious bodily harm (*R v Nedrick* [1986]).

It is worthy of note, in its report on manslaughter, *Legislating the Criminal Code: Involuntary Manslaughter*, the Law Commission recommends that the offence of 'unlawful act manslaughter' (constructive manslaughter) be abolished (Law Commission, 1996, p. 46).

## Manslaughter by Recklessness or Gross Negligence

This type of offence is generally more applicable to corporate homicide. The *mens rea* for this offence is largely governed by a principle of *objective* culpability. So a defendant may be convicted for an offence requiring *Caldwell* recklessness[13] even if s/he did not personally appreciate a risk that would have been recognised by an ordinarily prudent person in the defendant's position and, if relevant, occupation. This departs from what was at one time an elementary principle of criminal law – that the defendant must have been independently wicked or culpable, e.g. by consciously taking an unjustified risk. The justification for the objectification of guilt in some areas of criminal law is the imposition of basic standards of care for life, limb and property (Smith and Hogan, 1992, pp. 60–6). The concept of recklessness is not quite as severe as the imposition of guilt for criminal negligence. This is because for recklessness, D may not be liable if s/he *has* considered whether or not there is a risk and concluded wrongly and unreasonably that there was no risk, or so small a risk that it would have been justified to take it.[14]

Companies and employers owe a duty of care to their employees and to members of the public. Since 20 May 1993, when the Court of Appeal gave its judgement in *R v Prentice and others*, the appropriate charge in respect of manslaughter by an employer (through the operation of business) will be one of involuntary manslaughter by breach of duty such as can be characterised as grossly negligent. This formula was upheld by the House of Lords in *R v*

*Adomako* (one of the four defendants appealing in *Prentice*). Prior to that, going back to *R v Seymour* in 1983, the appropriate charge in the same circumstances was one of involuntary manslaughter by recklessness.

In *R v Prentice and others*, the Court of Appeal has the opportunity to review the law of involuntary manslaughter. Three appeals against convictions for manslaughter were considered together. Two of the cases (*Prentice and Sullman* and *Adomako*) involved doctors administering treatment in hospitals, and the third concerned an electrician who had wired a domestic heating system. The questions to be addressed in this appeal were: 1) was *Seymour* now to be treated as the main authority on the law of reckless manslaughter; 2) if not, what precisely was the law that it had tried to replace, and did that constitute the current law; and 3) has gross negligence manslaughter survived *Caldwell* and *Lawrence*?

In *Prentice*, the Court stated (937C, E–F, 943B, 948A–D, 952F–G) that, except in cases of motor manslaughter, the ingredients of involuntary manslaughter by breach of duty which need to be proved are: 1) the existence of a duty; 2) a breach of the duty causing death; and 3) gross negligence which the jury consider justifies a criminal conviction. The court ruled that it would be possible to prescribe a standard jury direction appropriate in all cases. It stated simply that proof of any of the following states of mind in the defendant might properly lead to a conviction: a) indifference to an obvious risk of injury to health; b) actual foresight of the risk coupled with the determination nevertheless to run it; c) an appreciation of the risk coupled with an intention to avoid it, but also coupled with such a high degree of negligence in the attempted avoidance as the jury considered justified conviction; d) inattention or failure to advert to such a serious risk which went beyond 'mere inadvertence' in respect of an obvious and important matter which the defendant's duty demanded he should address.

In *Adomako* the House of Lords largely agreed with this formula and has thus restored gross negligence rather than recklessness as the essential basis of liability (although by overruling *Seymour* it effectively precludes future cases of motor manslaughter as a distinct category). The *Prentice* decision was, however, narrowed in one respect; the risk to which the defendant must have exposed the victim must be one of death (or arguable serious injury), so exposure to risk of minor injury or injury to health will no longer suffice.[15] Henceforward it will be open to a trial judge to use the word 'reckless' in its ordinary meaning if it is thought that the word will assist the jury, but the words must not be given any special or technical definition. I now turn briefly to consider the developments which led to this current state of the law.

In earlier editions of *Criminal Law,* Smith and Hogan stated that there were two distinct categories of involuntary manslaughter. Gross negligence manslaughter, which required gross negligence as to whether death or serious injury was caused, and reckless manslaughter, where the recklessness might be as to death or injury (even slight) and possibly, following *Stone and Dobinson* [1977], any injury to 'health or welfare'. To equalise the difficulty of proof in each case, there operated a sort of trade-off: gross negligence is a harsh objective test so the defendant is given some benefit by keeping the relevant risks limited to death or serious injury. The defendant charged as 'reckless', on the other hand, does have a possible escape route through the so-called lacuna (i.e. if s/he considered whether there was a risk and concluded wrongly, that there was none[16] so the scope of the relevant risk can be larger, even extending to risks to 'health'.

The central question posed by the appeal in *Prentice* was that identified in *Archbold Criminal Pleading, Evidence and Practice* (1992, para. 19–97): whether gross negligence manslaughter had survived *R v Caldwell* [1982] and *R v Lawrence* [1982]. It is important to look at how the Court of Appeal came to be addressing the choice between gross negligence and reckless manslaughter in 1993. A classic statement of gross negligence manslaughter is that given by Lord Hewart CJ in *R v Bateman* [1925], a case involving negligent medical treatment causing death. He observed, that whatever epithet is used by the trial judge to direct the jury as to when negligence becomes criminal (e.g. gross, wicked etc.):

> in order to establish criminal liability the facts must be such that, in the opinion of the jury, the negligence of the accused went beyond a mere matter of compensation between subjects and showed such disregard for the life and safety of others as to amount to a crime against the State and conduct deserving of punishment.

In *Andrews v DPP* [1937], a case involving a death from a road traffic incident, Lord Atkin quoted the passage from *Bateman* (above) and introduced the word 'reckless' to denote the degree of negligence required. He conceded, however, that the word could not cover all cases and that there was still scope for manslaughter by a high degree of negligence. He excluded 'mere inadvertence' (p. 582) but said that some forms of inadvertence might suffice. Conviction for manslaughter should follow if the defendant was proved to have had a 'criminal disregard' for the safety of others (p. 582).

In *Stone and Dobinson* [1977], a ghastly case involving an anorexic woman who was allowed to degenerate to death (she died of toxaemia from infected bedsores) by two relatives with whom she lived, the modern formula for reckless manslaughter emerged in embryonic form. Lord Justice Lane quoted from *Andrews* and then stated (p. 363):

> It is clear from that passage that indifference to an obvious risk and appreciation of such risk, coupled with a determination nevertheless to run it are both examples of recklessness ... mere inadvertence is not enough. The defendant must be proved to have been indifferent to an obvious risk of injury to health, or actually have foreseen the risk but to have determined nevertheless to run it.

The law seemed to have become relatively settled after the decisions in *Caldwell*, *Lawrence*, and *Seymour*. The *actus reus* of this type of involuntary manslaughter consisted of the defendant creating an obvious and serious risk. The *mens rea* entailed someone proceeding with a course of action 'without having given any thought to the possibility of there having been any such risk or, having recognised that there was some risk involved, [to have] nevertheless gone on to take it' (*R v Seymour*, p. 1063).

Aspects of the decision in *R v Seymour* and the Privy Council case *R v Kong Cheuk Kwan*[17] posed potential serious latent problems concerning the precise legal meaning to be given to the words 'reckless' and 'obvious'[18] (Slapper, 1993a). These problems could have been resolved by clear guidance on each area of difficulty. The applicability of the gross negligence test appeared to have been rejected by the courts arguably since *Kong Cheuk Kwan* in 1985; all that was perhaps required was lucid and authoritative guidance from the House of Lords on aspects of the principle like the meaning of 'obvious'. Instead, the Court of Appeal in *Prentice* resurrected the gross negligence test but only in cases where death has resulted from 'a breach of duty'. This has not been a notion traditionally employed in this area of law as it has now been adopted by the Lords in *Adomako* (p. 86 h–j). It will no doubt take a number of test cases to establish the nature of the duty in the criminal context.

The new guidance in the Court of Appeal's decision in *Prentice* stated that Lord Roskill's statement in *Seymour* that 'reckless' was to be given the same meaning in relation to all offences was in fact *obiter* and should not be followed in the class of manslaughter involved in the cases under appeal; then the House of Lords cleared up the mess, completely overruling *Seymour*.

The gist of the Court of Appeal's new test was to leave it to the jury to decide whether the risk that the defendant took in the course of his or her duty was one which they (the jury) consider justifies a criminal conviction. Juries will now, therefore, be more responsible for determining the boundaries of the crime. The public attitude to defendants who have, through indifference or gross negligence, caused death in the course of their professional duties, is not notably sympathetic, especially where commercial considerations have led to fault (Law Commission, 1994a, p. 89; Wells, 1993b, p. 553).

The Court of Appeal decision was upheld by the House of Lords in *R v Adomako*. Lord Mackay took the opportunity to iron out some of the creases left by the Court of Appeal's judgement: in particular he ended the separate category of 'motor manslaughter'.[19] The case arose from an eye operation at the Mayday Hospital, Croydon in 1987 at which the defendant was the anaesthetist in charge of the patient. During the operation a disconnection occurred at the endotracheal tube connection. The supply of oxygen to the patient ceased and led six minutes later to cardiac arrest. The patient was going blue, his chest was not moving and an alarm sounded on the blood pressure monitor but the appellant failed to notice or remedy the disconnection. The defendant's conviction for manslaughter was upheld but the test of 'gross negligence' was confirmed to be something, effectively, in the hands of the jury. Lord Mackay stated that how far conduct must depart from accepted standards to be characterised as criminal was necessarily a question of degree. Any attempt to specify that degree more closely was likely to achieve only a 'spurious precision'. The essence of the matter was 'supremely a jury question' – it was whether, having regard to the risk involved, the conduct of the defendant was so bad in all the circumstances as to amount in their judgement to a criminal act or omission.

Lord Mackay approved the use of *Andrews v DPP* ('it remains the most authoritative statement of the present law which I have been able to find' ( p. 86J)). He stated that the ordinary principles of the law of negligence will apply to ascertain whether or not the defendant has been in breach of a duty of care towards the victim who had died. If such a breach of duty is established the next question is whether it caused the death of the victim. If so, the jury must go on to consider whether it should be characterised as gross negligence and therefore a crime. He states (87B–D):

> It is true that to a certain extent this involves an element of circularity, but in this branch of law I do not believe that it is fatal to its being correct as the test of how far conduct must depart from accepted standards to be characterised as criminal. This is necessarily a question of degree and an attempt to specify that degree more closely is I think likely to achieve only a spurious precision. The essence of the matter, which is supremely a jury question, is whether, having regard to the risk of death involved, the conduct of the defendant was so bad in all circumstances as to amount in their judgement to a criminal act or omission.

Lord Mackay goes on to say that the law as expressed in *Seymour* should no longer apply as the law on which it was based has been repealed by the Road Traffic Act 1991. He said he thought it appropriate for the word 'reckless' to be used in cases of involuntary manslaughter but only 'in the ordinary connotation of the word'. It was not necessary to elaborate upon its meaning in the way that had been done by the Lords in *Lawrence.*

It is possible to distil from the *Seymour* and *Adomako* decisions an essence of criminal culpability for involuntary manslaughter, proof of which (beyond reasonable doubt) would convict an employer. An employer will thus be guilty of manslaughter if:

a) he creates or condones a risk of death or serious physical injury to his employees or members of the public; and

b) that risk is serious and obvious – serious in the sense it cannot be dismissed as insignificant, and obvious in the sense that it would be obvious to any ordinarily prudent person in the employer's position; and

c) he determined that the risk should be run either by being indifferent to it through gross negligence, i.e. negligence so bad it went beyond a mere matter of compensation between parties; or by intending to avoid it but with such a high degree of negligence or recklessness that a jury thought justifies a criminal conviction for manslaughter.

There are, however, few appellate cases dealing with *reckless* or *gross negligence manslaughter*, rather than killing by an unlawful act. One example is *Morgan* (1990). An engine driver inexplicably ignored yellow and red track warning signals, with the result that his train crashed into another. Five people were killed and 87 were injured. He pleaded guilty, was a person of good character and there was no suggestion that he had been drinking at the time of the crash. The Court of Appeal, attempting to 'reconcile the irreconcilable' (p. 508) by balancing the need to express public disapproval with the reality that prison could achieve nothing in this case and that the crime would trouble the offender's conscience for the rest of his life, reduced a sentence of 18 months imprisonment, with six months to serve and the balance suspended, to four month's imprisonment. Another example is *Saha* (1994), where a sentence of 21 months imprisonment was upheld on a doctor who recklessly prescribed, over a 10-day period, increasing doses of largactil and methadone, causing the death of a patient in his care. A third is *Kite* (1994), where the offender was the manager of a company organising leisure activities for young people, four of whom were drowned while taking part in a canoeing trip. The defendant was convicted of manslaughter by gross negligence, on the basis that he had failed to establish adequate safety procedures. Two years' imprisonment was imposed (Blackstone, 1996, p. 118).

## The Crown Prosecution Service

Until 1886, England and Wales was one of the few jurisdictions which allowed the police to prosecute rather than hand over this task to a state agency such as the district attorney in the USA. The Crown Prosecution Service (CPS) was established by the Prosecution of Offences Act 1985 and the police now play no further part in the prosecutions beyond the stage of charging the suspect.

Since its inception in 1986 the CPS has been criticised for a variety of alleged faults, principally that it is inefficient and has a low rate of prosecutions. Many police officers have expressed doubts about the rigour with which cases are handled by it, and have dubbed it the 'Criminal Protection Society'. The Bar Council passed a motion in 1993 condemning the service for being too ready to abandon cases 'fearing defeat or cost'.

The former Director of Prosecutions, Barbara Mills QC, who headed the CPS until April 1998, laid much of the responsibility for poor conviction rates at the door of the police. In one public statement, she blamed lack of proper preparation by the police for two-fifths of the 185,824 cases dropped in the magistrates' court in 1992/93. Another 8,046 were dropped at the Crown Court. Mrs Mills claimed that in a quarter of cases that had to be dropped, CPS lawyers had no option because witnesses were missing or refused to give evidence or because the case was being considered elsewhere in the justice system so the 'double jeopardy' rule applied. Between 1994 and 1997 crime figures fell but arrest rates remained static reflecting what police claim was increasing success against offenders but the percentage of magistrate-level cases discontinued by the CPS crept up. Again the reasoning for dropping or downgrading cases was found wanting.

To answer criticism, the CPS commissioned an analysis sample 10,000 cases that it had to drop in 1992/93. The results show that 43 per cent were abandoned on the ground of insufficient evidence to provide a realistic prospect of conviction. In 31 per cent of cases, prosecutors abandoned them because it was 'not in the public interest' to proceed, for example, where the defendant had already been convicted and sentenced on another matter (9 per cent) or only a nominal penalty was likely (6 per cent). Much criticism of the CPS has come from police officers who object to its not continuing to pursue cases for these very reasons.

A highly critical report published by a review body headed by Sir Iain Glidewell in June 1998 concluded that the CPS had failed to achieve the expected improvements in the prosecution system since it was set up in 1986 and had become bureaucratic and over- centralised. The report depicts a service where charges are thought to be 'inappropriately downgraded' and a disproportionately large number of serious violent crimes not prosecuted. Proposals for a complete overhaul have been strongly backed by many in the criminal justice system (*The Times*, 2 June 1998).

## The Code for Crown Prosecutors

This code is issued under s.10 of the Prosecution of Offences Act 1985. It explains the principles used by the CPS in its work. It says, 'police officers should take account of the principles of the Code when they are deciding whether to charge a defendant [sic; i.e. not 'suspect'] with an offence'. The latest Code for Crown Prosecutors, (June 1994) retains the two previous tests which determine whether a prosecution should be brought: the evidential test – there must be a 'realistic prospect of conviction' and the public interest test – the prosecution must be in the public interest.

Regarding the evidential test, the Code says (5.1) that in considering whether there is a 'realistic prospect of conviction' prosecutors must consider what the defence case may be and how that is likely to affect the prosecution case. The test is objective (5.2) and means that a jury or bench of magistrates, properly directed in accordance with the law, is more likely than not to convict the defendant of the charge alleged. In a commentary on the Code, Barbara Mills, the DPP, stated (1994, p. 900) that:

> ... Crown Prosecutors should not be looking for the same high standard of proof that a jury or bench of magistrates needs to be satisfied about before it convicts. That is too high a standard for the Crown Prosecution Service to require and it would arguably, usurp the role of the court. A test based on 'more likely than not' means just that.

When evaluating the case, prosecutors should consider whether the evidence is reliable, for example: 'is the witness's background going to weaken the prosecution case ... does the witness have any dubious motive that may affect his or her attitude to the case?' (5.3).

As Glanville Williams (1985, p. 115) and Andrew Sanders (1994, p. 946) have argued, this test favours people like police officers and business men who are well-respected in society – in whose favour juries and magistrates might be biased. It also disfavours the sort of victims who are unlikely to make good witnesses. Sanders proposes a better test: whether, on evidence, a jury or bench ought [morally] (on the balance of probabilities) to convict.

The public interest test is prefaced with a quotation from Lord Shawcross, the former Attorney-General who in 1951 said: "It has never been the rule of this country – I hope it never will be – that suspected criminal offences must automatically be the subject of prosecution' (House of Commons Debates, vol. 483, col. 681.29 January 1951).

The Code states that even where there is enough evidence to provide a realistic prospect of conviction, the public interest must be considered (6.2). One innovation[20] in the new Code is the listing of some 'public interest factors in favour of prosecution' (para. 6.4) and some against (para. 6.5). The former includes cases where:

a) a conviction is likely to result in a significant sentence;
b) a weapon was used or violence threatened during the commission of the offence;
c) the offence was committed against a person serving the public like a police officer or a nurse;
d) *the defendant was in a position of authority or trust;*
k) *the defendant's previous convictions or cautions are relevant to the present offence;*
m) there are grounds for believing that the offence is likely to be continued or repeated, for example, by a history of recurring conduct [emphasis aded].

A prosecution is likely to proceed we are told, where:

a) the court is likely to impose a very small or nominal penalty;
b) the offence was committed as a result of a genuine mistake or mis-understanding (these matters must be balanced against the seriousness of the offence);
c) the loss or harm can be described as minor and was the result of a single incident, particularly if it was caused by a misjudgement.

The parts emphasised are those possibly applicable to cases of work-related deaths. The Code states that 'the factors that apply will depend on the facts in each case' and Barbara Mills has reminded observers of CPS practice (1994, p. 900) that:

> decisions in the public interest are not simply matters of adding up the factors for and against and arriving at a decision. It is not a question of seeing which side of the balancing scales is numerically heavier.

The decision-making process concerning whether to prosecute therefore turns to the use of discretion.

## The Police

The instructions framed by Rowan and Mayne, the first commissioners of the Metropolitan Police, for the first recruits to the service are still used in police training and provide a good indication of the constitutional role of the police:

> The primary object of an efficient police is the prevention of crime; the next that of detection and punishment of offenders if crime is committed ... It should be understood at the outset that the object to be attained is the prevention of crime. To this great end every effort of the public is directed. The security of the person and property, the preservation of public tranquillity, and all other objects of a police establishment will thus be better effected than by the detection and punishment of the offender after he has succeeded in committing the crime .... Every member of the Force must remember that his duty is to protect and help members of the public no less than to apprehend guilty persons. Consequently, while prompt to prevent crime and arrest criminals, he must look upon himself as a servant and guardian of the general public and treat all law-abiding citizens, irrespective of their social position, with unfailing patience and courtesy (Whitaker, 1964, p. 9).

The Royal Commission on the Police (1962) outlined the main functions of the police as follows (Hood Phillips and Jackson, 1987, p. 408):

(i)   The duty to maintain law and order, and to protect persons and property;
(ii)  The duty to prevent crime;
(iii) Responsibility for the detection of criminals ...

There was still no significant change in responsibilities by the time Patrick Sheehy reported on the functions and operation of the police in 1993.[21]
Because they are sudden and unnatural, deaths at work are reported to the

police either by the employer or the ambulance crews who attend the scene. Occasionally, it is an HSE inspector who notifies the police. Where the victim is seriously injured at the workplace and taken to hospital where s/he dies, the police will not always attend to take statements until after the death. In the case studies undertaken by the author, although the victim did not die at the scene in seven (18 per cent) of the cases, an officer was in attendance at each of the incidents.

The attending officer is bound to satisfy him- or herself that the death was not the result of a serious crime beyond the prosecutorial powers of the HSE. There is a constitutional duty for the police to enforce the law,[22] but Hood Phillips and Jackson (1987, p. 409) note that:

> Although the police are described as being under a duty to maintain law and order to prevent crime, in most cases that duty involves a large element and judgement of discretion ... usually, even the ordinary constable is possessed of a wide discretion; should he arrest wrongdoers or merely warn them; arrest all or some of the participants in a brawl?

Thus, *a fortiori*, a constable has a wide discretion about whom he or she should question after a workplace death, what sort of inquiries should be made and with what sort of tenacity. Apart from this there is the doctrine of constabulary independence (see *Fisher v Oldham Corporation* [1930]) which regards the constable as an independent office holder under the Crown who cannot be instructed by organisational superiors or by governmental agency about how he or she exercises his or her powers. The constable is accountable only to law.

An interesting instance of the courts being used to attack a use of police discretion is *R v Coxhead* [1986]. The appellant was a police sergeant in charge of a police station. A young man was brought into the station to be breathalysed and the sergeant recognised him as the son of a police inspector at that station. The sergeant knew the inspector to be suffering from a bad heart condition. In order not to exacerbate this condition the sergeant did not administer the test and allowed the motorist to go free. The sergeant was prosecuted and convicted for conduct tending and intended to pervert the course of justice. The sergeant's defence was that his decision came within the legitimate scope of discretion exercised by a police officer. The trial judge said the matter should be left for the jury to determine; they must decide the extent of any police discretion in accordance with the facts. The jury convicted the sergeant and this was upheld by the Court of Appeal. In minor cases the police had a very wide discretion whether to prosecute and in major cases they had no discretion or virtually none. It is odd, however, that this is left for the jury to decide after the event rather than being subject to clear rules.

## The Health and Safety Executive

The aims of the Health and Safety Commission and Executive, whose evidence and function derive from the Health and Safety at Work Etc. Act 1974, are to protect the health, safety and welfare of employees, and to safeguard others, principally the public, who may be exposed to risks from industrial activity. The Robens Report, whose creature the HSE is, concluded that the criminal law had a 'very limited' role to play after deaths and injuries at work. The report states (1972, p. 82):

> Our deliberations over the course of two years have left us in no doubt that the most important single reason for accidents at work is apathy ... The fact is – and we believe this to be widely recognised – that the traditional concepts of the criminal law are not readily applicable to the majority of infringements which arise under this type of legislation. Relatively few offences are clear-cut, few arise from reckless indifference to the possibility of causing injury, few can be laid without qualification at the door of a particular individual. The typical infringement ... arises rather through carelessness, oversight or lack of knowledge or means, inadequate supervision or sheer inefficiency.

This is a puzzling piece of reasoning on several counts. The majority of people who acquire too much change from a cashier at a supermarket checkout do not do so by deception, but it would be odd to use such an observation to argue that there should not be a law of theft applicable to those who do get money dishonestly in such circumstances. Similar reasoning, however, appears to be used by Robens. Again, there is a disturbing circularity in his contention that 'the traditional concepts of the criminal law are not readily applicable to the majority of infringements which occur under this type of legislation': if the legislation under review (like the Factory Acts) is not part of the ordinary criminal law then, *ipso facto*, violations of it that are processed and thus come to the attention of the committee will not be the sort of thing normally associated with crime. There may doubtless be a few serious cases among such a collection as was examined by Robens, but the defining characteristic which classes them together is violation of a regulatory law, so it was a foregone conclusion that he would not find most of them to be very serious cases. No one has argued that most safety violations result from a degree of recklessness commonly associated with the criminal law.

Significantly, the enforcement and prosecutorial roles of the HSE were ranked below *seven* other purposes in a 1993 (iii) HSE publication, which stated [emphasis added] that:

> The Commission and Executives are there to inform, stimulate and guide those with duties of care, and others concerned with health and safety, in actions leading to higher standards; and in particular to:
>
> (a) *define standards* [1] particularly by:
>    (i) *proposing reform* [2] of existing legislation, through regulations and approved codes under the 1974 Act;
>    (ii) *issuing guidance* [3]; and
>    (iii) *co-operating with other standard-setting bodies* [4];
> (b) participate, through *negotiation* [5], in relevant standard-setting in the European Community and in other international bodies, taking account of the principles of the 1974 Act;
> (c) promote compliance with the Act, and other legislation as relevant, in particular by:
>    (i) *inspection* [6], *advice* [7] and enforcement in undertakings where HSE is the enforcing authority; and
>    (ii) proposing arrangements for the allocation of enforcement responsibility as between HSE and other enforcement bodies; and keeping their effectiveness under review ...

In the same publication, the HSE did not purport to achieve the highest possible standards of safety. It admitted to balancing economic and cost considerations against those of safety:

> The Commission and Executive's business is to see that risks from economic activity are controlled effectively, in ways that allow for technological progress *and pay due regard to cost as well as benefits* [emphasis added] (HSE, 1993, p. iii).

Thus, up until 1993 there was no significant shift in approach since Alexander Redgrave, reviewing his 30 years of work with the factory inspectorate, could openly state in 1876:

> In the inspection of factories it has been my view always that we are not acting as policemen, ... that in enforcing this Factory Act, we do not enforce it as

policemen would check an offence which he is told to detect. We have endeavoured not to enforce the law, if I may use such an expression, but it has been my endeavour ... that we should simply be the advisers of all classes, that we should explain the law, and that we should do everything we possibly could to induce them to observe the law, and that a prosecution should be the very last thing we take up (cited in Carson, 1979, p. 53).

In 1995, in response to changes in the labour market, the way in which industry is organised and in public expectations, a series of organisational reviews was carried out with the aim of improving the HSE's efficiency and effectiveness. As a result, the mainstream work, which originates from statutory functions under the 1974 Act, remains broadly the same. Securing compliance with the law and consistency of enforcement is now ranked second as one of the HSC/E's principal activities and is described as lying at the core of their work. However, the changing patterns of accidents and occupational ill health revealed by the statistical analysis published for the first time in the HSE's *Safety Statistics Bulletin for 1996/97* show the current state of affairs is not entirely unproblematic. Although fatal accident rates were at an historically low level the picture is not encouraging. It is uncertain whether current figures indicate only a brief rise in the country's previously improving safety record (HSC Annual Report 1996/7, p. xi). The provisional figures for 1996/97 show that 302 workers (employees and self-employed combined) were killed in workplace accidents compared to 258 the previous year. The rate of fatalities per 100,000 workers is estimated to rise from 1.0 to 1.2. There is also a rise in fatalities in the manufacturing industry and the estimated figures show an increase in the number of fatal accidents to members of the public. The Chairman of the Board states (HSC Annual Report 1996/97):

We need to be seen to be acting and *enforcement* action but have bite. But the main duty is with people in industry – they have a legal obligation to manage safety and operate safely and they need to do better [emphasis added].

The Health and Safety at Work Etc. Act 1974 deals with enforcement in sections 18–26 arrangements for the enforcement of the relevant statutory provisions, except to the extent that some other authority or class of authorities is made responsible for them by the Secretary of State. The Secretary is given authority to make regulations enabling local authorities responsible for enforcing some of the regulations. The division of responsibility is currently governed by the Health and Safety (Enforcing Authority) Regulations 1989 (S.I. 1989 No. 1903) and broadly, these regulations allocate responsibility to local authorities. The regulations operate some fairly complicated principles where the level of danger is a key factor. For example, the local authority is responsible for activities concerning the storage of goods *except* '(1)(b) at container depots where the main activity is the storage of goods in the course of transit to or from dock premises, an airport or a railway'. In general the HSE is responsible for the inspection and investigation of the majority of workplaces including those involved with manufacturing, construction and agriculture. Local Council Environmental Health Departments (EHDs) are responsible for the inspection of all other workplaces including offices, shops, warehouses and the service sector in general. The attitude of the EHD officers to fatal incidents at work and their investigative approach does not seem to differ significantly from those of HSE inspectors (see chapter 2).

An HSE inspector is always summoned to the scene of a work fatality either by the employer or by the police, if they have arrived at the scene before the employer is aware of the incident. The HSE argues that thorough police investigations from the outset are superfluous because it will refer any suitable case to the CPS or the police. John Rimington, former Director-General of the HSE, has said that his inspectors:

> receive thorough training in all aspects of criminal law which they need for their work including guidance on when to refer a case to the police ... Discussions between the HSE inspectors and the police or the Crown Prosecution Service will take place if the most appropriate charge is one not available to an HSE inspector (*New Statesman*, 10 August 1990, p. 21).

Inspectors can prosecute only offences under health and safety legislation whereas manslaughter is a common law crime. Another HSE publication states (1992, p. 131) that:

> when investigating workplace deaths, inspectors have in mind the circumstances in which manslaughter charges might be appropriate. HSE liaises with police and coroners' officials and, if they find evidence suggesting manslaughter, pass it on to the police or in some cases the Crown Prosecution Service.

In the past the operation of this procedure has been called into question (Bergman, 1991, pp. 25–9) because, before 1990, the HSE appeared unable to cite any cases where referrals had been made. Subsequently the position changed and the HSE was able to allude to 12 referrals made between 1990 and 1994, although none of these cases resulted in any prosecution action (Bergman, 1994, p. 8). The first prosecution for corporate manslaughter by the CPS in cooperation with the HSE (who prosecuted certain breaches of health and safety law) finally took place in 1996 (*R v Jackson and Jackson Transport (Ossett) Limited*, Bradford Crown Court, November 1996). Allan Jackson was the Managing Director of the defendant company, which transported and stored toxic chemicals. An employee died while attempting to free a blocked valve on a tanker without wearing the correct protective clothing and while using an inappropriate procedure. The company pleaded not guilty at first, but pleaded guilty part way through the two week trial. Mr Jackson pleaded guilty throughout and was convicted by the jury. He was sentenced to 12 months imprisonment, and the company was fined heavily (CPS Annual Report 1996–97).

The HSE has now agreed a protocol with the CPS for dealing with work-related deaths aimed at securing an effective liaison between the enforcing and prosecuting authorities. Where the former is the enforcing authority, both it and the police will attend the scene of the death and, if indicated, the police will conduct an investigation for general criminal offences while the HSE investigate possible offences under the HSWA. They will both assist and liaise with each other during the course of their separate investigations. In the case of some serious incidents, investigations may be jointly managed. The protocol also includes procedural guidelines to deal with cases where either the CPS or HSE prosecute and the other wishes to retain an interest, joint prosecutions, liaison at national and local level, agreeing arrangements for keeping relatives informed, responding to immediate enquiries, and making public announcements (Ecclestone, 1998, p. 910).

## The Coronial Inquest

About 650,000 people die in Britain each year.[23] In England and Wales, all violent and unnatural deaths and deaths of which the causes are either unknown or are in serious doubt and all deaths of person in custody are reported to coroners. The coroner's investigation is most often concluded without an inquest being held, usually after a post-mortem has enabled the coroner to determine the medical cause of death and to establish that the death was not one on which s/he is required by law to hold an inquest. In addition to those cases where the coroner is required by law to hold an inquest, s/he will proceed to an inquest, if, after the initial investigation, it appears that the death was not due to natural causes. The number of deaths reported to coroners in 1997 was 190,000 and inquests were held on just over 22,700 (*Home Office*

*Statistical Bulletin*, 11/98, p. 1043 6384).[24] Every county has to appoint one or more coroners, who are experienced doctors or lawyers, to do this.

There is no certainty about what were the origins of the ancient office of coroner. Although there is some evidence that the office existed before 1194, it is only because of Article 20 of the Articles of Eyre of that year that the office can be conclusively established (Matthews and Foreman, 1993, p. 3).[25] The Eyre system was the means by which royal power, including justice, travelled the country in the twelfth century. The Articles set out matters of financial interest to the king in local affairs, like a 'checklist' (Matthews and Forman) for the itinerant justices. Article 20 provided for the election of three knights and clerks by every county as 'keepers of the pleas of the Crown' who were to have custody of the records of the cases in which the Crown had an interest. It was particularly interested in the revenue to be obtained from the administration of criminal justice; a revenue which would include forfeiture of sureties, seizure of the possessions of felons and the confiscation of deodands[26] and treasure trove. Although coroners were not intended to be judges, they seem to have often sat to hear criminal cases. During the thirteenth and fourteenth centuries coroners were apparently 'the principal agents of the Crown in bringing criminals to justice' (Select Coroners' Rolls (Selden Society), vol. 9, p. xxiv, cited in Jervis, 1993, 1829, p. 4).

Apart from the inquest into violent deaths, the coroner had certain criminal jurisdiction in connection with abjurations, outlawries and accusations of felony, which were called appeals (Thurston, 1976, chapter 1).

Today, the cost of the coronial service is met from local taxation, but coroners are judicial officers who are independent of both local and central government. They have to be available (or arrange for suitably qualified deputies to be available) at all times. Not all deaths are reported to the coroner. In most cases the deceased's own doctor or a hospital doctor who has been treating the deceased is able to give a medical certificate of the cause of death. Deaths must be reported to the coroner in the following circumstances: when no doctor has treated the deceased during his or her last illness; or when the doctor attending the patient did not see him or her within 14 days before or after death; or when death occurred during an operation or before recovery from the effect of an anaesthetic; or when death was sudden or unexplained or attended by suspicious circumstances; or when the death might be due to an industrial injury or disease, or to accident, violence, neglect or abortion, or to any kind of poisoning; or when the death occurred in prison or police custody.[27]

A death occurring in any of these circumstances is usually reported to the coroner by the police or a doctor called to the death if it is sudden or accidental. Where no such report has been made then a duty falls upon the Registrar of Deaths to make the report. If the coroner cannot establish that the cause of death was natural then he is obliged to hold an inquest. One Home Office publication (7/92 11210/A. 1984) explains the inquest thus:

> The purpose of the inquest is to ascertain the identity of the deceased, when, where and how the death occurred, and to establish the particulars which have to be registered with the Registrar of Deaths. The inquest does not attempt to allocate responsibility for the death, as a trial would do. In the few cases where an enquiry shows that the death might be due to murder, manslaughter or infanticide, the Coroner must send the papers to the Director of Public Prosecutions ... The inquest may be of help to the family of the deceased in finding out what happened. In the case of a death due to an accident at work, etc. ..., it can also help to avoid similar accidents in the future.

This is a rare example of inquisitorial proceedings in England and Wales. The character of such a process was addressed by Lord Lane CJ in *R v South London Coroner, ex parte Thompson* [1982]:

> Once again it should not be forgotten that an inquest is a fact finding exercise and not a method of apportioning guilt. The procedure and rules of evidence which are suitable for one are unsuitable for the other. In an inquest it should never be forgotten that there are no parties, there is no indictment, there is no prosecution, there is no defence, there is no trial, simply an attempt to establish facts. It is an inquisitorial process, a process of investigation quite unlike a trial where the prosecutor accuses and the accused defends, the judge holding the balance or the ring, whichever metaphor one chooses to use.

Then, explaining the purpose of the inquest, the Lord Chief Justice said that: 'The function of an inquest is to seek out and record as many of the facts concerning the death as public interest requires'. The Brodrick Committee (1971) exhaustively considered the role of the coroner's inquest in modern society and identified the following functions:

(i)   To determine the medical cause of death;
(ii)  To allay rumours or suspicion;
(iii) To draw attention to the existence of circumstances which, if unremedied, might lead to further deaths;
(iv)  To advance medical knowledge;
(v)   To preserve the legal interests of the deceased person's family, heirs or other interested parties.

Nevertheless, the inquest cannot be used to assist contemplated litigation: 'It is not the function of a coroner's inquest to provide a forum for attempts to gather evidence for pending or future criminal or civil proceedings'.[28]

It used to be the duty of the coroner's jury, where they found death to have resulted from murder, manslaughter or infanticide, to state in their verdict the name of the person or persons responsible or of being accessories before the fact. Here, the inquisition (the document containing the jury's findings and verdict) would be tantamount to a bill of indictment and would commit the named person to the next assizes to stand trial. This power was abolished by SS.56 and 65 of the Criminal Law Act 1977.

Originally all inquests were held with a jury. Today, a coroner may hold an inquest without a jury (Coroners Act 1988, s.8 (1)) and the majority of inquests are held without juries. Of the 22,700 inquests in 1997, just over 1,900 were held with juries, 4 per cent of the total.[29] In certain cases the inquest must be held with a jury. These are (Coroner's Act, 1988, s.8) where the death may have been caused by an accident or disease of which notice has to be given to the government (e.g. an industrial accident[30]) or if the deceased died in prison or police custody or if the death may have been caused by a police officer in the purported execution of his duty. In other cases the coroner can call a jury if he thinks that it would be of assistance. A jury must be not less than seven and not more than 11 people and the verdict can be by majority where the minority is no more than two.[31]

The coroner decides which witnesses to call to the inquest and in which order they should give evidence (Jervis, 1993, 1829, pp. 172 et seq.), although the coroner's decision is not unassailable and failure to call or hear relevant witnesses can result in the verdict being quashed.[32] Anyone who can give evidence is entitled to come forward at an inquest without being summoned by the coroner. Any person who has a proper interest may question a witness. He or she may be represented by a lawyer or, if preferred, ask questions themselves. But the questions must be relevant, and incriminating questions do not have to be answered.[33] A 'properly interested person' includes a parent, spouse, child, any personal representative and a trade union representative from the union of which the deceased was member if he died at work (Coroners Rules, 1984, r.20).

After the coroner's summing up to the jury, they must consider what verdict is to be returned. Strictly, the 'verdict' is the entirety of the answers required to enable the form of inquisition to be completed, i.e. who the deceased was, where, when and how he came by his death (Coroners Act, 1988, s.11). 'How' means 'by what means' rather than 'in what broad circumstances': *R v*

*Birmingham Coroner, ex parte Home Secretary* [1990]. The inquisition is now required in a standard form in which the following have to be recorded: 1) the name of the deceased; 2) the injury or disease causing the death; 3) the time, place and circumstances at or in which injury was sustained; 4) the conclusion of the coroner or jury (as the case may be) as to death; 5) the registration particulars.

The inquest 'verdict' usually referred to by lay persons consists of the answer to item (4). Note 4 to the prescribed form of inquisition[34] gives a comprehensive list of suggested conclusions.[35] The purpose of the list of suggested options is to standardise the annual returns made by coroners to the Home Office; returns from which the annual statistics are compiled. The list is as follows: natural causes; industrial disease; dependence on drugs/non-dependent abuse of drugs; want of attention at birth; suicide; attempted/self-induced abortion; accident/misadventure; sentence of death; lawful killing; open verdict; unlawful killing; stillbirth.

Some of these have a self-evident meaning. In the context of deaths at work, however, points concerning the legal meaning of four of these options must be made. It should be remembered that the verdict has a social meaning, a meaning on the public record and a meaning for the bereaved, but it cannot be used to assist either side in a criminal or civil court.[36]

First there is no significant difference between 'accident' and 'misadventure'. It has been suggested that 'accident' connotes something over which there is no human control, or unintended act, while 'misadventure' indicates some deliberate (but lawful) human act which has unexpectedly taken a turn with fatal results (Burton, Chambers and Gill, 1985, p. 84). The practitioner's work does not favour this dichotomy and notes that 'even if this distinction exists in logic, it is clear that coroners have not observed it in practice' (Jervis, op. cit., p. 250). For statistical purposes the verdicts are treated as the same; thus in the figures for verdicts returned in 1993, there were 9,273 deaths by accident or misadventure.[37]

Second, 'unlawful killing' covers all cases of homicide, i.e. murder, manslaughter and infanticide.[38] Jervis also states (ibid., p. 252) that:

> Since there is no rule that a corporate body cannot be guilty of involuntary manslaughter, it is possible for an unlawful killing conclusion to be recorded when a corporate body would be so liable.[39]

Third, an 'open verdict' is only appropriate if the jury believe that there is insufficient evidence to record any of the other suggested conclusions, or where the evidence fails to reach the required standard of proof. The standard of proof is the same as for civil cases (i.e. the jurors must be satisfied on the 'balance of probabilities') except for the verdicts of 'unlawfully killed', and 'suicide' which require satisfaction to the criminal standard of sureness 'beyond reasonable doubt'.[40]

Fourth, the words 'lack of care' can be used as a free standing conclusion or as a qualification to another verdict, e.g. 'Natural causes aggravated [sic] by lack of care ...' (ibid., p. 255). As Jervis indicates, following *R v Southwark Coroner ex parte Hicks* [1987]:

> It cannot be over-emphasised that 'lack of care' has nothing to do with the concept of civil negligence, and does not, and cannot be used to indicate a breach of duty by anyone.

In a landmark judgement *R v HM Coroner for North Humberside ex parte Jamieson* [1994], the Court of Appeal reconsidered the verdict and appeared to set out to abolish 'lack of care' as a verdict, setting up 'neglect' as a replacement on a much narrower basis. The court followed argument from precedent that lack of care meant narrowly, a failure to provide care for another who was dependent on it and took this as their basis for the verdict of neglect. A clear and direct causal connection must be established between the neglect and the death. The Court reaffirmed however, that it is no part of the coroner's function to determine any question of civil or criminal liability, or appear to do so, or to attribute responsibility. The coroner and his jury may *explore* facts bearing on civil and criminal liability: the prohibition of determining any question of liability on the part of a named person applies only to the *verdict*.

Once all the evidence has been given and all the legal submissions made, the coroner must sum up the evidence for the jury and direct them on the relevant law. The coroner must warn the jury not to add any rider to their verdict,[41] nor to appear to determine any matter of criminal liability of a named person nor civil liability generally.[42] The various conclusions that might be returned by the jury should be described by the coroner but it should be made clear that the jury are the final arbiters on the matter (ibid., p. 240) and that they are free to come to whichever of the described conclusions they choose.

How much evidence in favour of a particular conclusion is legally required before the coroner is obliged to put that conclusion as an option to the jury? The level required seems simply evidential, i.e. some factual foundation but that is all. The Divisional Court has decided[43] a verdict of unlawful killing should be left to the jury where there is evidence which cannot be rejected as incredible or worthless. A coroner will therefore be obliged to offer the 'unlawfully killed' conclusion to the jury at an inquest into a death at work where there is believable evidence (no more) that the deceased died as a result of the employer's gross negligence.

## Notes

1    *Proprietary Articles Trade Association v Att Gen for Canada* [1931] at 324.
2    One difficulty with this formula, as Smith and Hogan note, is that there are many crimes which have, in fact, ceased to be a threat to the well-being of society but have simply not been abolished.
3    There is though provision in s.24 of the Prosecution of Offences Act, 1985 for the High Court, on the application of the Attorney-General, to restrain a vexatious prosecutor.
4    *R v Wood* [1832] B & Ad 657.
5    *per* Hewart LCJ in *R v Bateman* [1925] 19 Cr. App.R.8 at 11.
6    While the state was undeveloped in early society compensation and retribution were enforced at the insistence of the wronged party and his/her kin. There was either a feud between one family and another or this was averted by customary arbitration process which resulted in payment of a sum of money by way of an 'emendation'. This payment appears to have served both retributive and compensatory purposes.
7    'To say truth, although it is not necessary for counsel to know what the history of a point is, but to know how it now stands resolved, yet it is a wonderful accomplishment, and, without it, a lawyer cannot be accounted learned in the law' (Roger North, quoted in Holdsworth,1936, Vol.1 II i.
8    Apart from the benefits of augmented power that were given to the king by the geographical expansion of the 'King's Peace' through the twelfth century, it was also a very useful source of revenue – 'the fiscal profits of punishment' (Baker, 1971, p. 275).
9    Thus compare Pashukanis (1983, 1924, p. 174):

> In reality, we are faced only with classes, with contradictory, conflicting interests. Every historically given system of penal policy bears the imprint of the class interests of that class which instigated it.

with Norrie (1993, pp. 26, 29):

> The logic of the law … is a logic which masks and mediates underlying realities of class and conflict. It is this contradictory location that gives rise to the problem of grasping law's peculiar character …. Thus, the character of the law, its means of interpretation and its practical application all reflected the social conflict between rich and poor that the law was designed to control.

Norrie's work is 'subtler and more sensitive' regarding the historical origins and development of English criminal law. Pashukanis's work although criticised for its curiosities (e.g. how can property historically pre-date law? How can his mechanical, economic determinism account for consumer legislation, the Rent Acts, trade union protection, etc.?)

(see Warrington, 1983, pp. 43–68) is a much wider (although briefer) work than Norrie's and I make no general judgement about it here.

10  Benefit of Clergy – the privilege of clergymen from temporal punishment. It became widely extended through various fictions as a method of avoiding a mandatory death sentence. When certain serious offences were man 'non-clergiable', the residue became known as 'clergiable' offences. The privilege was not abolished until 1927.

11  *Andrews v DPP* [1937].

12  *R v Lowe* [1973] – the case has since been overruled by *Sheppard* [1980] 3 All ER 899, but not on this point.

13  There was a way in which the notions of criminal recklessness and criminal negligence had been 'dovetailed' (McColgan, 1994, p. 548) recently by the House of Lords in *R v Reid* [1992] 1 WRL 793 so that the differences remaining 'are those of form rather than substance'. This argument rests on the closure of the *Caldwell* 'lacuna' to the extent that the defendant who makes an unreasonable mistake in the face of an obvious and serious risk will be considered to be reckless.

14  *Kong Cheuk Kwan v R* [1985].

15  See Lord Mackay's opinion: [1994] 2 All ER 79 at 87 a–c. The reference to death alone (i.e. without reference to serious injury) is arguably confined to the facts of the particular case under appeal. Lord Mackay, when he formulates the law elsewhere in the opinion, does not underline that he is proposing to restrict the long-established rule that manslaughter can result from gross negligence in respect of serious injury.

16  This was altered by the House of Lords in *Reid* [1992], which went some way to closing the *Caldwell* lacuna by saying that the defendant who makes an unreasonable mistake in the face of an obvious and serious risk will be considered 'reckless'.

17  [1985]. This case arose from a collision on a clear sunny day between two hydrofoils carrying passengers to Hong Kong from Macau. The defendant had been in command of one of the vessels.

18  The meaning of the word 'obvious' given by the trial judge in the prosecution of P&O European Ferries (Dover) Ltd. was highly contentious and instrumental in allowing that case to collapse. The judge ruled that the case should not continue before the jury because it was not legally 'obvious' that doors might be left open even though there was no fail-safe system of reporting or indicating whether they were open or not. The judge accepted the meaning of the word argued by the defence counsel as 'something which stares one in the face'. Mrs Margaret de Rohan, who lost a daughter in the disaster, wrote to the Lord Chancellor with the view that a better meaning of the word 'obvious' is conveyed by the *Oxford Advanced Learners Dictionary of Current English* – 'easily understood, clear; plain' ('Business News', *Private Eye*, 4 January 1991, p. 26; personal communication, January, 1991).

19  The reason the Court of Appeal awkwardly excepted cases of 'motor manslaughter' from the generality of its formula was the decision of the House of Lords in *Seymour* [1983], by which it was bound, in which it was held that where manslaughter was charged and the circumstances were that the victim was killed as a result of the reckless driving of the defendant on a public highway, the trial judge should give the jury the direction approved in *Lawrence* [1981], but that it was appropriate to also point out that in order to constitute the offence of manslaughter the risk of death being caused by the manner of the defendant's driving must be very high.

20  Note that the innovation is the listing of these factors themselves (see note above on Barbara Mills' commentary on the new code).

21  The committee commended the Police Service Statement of Common Purposes and Values which provides a framework definition of the objectives of police forces in the UK. The aims are very similar to those expressed in the Rowan and Mayne, and Royal Commission statements, although they do recognise a wider role which includes the undertaking: 'to reflect [the public's] priorities in the action we take' (Appendix V1) characterised by Sheehy as: 'the enhanced priority the police service has given in recent years to establishing and meeting priorities and expectations of the community' (Sheehy, 1993, p. 15).

It was perhaps in this context that, following a delegation of union officials and lawyers in 1991, the Metropolitan Police agreed to respond to construction site deaths with more rigorous investigations. I look at this in chapter 3.

Public feeling against corporations that apparently risk life in the quest of profit is also relevant here. The Law Commission notes (1994, p. 89):

> a widespread feeling among the public that in cases where death has been caused by the acts or omissions of comparatively junior employees of a large organisation, such as the crew of a ferry boat by a leading public company, it would be wrong if the criminal law placed all the blame on those junior employees and did not also fix responsibility in appropriate cases on their employers who are operating, and profiting from, the service being provided to the public.

According to their adopted declaration of intent, the police will be bound to act on such public concern and investigate senior public officials, and company records (like accident books) following a death at work.

22  *R v Metropolitan Police Commissioner ex parte Blackburn* [1968], although as Lord Denning noted in this case:

> ... it is for the Commissioner of the Police of the Metropolis, or the chief constable as the case may be, to decide in any particular case whether inquiries should be pursued, or whether an arrest should be made or a prosecution brought. It must be for him to decide on the disposition of his force and the concentration of his resources on any particular crime or area. No court can or should give him directions on such a matter.

23  *Annual Abstract of Statistics* 1994–97, London, HMSO; *Social Trends*, London, HMSO.

24  *Statistic of Deaths Reported to Coroners: England and Wales* 1997, Issue 11/98 (23 April 1998) Home Office Research and Statistics Department, London.

25  I rely on the historical accounts in Jervis (1993), the Brodrick Report (1971), and Thurston's work on coronership (1976) for much of the material here.

26  A 'deodand' was an instrument found by the coroner's jury to have been used to kill a person. It was then forfeit to the Crown supposedly to be put to 'pious uses' by the king's almoner. The law of deodand – which even extended to animals like pigs – was abolished in 1846 but only after the Crown had benefited from several expensive railway engines which had run over and killed people (Matthews and Foreman, 1993, p. 4).

27  These are listed in the Registration of Births and Deaths Regulations 1987, reg. 41(1). See also Jervis, 1993, pp. 68–9.

28  *per* Dillon LJ, *R v Poplar Coroner's Court, ex parte Thomas* [1993] at p.553. The trouble here often is that in soliciting information and answers which would go to the quite proper verdict of 'unlawful killing', advocates are often stopped in their tracks by over-vigilant coroners who presume that the motive for the questions is concerned with the ulterior, exogenous matter to be examined later in civil and/or criminal litigation. Surprisingly, as I

explain in chapter 3, these curtailments of particular lines of questioning are not often properly resisted by advocates.

29  *Statistics of Death* (above).
30  Work deaths must be notified to the HSE according to The Reporting of Injuries, Diseases and Dangerous Occurrences Regulations 1985, S.I 1985 No. 2023.
31  Coroners' Act 1998, s.12(2).
32  *R v Inner North London Coroner ex parte Linnane (no. 2)* [1990].
33  Coroners' Rules 1984, Sched. 4, Form 22.
34  Coroners' Rules 1984, Sched. 4, Form 22.
35  The Notes are not part of the Coroners' Rules: *R v Turnbull, ex parte Kenyon*, 15 March 1984 (DC) unreported.
36  *Hollington v Hewthorn & Co Ltd* [1943]; this view is supported by Keane, 1994, p. 500.
37  Home Office figures (above).
38  There is authority to show it excludes complicity in the suicide of another: *R v Turnbull ex parte Kenyon* [1984]. It has also been suggested it excludes death by dangerous driving (Jervis, 1993, pp. 271–3).
39  A view supported by *Re Herald of Free Enterprise, The Times*, 10 October 1987. See also *Re Towy Rail* (unreported), *The Independent*, 22 July 1988.
40  See *R v West London Coroners Court ex parte Gray* [1988].
41  A power which was abolished by the Coroners (Amendment) Rules 1980, r.11 following recommendation by the Brodrick Report.
42  Coroners Rules', 1984, r.42.
43  *R v Inner North London Coroner ex parte Diesa Koto* [1993].

# 2 The Development of Corporate Liability and the Scale of Corporate Risk-Taking

In its incipient form, in the twelfth century, criminal law was focused exclusively on individual wrongdoers. It was not until the middle of the nineteenth century that the malfeasance of corporations was within its scope. The extent of corporate criminal liability has been extended both by parliament and the courts. This chapter begins by examining the development of the corporation in its social and historical settings and tracing the evolution of its legal liabilities. It then explores the scale of corporate risk-taking resulting in death.

In primitive times sanctions tended to be collective. The breaking of a taboo was sanctioned, in many societies, to appease the supernatural, and punishment was by and for the whole group. Even individual disputes produced a collective response (Plucknett, 1956, pp. 410–6). By contrast, feudal sanctions were individualistic. While the emergent criminal justice system was becoming more formalised, other major socioeconomic changes were taking place. Late feudal Europe saw the development of shipping, at the heart of the trading economy, begin to flourish. The vessels built for exploration and trade became larger, faster and more profitable. They also became much more expensive to finance. The prevalence of piratical attacks made the dangers of the sea even greater. Merchants were pressured to pool their resources and investments and collective ventures gradually became more common. The earliest joint stock companies can be traced to these circumstances (Hadden, 1977, p. 13; Gower, 1992, p. 21).

During the period when mercantile capitalism was growing from the old feudal order, there was a transfer of power from the aristocracy to the boroughs and counties. The Crown could tax the authorities and grant or withhold business privileges. It extended its control over the towns and boroughs and their mercantile interests by using the Royal Charter, an official grant which conferred a distinct legal status and existence. From even earlier, since the twelfth century, the Crown had sought to limit blood feuds by usurping the process of prosecution (Baker, 1971, pp. 252–7).

It was during the late medieval period that the concept of legal personality really began to be elaborated. Much of this theory derived from the Roman Law principle of *societas*, an association of persons with legal rights and duties distinct from those of its constituent members (ibid., p. 10). One of the earliest cases of legal recognition of a collective entity in England and Wales arose from a problem related to the ownership of churches. Traditionally, the feudal lord had erected the church on his estate and had enjoyed property rights in it. He also had the authority to select the priest and the religious rites of the church. But the power of such lords had begun to diminish by the late thirteenth century. The question arose as to who owned the churches. A number of legal fictions were used at first, but the ultimate solution was for the Church (*in abstracto*) to own the buildings, property and income which they generated. The highest officials of the Church could thence transact business in its name. The church had become a juristic person.

By the fourteenth century the concept had been extended to boroughs and towns. They were bestowed rights, including those of levying tolls and selling franchises, but they also had responsibilities, often to pay money to the Crown. The capacity to generate revenue required the status of a juristic person and this was the Crown's prerogative to grant, as Cullen et al. (1987) have observed, these collective entities developed largely at the pleasure of the state and during this time the corporations often acted in quasi-governmental capacities by collecting tolls. This can explain the frequently preferential treatment enjoyed by corporations. The corporation was a 'child of the State and in many instances performed the duties of the State' (Coleman, 1982, pp. 39–40).

The trading company emerged in sixteenth century England as a commercial arrangement that allowed merchants to engage in joint ventures. At first they resembled partnerships where the constituent members acted legally as individuals but as their ventures grew larger they traded as joint stock companies (Hadden, 1977); initially for single ventures and then later as permanent enterprises.

Although business was the *raison d'être* of these companies, they were also assisting the government from quite an early stage in their development. With burgeoning overseas trade and colonisation in the sixteenth century, companies would operate in a political capacity in new territories until the government could formally establish a colonial government (Cullen et al., 1987, p. 112). Such companies were created by Royal Charter based on the constitutions of the earlier boroughs and towns which had been authorised to perform governmental functions like the levying of tolls. The government was generally keen to foster the symbiotic relationship between itself and these companies as is evidenced by legislation like the so-called 'Bubble Act' of 1720. The South Sea company had been founded by statute in 1710 with the joint objectives of exploiting the opportunities for trade with South America and serving as a means of relieving the government of the burden of the national debt. The 1720 Act declared unlawful the operation of unchartered joint stock companies and was part of an effort to shore up the market for South Sea shares by suppressing some of its competitors. A House of Commons Resolution of 27 April 1720 emphasised the effects of rash speculation by drawing attention to the numerous undertakings which were purporting to act as corporate bodies without legal authority, practices which 'manifestly tend to the prejudices of the public trade and commerce of the Kingdom' (Gower, 1992, p. 26). This Resolution was followed by the Act, s.18 of which made the conduct of business along the lines described in the resolution illegal.

The 1720 Act, however, produced a financial panic,[1] causing the collapse of many companies. The demand for charters declined rapidly as a result of the panic and lawyers began to devise ways to circumvent the Act. Companies were created with contractual agreements using a deed of settlement modelled on the fourteenth century trust. The trust had worked on the principle that trustees were obliged to administer the trust property on behalf of the *cestui que trust* (beneficiary) and the trustees were deemed to hold the property as trustees, a continuing and distinct legal entity. These 'deed of settlement' companies shared the status of corporations in that they both enjoyed the asset of transferable shares. Unlike corporations, but like partnerships, the trust companies had no distinct legal personality, although they could limit liability through contract: *Hallet v Dowdall* [1852].

In their early stages of development, companies pioneered new areas of trade and governments had an interest in supporting these corporate activities. Much later, in the nineteenth century, such principles were still at work. The rapid economic changes of industrialisation entailed the rapid expansion of many companies. Many workers were sacrificed on the altar of frenetic economic expansion (Marx, 1954, 1887, ch. 10; Engels, 1969, 1845; Ward, 1962; Hobsbawm, 1968). Deaths and serious injuries at work were prevalent in many industries, such as the great railway enterprises. There were, in the early nineteenth century, a growing number of civil actions against companies for compensation where workers had been injured in the most appalling circumstances. The number and gravity of injuries was such that if a doctrine of negligence allowing such claims had been clearly formulated at that time the companies would have had to pay such huge sums in damages to so many maimed workers or alternatively spent what they claimed were prohibitively high sums on safety, that they would have become inviable or insolvent. Consequently, a number of legal doctrines were constructed which obviated the possible success of any such litigation.

One defence afforded to company defendants was that of *volenti non fit injuria* (no legal injury can be done to someone who volunteers to the risk). This defence meant that injured workers were not entitled to damages for injuries resulting from dangerous work which they were deemed to have consented to by accepting the employment. Thus even though it was 'his poverty, not his will, consented to the danger' (*per* Hawkins J, *Thrussell v Handyside* [1888], p. 364), it was often held that:

> The master says here is the work, do it or let it alone ... The master says this, the servant does the work and earns his wages and is paid but is hurt. On what principle of reason or justice should the master be liable to him in respect of that hurt? (*per* Lord Bramwell in *Memberry v Great Western Railway* [1889], p. 188).

Another defence protecting corporations was that of contributory negligence. Under this principle, until 1945, an injured employee or any other plaintiff could not sue for damages if s/he had contributed to his or her own injury by carelessness even of the smallest degree (Brazier, 1988, p. 238). As this could usually be proved against a plaintiff working often under great stress, many claims failed on this point.

A third type of shield given to corporate defendants in personal injury cases was the doctrine of common employment. Under this doctrine, an injured worker was not able to sue if his/her injury was actually inflicted through a co-worker (ibid., p. 282). Many injuries were of this sort even though the causation seen in a wider context was directly related to the conditions or system of work insisted on by the employer. As Fleming has argued (1983, p. 7) it was felt better in the interests of an advancing economy to subordinate the security of individuals, who happened to become casualties of the new machine age, rather than fetter the enterprise by loading it with the costs of inevitable accidents.

The civil law was thus being developed to offer support and protection to companies. The policy was created on an *ad hoc* basis, judgement by judgement, not as part of any grand conspiracy but its effects were clear. Gobert (1994a) points out, the same phenomenon was to be found in the law of contract where the courts invoked technical doctrines such as privity of contract to limit the scope of a company's liability (*Winterbottom v Wright* (1842) 10 Meeson & Welsby 109).

The criminal law, as it touched corporations, was equally as sensitive to the needs of expanding business (Gobert, 1994a, p. 397) but for the early part of its history the corporation lay outside the criminal law. 'It had no soul to damn and no body to kick' (attributed to Lord Thurlow, quoted in Leigh, 1969, p. 4). If a crime was committed by the orders of a corporation, criminal proceedings for having thus instigated an offence could only be taken against the separate members in their personal capacities and not against the corporation itself (Stephen, 1883, Vol. II, p. 61).

In 1701 Lord Holt CJ is reported as having said that '[a] corporation is not indictable but the particular members are' (12 Mod., p. 559). This was a consequence of the technical rule that criminal courts expected the prisoner to 'stand at the bar' and did not permit 'appearance by attorney' (a problem later solved by s.33 of the Criminal Justice Act 1925 which allowed for a company to appear by representative). The old idea was supported by Roman Law. It was reasoned that as it did not have an actual existence, a corporation could not be guilty of a crime because it could not have a guilty will. Furthermore, even if the legal fiction which gives to a corporation an imaginary existence could be stretched so as to give it an imaginary will, the only activities that could be consistently ascribed to the fiction thus created must be such as are connected with the purposes which the corporation was created to accomplish. A corporation, could not, therefore, commit a crime, because any crime would necessarily be *ultra vires* the corporation. Moreover, it is devoid not only of mind but also of body and therefore incapable of receiving the usual punishments: 'What? Must they hang up the common seal?' asked an advocate in 1682 (*R v City of London* [1682], p. 1138).

The proliferation of companies in modern times and the extent of their influence in social life has necessitated accountability within the criminal law. As Turner noted (1966, p. 76):

> ... under the commercial development which the last few generations have witnessed, corporations have become so numerous that there would have been grave public danger in continuing to permit them to enjoy [the old] immunity.

This reasoning was also followed by Mr Justice Turner in the course of his preliminary ruling in 1990 in the *Herald of Free Enterprise* case. He examined the history of corporate liability and noted that:

> Since the nineteenth century there has been a huge increase in the numbers and
> activities of corporations whether nationalised, municipal or commercial, whose
> activities enter the private lives of all or most of 'men and subjects' in a diversity
> of ways. A clear case can be made for imputing to such corporations social
> duties including the duty not to offend all relevant parts of the criminal law.[2]

The first time corporations were brought within the jurisdiction of the
criminal law was for failure to satisfy absolute statutory duties. Thus the courts
were not taxed with the problems of finding any mental element (in legal
terms, a *mens rea*) in a non-human entity. Developing commerce required
that there should be no serious interruption or damage to parts of the economic
infrastructure (such as roads and bridges) which would impede the expedition
of all sorts of commercial activities and thus be a cause of financial loss and
annoyance to many enterprises. It was in this context that obligations were
statutorily imposed on companies, and where the earliest prosecutions against
companies would follow if they did not meet those obligations. In *R v
Birmingham and Gloucester Rly* Co. [1842] a company was prosecuted for
failing to construct connecting arches over a railway line built by it, in breach
of a duty imposed by the statute which authorised the incorporation of the
company. It was argued that an indictment would not lie against a company
but Mr Justice Patterson rejected that claim, stating (p. 232) that: 'a corporation
may be indicted for breach of duty imposed on it by law, though not for a
felony, or for crimes involving personal violence as for riots and assaults'.

The prosecution there relied on non-feasance (not performing an
obligation, as opposed to misfeasance – performing an obligation badly) as
the basis of liability. Subsequently, the misfeasance/non-feasance distinction
was dismissed as arbitrary and in *R v Great North of England Rly Co.* [1846],
Lord Denman CJ confirmed that a company could be indicted for misfeasance.
The company had obstructed a highway during its construction work on a
railway, and failed, contrary to a duty imposed on it by statute, to build a
bridge for other traffic. Liability for omissions as in the *Birmingham* case
(above) was now extended to liability for positive acts. Denman LCJ said (p.
325):

> It is as easy to charge one person *or a body corporate*, with erecting a bar across
> a public road as with the non-repair of it; and they may as well be compelled to
> pay a fine for the act as well as for the omission [emphasis added].

Disposing of an argument that it was unnecessary to prosecute the company when a culpable individual could be identified and proceeded against, the Lord Chief Justice said (p. 327):

> There can be no effectual means for deterring from an oppressive exercise of power for the purpose of gain, except the remedy by an indictment against those who truly commit it, that is, the corporation acting by its majority: and there is no principle which places them beyond the reach of the law for such proceedings.

Gradually companies were being successfully prosecuted and those found guilty were fined. Delivering his opinion in a case in 1880 (*The Pharmaceutical Society v London and Provincial Supply Association* [1880]), Lord Blackburn stated, in passing, that a corporation can commit crimes for which it could be suitably punished. The courts agreed, however, that while companies could be criminally prosecuted they could not be prosecuted for offences requiring intent. In *R v Cory Bros* [1927] a coal company was indicted, *inter alia*, for manslaughter after it had instructed, during the 1926 miners' strike, that one of its fences should be electrified to prevent coal being pilfered. An unemployed collier was killed when he stumbled accidentally against the fence in the course of a ratting expedition. Mr Justice Finlay held that the indictment could not properly lie against a corporation for a felony or for a misdemeanour involving personal violence.

If the criminal liability of corporations was to extend beyond this point, two difficulties had to be overcome. First, a corporation having no social duties was generally unable to form that state of mind that is required for the *mens rea* of crime. The only crimes it could commit were strict liability offences. The second problem was the means by which the 'mind' of the corporation could be identified or ascertained.

In 1944 a trio of cases were decided which were to have a lasting effect on this area of law. Indeed, Welsh has argued (1946, p. 346) that the effect was 'revolutionary' in the way that it established the notion that a company could have an ordinary *mens rea*. The reason for such a dramatic watershed in three decisions all within a few months of each other is not certain, but Leigh has suggested (1969, p. 2) that it was in response to violations of wartime regulations. The cases established that a corporation could be guilty of a crime in circumstances where the principles of vicarious liability would not apply (Smith and Hogan, 1996, pp. 183–90). In these decisions we find the genesis of the doctrine of identification.

The offence in question in the first case, *DPP v Kent and Sussex Contractors* [1944], was one under the Motor Fuel Rationing Order. The Divisional Court held that a company could commit a crime requiring intent to deceive. Mr Justice Hallett states (p.158):

> With regard to the liability of a body corporate for ... crimes ... there has been a development in the attitude of the courts arising from the large part played in modern times by limited liability companies.

Giving judgement in the same appeal, Lord Caldecote said (pp. 155–6):

> The real point which we have to decide ... is ... whether a company is capable of an act of will or a state of mind, so as to be able to form an intention to deceive or to have knowledge of the truth or falsity of a statement ... Although the directors or general manager of a company are its agents, they are something more. A company is incapable of acting or speaking or even of thinking except in so far as its officers have acted, spoken or thought ... the officers are the company for this purpose.'

In the second case, *R v ICR Road Haulage Ltd.* [1944] it was held that an indictment will lie against a company for common law conspiracy to defraud. Mr Justice Stable said (p. 556), referring to the decision in *R v Cory Bros* [1927], '... if the matter came before the court to-day, the result might well be different'.

The last of the trio of cases, *Moore v Bresler* [1944] followed the earlier decisions, and a company was successfully prosecuted for using a document with *intent* to defraud. Although the ratios of these three cases are far from clear, they manage to surmount the theoretical difficulties of attributing *mens rea* to a company.

The observations of Hallett and Stable JJ were fully vindicated 21 years later in the unreported Glamorgan Assizes case of *R v Northern Strip Mining Construction Company* [1965] (*The Times*, 2, 4 and 5 February; *Western Mail*, 4 and 5 February). The defendant company was indicted for manslaughter. Neither eminent counsel (Mr Philip Wien QC for the Crown; Mr W.L. Mars-Jones for the defendant), nor the very experienced presiding judge, Mr Justice Streatfeild appeared to have any doubt about the validity of the indictment. Indeed, Mr Mars-Jones, for the defendant, directly conceded the propriety of such an indictment when he said:

> it is the prosecution's task to show that the defendant company, in the person of

Mr. Camm, managing director, was guilty of such a degree of negligence that amounted to a reckless disregard for the life and limbs of his workmen (*The Times*, 2 February 1965).

Glanville Evans, a welder employee of the company, was drowned when a railway bridge he was helping to demolish collapsed and threw workmen into the Wye. The victim had been instructed to start the demolition work in the middle of the bridge. The man whom the company managing director had selected to supervise this demolition had no relevant training nor any substantial experience of this type of work. The Crown argued that the instructions given were an act of folly and would have inevitably led to the collapse of the bridge:

there was such a complete disregard for the safety of the workmen that it goes beyond the mere matter of compensation and amounts to a crime against the state (*The Times*, 4 February 1965).

Although the company was found not guilty on the merits of the case, Leigh, writing in 1969, was clear that liability for manslaughter had been established as a crime for which a corporation could be indicted.

Following the decisions of the 1944 trio of cases, corporate intention was found by treating the *mens rea* of certain employees of the company as the *mens rea* of the company itself. It was not every employee whose *mens rea* was also that of the company however. The test was wide and flexible, one of mixed fact and law (Burles, 1991, p. 610). However, as a company has no physical existence and cannot think or act, a fiction has to be applied to convert the acts and thoughts of a human into those of the corporation, thereby attributing personality to it. This is known as the identification principle and a variety of criteria and phrases for determining who in a company thinks and acts *as* that company have been suggested in the leading case of *Tesco Supermarkets Ltd v Nattrass* [1972]. Viscount Dilhorne (p. 171) thought that it would have to be someone

... who is in actual control of the operations of a company or of part of them and who is not responsible to another person in the company for the manner in which he discharges his duties in the sense of being under his orders.

In determining who are the people representing the 'controlling minds' of the corporation, a dictum of Lord Denning, in *H.L. Bolton (Engineering) Co. Ltd v T.J. Graham & Sons* [1957] (p. 172) was approved:

A company may in many ways be likened to a human body. It has a brain and a nerve centre which controls what it does. It also has hands which hold the tools and act in accordance with directions from the centre. Some of the people in the company are mere servants and agents who are nothing more than hands to do the work and cannot be said to represent the mind or will. Others are directors and managers who represent the directing mind and will of the company and control what it does. The state of mind of these managers is the state of mind of the company and it is treated by the law as such.

This formula does not include all 'managers' since not all such persons 'represent the directing mind and will of the company and control what it does'. The wide and flexible test of the 1944 cases was disapproved and replaced by a far stricter one known as the 'controlling officer' test.

In any event, it is a question of *law* whether a person is to be regarded as having acted as the company or merely as the company's servant or agent (*per* Lord Reid, in *Tesco*, ibid., p. 173).

Thus corporations can be liable in two different ways. For some offences – in the main regulatory, strict liability offences – a company is liable whenever one of its servants commits an offence. This is the *vicarious liability* route – a form of strict liability arising from the master-servant relationship without reference to any fault of the employer.

For crimes involving blameworthiness, i.e. those offences requiring *mens rea*, the criminal liability of corporations is subject to the much more restrictive identification doctrine. A corporation can only act through individual persons. If there is an individual who has committed the *actus reus* of a crime with the appropriate *mens rea* and who is sufficiently important in the corporate structure for his or her acts to be identified with the company itself, the company as well as the individual can be criminally liable (unless the statutory provision creating the offence precludes this).

A weakness inherent in the *Tesco Supermarkets* case is that there are myriad regulatory offences which do not fall neatly into either the strict liability or the *mens rea* category. These offences mitigate the potential severity of strict liability by allowing for defences such as due diligence or lack of knowledge by the master or principal or in the case of a company, by an officer who constitutes the directing mind of the company. The due diligence defence provided in the legislation requires the defendant to prove that the commission of the offence was due to the default of one of its non-directing mind employees and that they (the defendant) had taken reasonable precautions to avoid it or exercised due diligence to avoid the commission of the offence by a person under their control (Wells, 1997a, p. 8). The majority of their Lordships in

*Tesco* took the view that the identification doctrine applied to this sort of hybrid offence common in regulatory legislation and that a rational and fair system of justice generally required that a company only be criminally liable for the wrongs of those who formed its directing mind. In fact this approach of presuming that statutory offences did not intend to impose strict liability – but required *mens rea* – continued for over 20 years. It has been suggested that the directing mind test which finally triumphed in the *Tesco v Natrass* case has to be viewed as arising in a more liberal atmosphere concerning the criminal liability of employers. Ironically, a case involving a store from the same corporate group, *Tesco Stores v Brent LBC* [1993] seems to have been the first indication of judicial dissatisfaction with the directing mind theory and the inappropriateness of the identification doctrine to hybrid offences.

*Tesco Supermarkets* has in effect been distinguished in four major decisions, namely, *Tesco Stores* [1993], *Re Supply of Ready Mixed Concrete (No 2)* [1995], *Meridian* [1995] and the *British Steel* [1995] case. The courts appear to have retreated from the policy aspects of *Tesco Supermarkets* in favour of reverting to a stricter regulatory regime suggesting that companies should not be treated any differently from other employers. In *Meridian*, Lord Hoffman acknowledged that the 'directing mind' model was not always appropriate. He stated that in considering whether to attribute *mens rea* to a company it was relevant to examine the language of any appropriate statute, and to consider its policy and content. The approach taken by Hoffman appeared to be stretching the identification model rather than taking the offence into the vicarious category. What is not clear, however, is how the more flexible test is to be determined and applied.

While the latest authorities seem to have thrown the law into considerable confusion, what all these developments seem to have in common is that a fundamental shift in direction has occurred away from notions of director and officer control towards establishing realist notions based on an understanding of the complexities of modern organisational attitudes and practices as the fundamental paradigm in matters pertaining to corporate liability. Certainly commentators (Burles, 1991, p. 609; Wells, 1997a, p. 5; Wickins and Ong, 1997, p. 554) have accepted that the *Tesco Supermarkets* case was a major obstacle to a stricter regulatory approach. It might be that the erosion of the directing mind theory is attributable to the spate of recent physical and financial disasters in the corporate field and the resulting public outcry. Other reasons may be changes in perceptions of work safety including significant increases in maximum penalties, now £20,000 on summary conviction, unlimited in the Crown Court (s.33, Health and Safety at Work Etc. Act (HSWA) 1994, ss.

17–24, Criminal Justice Act (CJA) 1991, as amended by s.65, CJA 1993). The demise of the *ultra vires* doctrine and the recognition of shadow directors and managers by the Companies Act 1985 has meant that the courts can be less precise and rigid in attributing acts of persons such as managers and employees to the company itself. Another reason may be an attempt to bring English company law into line with that of the European Community. (For comprehensive discussion see Wells, 1996 and 1997b: Wickins and Ong, 1997).

Neither of the two legal routes that have evolved to deal with corporate offenders, the vicarious liability and identification models, can be seen as satisfactory.

Such a narrow test as the identification doctrine has had considerable implications for prosecutors (Burles, 1991, p. 610). In his preliminary ruling in 1990 on whether a corporation could be properly indicted for manslaughter (arising from the charges brought against P&O European Ferries for the sinking of the *Herald of Free Enterprise*, above), Mr Justice Turner said (p. 84):

> ... where a corporation, through the controlling mind of one of its agents, does an act which fulfils the prerequisites of the crime of manslaughter ... it as well as its controlling mind or minds, is properly indictable for the crime of manslaughter.

However, in order to establish that P&O itself was guilty of manslaughter, the Crown had to prove that one of its directors was guilty of manslaughter. When the prosecution against five senior employees collapsed, the case against the company inevitably went too. Furthermore, certain restrictions on the criminal responsibility of corporations were set out in this judgement, precluding the aggregation of fault from several directors as being sufficient to incriminate the company.

In spite of a public outcry after the *Herald of Free Enterprise* trial, that no-one including the company itself was convicted of any criminal offence following the disaster, what the prosecution did achieve was the admission by the Court that a corporate body is capable of being guilty of manslaughter. Although this success was gratifying, the development of the law towards corporate manslaughter did not take place for a further five years.

On 8 December 1994, OLL Ltd became the first company in English legal history to be convicted of homicide (Slapper, 1997). Peter Kite, its managing director, also became the first director to be given an immediate custodial sentence from a manslaughter conviction arising from the operation of a business. Both defendants were found guilty on four counts of manslaughter arising from the death of four teenagers who drowned off Lyme Regis while on a canoe trip organised by the defendant leisure activity company. Mr Kite was sentenced to three years imprisonment, and the company was fined £60,000. The Lyme Regis conviction, argues Slapper (1997) may well have a symbolic significance, and have a chastening effect on businesses which currently adopt a cavalier attitude to safety. How far it will affect the number of prosecutions in future is questionable. The case was arguably atypical of corporate homicide scenarios. The company, OLL Ltd, was small, so it was relatively easy to find the 'controlling minds'; the risks to which the students were exposed were both serious and obvious and also, critically, they were not technical or esoteric in any way (anyone can see the dereliction of duty involved in not providing competent supervisors, flares, a look-out boat, in not notifying the harbour authority, etc.). For the prosecution there was also the serendipitous evidence of the letter from the former employees which indisputably made the managing director aware of the risks in question; risks which, as the prosecution was able to show, were not subsequently addressed with any seriousness.

Since the Lyme Regis case, another company has been convicted of manslaughter, along with one of its directors, James Hodgson. Hodgson was imprisoned for 12 months and fined £1,500, and the company, Jackson Transport (Ossett) Ltd, was fined £22,000. The case arose from the death of a 21 year-old employee who died after being sprayed in the face with a toxic chemical while cleaning chemical residues from a road tanker. The case centred on allegations of inadequate supervision, training, and protective equipment, (*The Health and Safety Practitioner*, December 1996, p. 3, cited in Slapper, 1997).

In 1972, immediately after the *Tesco* decision, the Law Commission considered the position of the law in this area. They examined possible reforms and questioned the moral justification for prosecuting corporate bodies. It concluded by generally approving the law as it then stood, i.e. immediately post-*Tesco* (Burles, 1991, p. 611). This was at the very beginning of the process by which companies were brought within the jurisdiction of the ordinary criminal law. The process, however, has been very slow with key developments separated by periods of 30 or 40 years.

A subsidiary development concerning corporate liability is the Company Disqualification Act 1986, which provides for the court to make a disqualification order against a person convicted of an indictable offence connected with the promotion, formation, management or liquidation of a company. It was perhaps thought, in some quarters, that the conduct at which the legislation was aimed, defined in section 2, was financial in nature. It is now clear, however, that the act will also apply in respect of health and safety matters. Speaking in the House of Lords in 1991, Viscount Ullswater said (*Hansard*, H.C., 22 November 1991, col. 1429–30):

> In our view section 2 of the Directors Disqualification Act 1986 is capable of applying to health and safety matters ... We believe that the potential scope of section 2(1) of that Act is very broad and that 'management' includes the management of health and safety.

The foregoing interpretation of the Act has enabled proceedings to be taken against the director of a company who with his consent, connivance or due to his negligence, has committed an offence. On 28 June 1992 at Lewes Crown Court, a director of a company was prosecuted by the Health and Safety Executive (HSE) under section 37 of the Health and Safety at Work Act 1974 (HSWA) and became the first director to be disqualified in connection with this sort of crime (Slapper, 1997, p. 225).

The philosophical and legal complexities of corporate attribution of knowledge, recognised by Lord Hoffman in the *Meridian* case, parallels the thinking of the Law Commission's report, *Legislating the Criminal Code: Involuntary Manslaughter* (1996). The Law Commission accords prominence in half of its report to the issue of corporate manslaughter and recommends that there should be a specific offence of 'corporate killing' broadly comparable to 'killing by gross negligence' on the part of an individual. If the proposals are implemented, a company would become liable for prosecution if a 'management failure' by the corporation results in death, and that failure constitutes conduct falling 'far below what can reasonably be expected of the corporation in the circumstances'. Thus, rather than use the ancient principle *actus non facit reum nisi mens sit rea* (conduct is not criminal unless accompanied by a culpable state of mind), and require a search for at least one person with a culpable mind, the new law would judge the corporation by the results of its collective efforts.

Interestingly, the report suggests that where a company is convicted of corporate killing the judge should have the power to both fine the company an unlimited sum, and order it to remedy the cause of death. It also suggests that the offence should apply to foreign corporations operating in this country (Slapper, 1997).

The full extent of the Law Commission's proposals (1996) are considered in more detail in chapter 6.

## The Scale of Corporate Risk-Taking

Evidence suggests that most people do not appreciate the existence of or true extent of corporate crime. (Sinden, 1980; Cullen et al., 1987). People are socialised to expect a criminal to appear as someone in a police mug shot, looking rough and aggressive. There is often an awareness that an apparently middle-class person could be an offender as a fraudster or dishonest car dealer but the idea that a corporation could be criminal is much more esoteric.

There is much evidence to suggest that a very high number of the 19,471 deaths occurring within a commercial setting during the last 27 years were classifiable, at least *prima facie*, as instances of reckless or gross negligence manslaughter. This study, which followed 40 cases of deaths at work through the legal process, suggests that 20 per cent of them were presented as *prima facie* cases of gross negligent manslaughter. In fact, none of these cases resulted in any person or company being prosecuted for manslaughter.

It is also possible that some deaths could have entailed prosecutions for 'unlawful act' or 'constructive' manslaughter. This crime occurs where death results from the defendant's unlawful and dangerous act, dangerous in the sense that it is likely to cause direct personal injury, though not necessarily serious injury (Smith and Hogan, 1992, p. 366). It was argued, in chapter 1, that such prosecutions may be problematic for several reasons, therefore discussion here does not rely on this species of homicide.

There are many cases where surgeons and anaesthetists have been prosecuted for reckless manslaughter in circumstances where they were engaged in trying to save or improve a patient's life (Slapper, 1994a).[3] However, whilst the prosecuting authorities have been so conscientious in the prosecution of individuals in what might be termed 'ordinary' manslaughter cases and also many arising from some quite unusual circumstances,[4] they have not been especially concerned to prosecute companies for the equivalent crime.

If there is a fault or anomaly in the state's prosecutorial policy it is not one which affects only a small, peripheral group of cases. However, the extent of the problem is difficult to quantify. Examining corporate misconduct in the USA, Reiman has given the issue a particularly dramatic perspective. He estimates that in 1972 the number of people in the USA dying from occupational hazards (diseases and accidents) was 114,000, whereas only 20,600 died as victims of personal homicide. Represented on a time clock for murder there would be one personal killing every 26 minutes but:

If a similar clock for industrial deaths were constructed ... and recalling that this clock ticks only for that half of the population that is the labour force – this clock would show an industrial death about every four and a half minutes! In other words in the time it takes for one murder on the time clock, six workers have died just trying to make a living! (Reiman, 1979, p. 68).

In Britain there is a similar discrepancy. Over any 12 month period, the number of deaths at work is, on average, about two and a half times the number of cases resulting in convictions for manslaughter (excluding 'diminished responsibility' cases – those under s.2 of the Homicide Act, 1957).

Over the decade, 1979–89, the number of annual convictions for manslaughter (excluding s.2 cases) fluctuated between 99 (1989) and 192 (1987). The number of people killed at work over a 12 month period is notably higher, for example: 558 during 1987/88, 730 during 1988/89, 681 during 1989/90 and 572 1990/91 (Health and Safety Executive, 1988, 1989, 1990 and 1991).

Equally alarming are the numbers of non-fatal accidents at work. During the 1993–94 period of review, the Health and Safety Executive recorded 379 deaths at work, and over 28,900 non-fatal major injuries (*HSE Annual Report* 1993–94). By 1995–96, the fatalities figure had fallen a little to 344, but the major injuries (involving amputations, loss of an eye, etc.) had risen to 30, 968 (*HSE Annual Report*). The 1996–97 Annual Report figures are more alarming – in the categories 'employed' and 'self-employed', a total of 44 more people were killed than the previous year. Apart, however, from that real rise using the same categories as the previous year, the overall annual death and major injury levels rose very sharply because new categories of death and injury (like railway deaths, and offshore oil and gas industry incidents) were also included. The figures for 1996–97 are 679 deaths and 63,937 major injuries.

Clearly, not all the work-related deaths and injuries at work are the result of criminal conduct (acts or omissions) on the part of companies and their directors. There is, however, considerable evidence that about 70 per cent of deaths and serious injuries at work to employees or members of the public result from managerial and systemic faults in operations (e.g. see HSE, 1985; HSE, 1986; HSE, 1988b; Slapper, 1998).

When one considers that these accidents only relate to the working population, which is less than 50 per cent of the whole (Box, 1983, cited in Williams, 1994, p. 54), it does give some idea of the extent of the problem.

The system of death registration and classification suggests that the annual figure for deaths through incidents at work could be higher than the official figure (quite apart, that is, from the exclusion of people 'at work' who are killed in road traffic incidents, which are considered below).

As a consequence of the historic duty of the coroner, before a death can be registered, a valid certificate giving the cause of death must be completed and signed by a registered medical practitioner who attended the deceased during his/her last illness. The cause of death, so certified, must be shown to be entirely natural. In every other case the death must be reported to the coroner and if a death is shown to be 'violent or unnatural', the coroner is required by law to conduct an inquest. The evolution of this 'fail-safe' system (Burton et al., 1985, p. 2) provides that the registration of every death shall be subject to scrutiny. The reason for the notification system is (Jervis, 1993, p. 289) that:

> certain types of accident and disease (usually, but not invariably, industrial in origin) are considered to be so serious that notification of their existence must be given to relevant Government bodies for the purpose of investigation and research.

Thus deaths arising out of or in connection with work must be so reported: S.I. 1985 No. 2023 – the Reporting of Injuries, Diseases and Dangerous Occurrences Regulations, reg. 2(1).

There is no higher duty imposed on doctors than upon any other person at common law to report a death to the coroner, although by virtue of their profession, doctors may be considered to be well placed to know which deaths should be reported and in practice the vast majority of cases are reported by doctors and the police. It is arguable, therefore, that the system stands or falls on the cooperation of the medical profession.

Two recent studies (Start et al., 1993 and 1995) highlighted the inability of both hospital clinicians and general practitioners to recognise some categories of reportable deaths. Buchanan et al. (1995, p. 145) argue that this is due to ignorance of the law and is the product of the minimal medico-legal teaching in English medical schools and of the free interchange of doctors from civil law jurisdictions of the European Community.

The dangers of failure to recognise a notifiable death undermine the safeguards provided to society by the coroner system and may cause administrative difficulties, unnecessary distress for bereaved relatives and 'cases may evade medico-legal investigation altogether because they are not recognised as death due to unnatural causes' (Start et al., 1993, p. 1038).

In the first study (Start et al., 1993) it was indicated that individual clinicians at all grades showed a variable appreciation of the different category of cases which should be reported with consultants consistently performing less well than their junior staff. When asked to assess medical histories and whether the resulting death should have been reported, anything up to 60 per cent in individual cases were wrong. Furthermore,

> most, but worryingly *not all*, clinicians reported the *cases involving allegations of negligence*, death in police custody, criminal death, suicide, and industrial disease. *Deaths resulting from accidents were often unrecognised and many clinicians did not seem to know that such deaths are reportable to the coroner, no matter how long a time had elapsed between injury and death* (ibid., p. 1039) [emphasis added].

Even when the lapse between an injury and consequential death is a period of many months or years, the matter could still be within the jurisdiction of English homicide law. Under the Law Reform (Year and a Day Rule) Act 1996, prosecutions for homicide may be brought at any time after the incident allegedly responsible for or accelerating death. However, to safeguard against oppressive prosecutions, any prosecution brought more than three years after the relevant incident (or where the perpetrator has already been convicted of an offence in relation to the incident) must have the consent of the Attorney-General.

In a second study involving general practitioners (Start et al., 1995), only 3 per cent recognised those deaths which should be reported for further investigation in all the case studies. Some doctors held disturbing misconceptions in relation to the coroner system that could have a wide range of outcomes, from serious crime going undetected to loss of industrial pension or other appropriate compensation for relatives. Deaths from industrial or domestic accidents were recognised as cases requiring referral by fewer than half of general practitioners.

Both of these studies indicate that certifying doctors consider only the eventual cause of death rather than the sequence of events leading to death (ibid., p. 193).

Although some of the unreported reportable deaths would be picked up later by other doctors signing cremation forms, by the local registrar of births, deaths, and marriages, or by coroners' officers when contacted for advice, other cases may receive no further attention.

Trade union research suggests that upwards of 10,000 people die every year from work-related medical conditions (Bergman, 1991, p. 3) and some research puts the figure at up to 20,000 (GMB, 1987, p. 5). These deaths result from multifarious chronic conditions and diseases, such as carcinoma arising from exposure to radiation, mesothelioma from construction work, and pneumoconiosis from working in mines.

In many cases it seems clear that employers knew of the risks to which their employees were being exposed. On current law, manslaughter could be proven against an employer where he or she (or the company) had shown 'indifference to an obvious risk of injury to health' or had an 'actual foresight of the risk coupled with a determination to run it'.

The asbestos industry provides some clear examples of appalling suffering and death caused to thousands of people when ample evidence, known to employers, demonstrated the health dangers. Asbestos was implicated in causing industrial disease as far back as the 1920s. There is documentary evidence that from the 1930s the English firm, and world leader in asbestos production, Turner and Newell set out to flout laws designed to protect workers. Recent research studies, by Professor Julian Peto, have shown that cancers from asbestos exposure are set to rise, for the next 30 years, to about 9,000 a year (*The Guardian*, 25 November 1994). Remembering that there are only about 500 ordinary homicide cases each year, the potential wrongdoing here is on an enormous scale.

Many serious injuries sustained while the victim is at work can result in death months later but are not classified as deaths arising out of work. It thus becomes important to consider the extent of serious injuries at work. There is clear evidence that there is considerable under-reporting of reportable injuries including major injuries:

> in contrast to the comprehensive information available on fatalities, a supplement to the 1990 Labour Force Survey (LFS) confirmed HSE's previous concerns that non-fatal injuries are significantly under-reported. The supplement revealed that only a third of reportable non-fatal injuries to employees are being reported, with marked variations between industrial sectors (from under a fifth in agriculture and only a quarter in the services sector to two fifths in manufacturing and construction and four fifths in the energy sector). For the self-employed, only one in twenty reportable injuries are reported (HSE, 1993, p. 83).

The self-employed sector is sufficiently large for even a tiny fraction of its fatalities and major injuries to be numerically important. According to figures from the Department of Employment, there are 2,978,000 in this category (*Annual Abstract of Statistics*, 1994, p. 105). Major injuries can occasionally be the cause of death many months later. Such deaths would technically be classifiable as deaths arising from work for HSE purposes;

they would also be prosecutable as manslaughter. It appears that a considerable number are not reported to (and thus not recorded by) the HSE. Taken together, this data suggests that the official annual figure of work accident fatalities may be an underestimate. The 'dark figure' of deaths at work may, therefore be higher than the officially-recorded statistic.

One study, by Bergman in 1994, further suggests that the level of corporate criminality is higher than official statistics suggest. The West Midlands Health and Safety Advice Centre (a non-governmental organisation) gained access to confidential documents relating to 28 workplace deaths in the West Midlands in the years 1988–92. The aim was to judge the level of criminal responsibility of the companies and the senior officers involved and evaluate the extent and rigour of the official investigations by the Health and Safety Executive and the Environmental Health Department. They concluded that in 13 cases the criminal responsibility of the companies and/or the senior officers was greater than suggested by the official action (in 11 cases there should either have been a prosecution for manslaughter or a referral for consideration to prosecute for manslaughter) and 11 others deserved further investigation. This suggests that the level of corporate criminality is considerably higher than statistics suggest and the enforcement agencies are not performing their function correctly. In particular they fail to take account of the previous history of the company and of the action of the officers involved and they fail to consider cases for a charge of manslaughter (and referral to the police) (cited in Williams 1994, p. 53).

Bergman (1994) also argues that part of the failure of the enforcement agencies to conduct adequate and competent investigations arises out of a starvation of resources supplied to the regulatory bodies but, he argues, part is also attitudinal – an apparent lack of will to criminalise employers' conduct, however culpable they may have been.

The abrupt end to the trial of the butcher's shop at the centre of the world's worst *E-coli 0157* food poisoning outbreak sparked anger from both politicians and victims of the epidemic (*The Times*, 21 January 1998). Twenty people died, 160 were admitted to hospital and altogether 400 people were affected. The first case against the owner of the shop collapsed because of lack of evidence. The new trial, which had taken almost a year to bring to court, was over within an hour when the Sheriff's Court was told the owner had changed an earlier not guilty plea. After hours of negotiations between the prosecution and the defence solicitors representing the firm, the four original charges brought against the firm and its three directors were dropped and two new charges, against the firm only, were agreed. Sheriff Lewis Cameron imposed a fine of £750 for breaches of food hygiene regulations, and of £1,500 for supplying and selling goods contaminated with *E-coli 0157*. The maximum penalty for the first charge was £5,000, and £20,000 for the second under the Food Safety Act 1990. One of the victims said, '[i]f you believe in the courts, then you think they will actually help you fight that battle'. She added, '[y]ou put your trust in the system to find the truth. What's £2,250? It's nothing.'

When considering the types of homicide other than what could be described as standard cases of voluntary and involuntary manslaughter, regard can be had to cases of road traffic deaths. There is evidence that there may be a high number of work-related deaths that are kept out of the annual HSE fatal injury statistics. Records of road traffic deaths are compiled by the Department of Transport, which publishes the annual statistics. This means that if someone is 'at work' in a motor vehicle when they are killed the death will not be processed by the HSE. There are many occupations which cause employees or the self-employed to be driving all or some of the time: cab drivers, minicab drivers, lorry drivers, van drivers (including plumbers, builders, etc.), commercial sales representatives, delivery drivers, police officers, business people, and maintenance engineers.

There are three million company cars on the roads in Britain travelling a total of 63 thousand million miles a year. In 1989 there was one death or serious injury per 41 company cars according to the insurance company General Accident (GA) (Maryon, 1993). These incidents are not just a matter of individual responsibility. David Crichton, the UK Commercial Underwriting and Claims Manager for GA, contends that management style and lack of training contribute to the death toll. He remarked that:

> Even a matter such as tight schedules or giving sales reps too big an area can have an effect on driving standards. Drivers and managers are ever optimistic about the time it will take to get from A to B and this can result in speeding and aggressive driving (quoted in Maryon, 1993).

Jim Horne, Director of the Sleep Research Laboratory at Loughborough University, has shown that the economy seems to influence road traffic behaviour as the quality of driving in a geographical area where he has conducted research has worsened with the recession. Between 1989 and 1993 accidents on the M5 involving driver fatigue have increased by 275 per cent, company car drivers being the largest group of victims. Professor Horne and the Automobile Association consider that the recession has led to more drivers, in fear of their jobs, travelling hundreds of miles without a break – between

four and six in the morning is the most likely time for a crash.[5] He has written
(letter, 5 December 1994) about research he is currently engaged in that:

> Our own work specifically looks at driving fatigue and we find that there is a
> substantial surge of sleep-related accidents between 5 and 7 in the morning.
> Many of these drivers are either on their way to work or are coming home after
> night shifts. In particular, I think that people driving home after their first night
> on shifts are very vulnerable to falling asleep at the wheel if the drive entails
> more than 20 minutes on a dull road.

Statistics available from the records of the Office of Population Census
and Surveys[6] show that over 200 people 'at work' die on the roads each year;
a figure which represents about half of deaths from all the other types of work
combined. For example, according to the 1993/94 *Annual Report* of the HSE,
the number of people who died in the construction industry during the year
under review was 65; the fatality figure for mining was seven; the figure for
agriculture, forestry and fishing was 16; for energy and water supply industries
it was 11; for quarrying and related work it was 17; in all manufacturing
industries it was 64; and in mechanical engineering it was 11. That is a total
of 191 industrial deaths,[7] less, over a 12 month period, than the number of
workers (perhaps socially regarded as enjoying safer work) who died while
'at work' on the motorways and roads.

A review by the International Transport Workers' Federation (1987) sought
to identify the main factors in work-related road traffic deaths. It found that
long working hours was one very common factor. The accident rate rose where
drivers had been on the road for more than five hours. It rises steeply with
driving duration. There were two and a half times as many accidents where
the driver had been driving for 13 hours (with short breaks) than where the
driver had been on the road for less than 10 hours. Many long-distance lorry
drivers are effectively required by employers to be on the road for longer than
EC regulations permit.

Reports of the HSE have consistently demonstrated that most occupational
deaths were avoidable and could have been prevented by the management of
the companies concerned. *Blackspot Construction* is an HSE report that
analyses the circumstances of 739 deaths in the construction industry between
1981 and 1985. Referring to these deaths, J.D. Rimington, the then Director-
General of the HSE said, '[t]hey represent a very saddening loss of life,
particularly *because most of the deaths could have been prevented*' [emphasis
added] (Health and Safety Executive, 1988b, p. 1). The report shows that the

immediate reasons for most deaths were lack of supervision, inadequate training and lack of attention to detail:

> The figures in this report clearly show that the basic causes of the deaths of 739 people from 1981–1985 have not changed over the last ten years. There were, on average, two deaths every week on construction sites. 90% of these could have been prevented. *In 70% of cases, positive action by management could have saved lives* [emphasis added] (ibid., p. 4).

In another report, *Agricultural Blackspot*, a study of 296 deaths between 1981–84 the HSE concluded that in 62 per cent of cases 'responsibility rested with management' (HSE, 1986, p. 12). Again, in *Deadly Maintenance*, a study into deaths at work in a range of industries, the HSE concluded that 'management were primarily responsible in 54% of cases' (1985, p. 8).

The HSE's case reports and allocation of responsibility in studies like *Blackspot Construction* further demonstrate that the criteria for reckless manslaughter appear, *prima facie*, to be present in many of the cases which, if they are prosecuted, are only charged as regulatory offences under the Health and Safety at Work Act 1974. For example, in its study of roofwork deaths we learn that 'In the vast majority of fatal accidents on roofs, management and those in charge of the work did not exercise sufficient control to ensure that relatively simple precautions were taken' (HSE, 1987, p. 27). Looking at demolition and dismantling, the HSE note that 95 people died doing this type of work during the period under review and says 'of the 95 accidents, 67 were caused by management allowing unsafe systems of work to be used' (HSE, 1988b, p. 31). It is worthy of note that in both of these statements, the word 'accidents' is used to describe deaths for which there are, on the HSE's own admission, identifiable persons who have played a substantial part in causing the deaths. In other contexts it would seem quite improper to refer to such cases as 'accidents'. Even if the word 'accidents' is used to convey the meaning of 'unintentional killing' this is unhelpful.

On 30 April 1981, Edward Seymour knocked down Iris Burrows with his lorry and killed her. In one sense this was an 'accident' because it was not an intentional killing. However, Mr Seymour was convicted of the serious crime of reckless manslaughter for this incident and was sentenced to five years imprisonment (*R v Seymour* [1983]). This use of the term 'accident' (and its grammatical variants) proliferates through the HSE literature and is very misleading. The point is of more than linguistic significance. The use of such terminology reflects a tacit assumption about the nature of these deaths (even when HSE evidence in the same sentence contradicts the suitability of such a word) and helps promote such an image in the public perception.

It can be argued that many thousands of instances of one of the most serious crimes on the criminal calendar are not being prosecuted as such. Some are left as 'accidents' whilst others are dealt with as administrative offences. The fact that there is no intention to kill in these cases should not lessen the aversion with which they are treated. In orthodox morality, intention to do wrong is regarded with greater abhorrence than recklessness as to whether or not harm occurs, but as Reiman has argued (1979, p. 60), a reverse formula can be just as cogent: if a person intends doing *someone* harm there is no reason to assume that s/he poses a wider social threat or will manifest a contempt for the community at large, whereas if indifference or recklessness characterises the attitude a person has towards the consequences of his or her actions, then s/he can be seen as having a serious contempt for society at large.

## Notes

1 The legislation did not produce a panic where before there was absolute calm. There was, before the Act, much anxious competition between rival corporations. There was evidence that many of the charters granted to companies were defective (and therefore invalid) and that trading entities were reluctant to pay the Crown the sums required for incorporation.
2 *R v Alcindor and others*, 5 June 1990, Central Criminal Court, Newgate Reporters transcript, p. 5; *P&O European Ferries (Dover) Ltd* [1991], p. 83.
3 See e.g. *The Guardian*, 13 March 1991 and 2 November 1991; *The Times*, 11 September 1990.
4 Doctors, dentists, a competing rugby payer, a couple of men who discharged a distress flare at a football match, and a female priestess who killed the subject of an exorcism have all recently been prosecuted for manslaughter. I cite these in endnote 12 in chapter 4.
5 *The Safety and Health Practitioner*, September, 1993, p. 4.
6 I am grateful to Nick Croll (Medical Support and Disease Classifications) for assistance in sifting through the raw data and in helping me piece together the figures. Reference was also made to the OPCS *Occupational Mortality* Decennial Supplement parts 1 and 2 1979–80, 1982–83.
7 These figures are from the *HSE Annual Report*, 1993/4, statistical supplement, table 1(a).

# 3 The Legal Process (1): The Police, the CPS and the HSE

Rules guide their subjects to act in certain ways; that is their purpose. Those who act officially in response to deaths at work do so within a framework of law. Their actions are governed by a quite complex matrix of regulations which flow from a raft of health and safety Acts; statutory instruments made pursuant to that legislation; legislation and regulations governing the coroner's jurisdiction, rights and duties; legislation governing the Crown Prosecution Service; the law of evidence and procedure; and the body of accumulated case law which determines other matters such as the limits within which coronial discretion must be exercised.

When people act officially, regulated by certain laws and rules, in response to a uniform and regular phenomenon – like deaths at work – then, *ceteris paribus,* they produce predictable outcomes.

As noted earlier (chapter 2), many deaths at work do not present themselves as possible cases for investigation as potential corporate manslaughter prosecutions. In the case studies undertaken by the author, 48 per cent of those investigated were not filtered out of the criminal justice system's prosecution of manslaughter processes by any systemic defect. The cases were simply not suitable for such a charge either because their essential facts presented as unsuitable for investigation along such lines or insofar as negligence could be established against employers, it was insufficient to pass the 'gross negligence' test; neither was there the necessary 'unlawful and dangerous act' for constructive manslaughter. Of the remaining cases which could, on their facts, have been better investigated for manslaughter, 20 per cent of them presented a *prima facie* case and should have properly been passed by police or HSE inspectors to the CPS. One of the main contentions of this study is that suitable cases are simply not reaching the proper stages of the criminal justice process – they are not being referred to the CPS and are, consequently, not coming to trial.

There are principally eight stages in the mechanical legal process that are geared to filtering out deaths at work cases from the criminal justice system.

The gearing, however, is not the conscious, conspiratorial work of the various types of personnel acting in concert. These people – coroners, coroners' officers, police officers, HSE inspectors, HSE directors, lawyers and prosecutors – are not *ad idem* about the overall policy that is eventually produced. Each is simply acting to solve his or her own problems in the way that seems most appropriate to them in their separate circumstances. The aggregate policy resulting from these constituent decisions is one largely consonant with the interests of capital, viz. avoiding too serious a deterrent to the risk-taking which is a part of competitive industry both under pressure to expand quickly in economic booms (Box, 1983, pp. 16–80; Carson, 1981) and, under increased pressure to cut corners during slumps (Clinard and Yeager, 1981; Box, 1987).

This chapter examines the first three stages of the legal process involving the police, CPS and HSE. As they however hinge primarily on the exercise of discretions which operate according to certain assumptions and perspectives of the relevant personnel, they are examined in detail in chapter five. The following chapter then considers the inquest procedure and how the role of the coroner, lawyers, and costs, resources and awkward law can affect the outcome of the inquest and help shape prosecutorial policy of corporate manslaughter.


## The Police Involvement

Following phraseology used by Robert Peel in his introduction, in the House of Commons, of what became the Metropolitan Police Act 1828 one of the primary purposes of modern police forces in Britain is the 'detection of crime'. Manslaughter is a serious crime. If, according to the definitions in contemporary criminal law, and the facts leading to and causing the deaths of many people at work, manslaughter is occurring in even 10 per cent of workplace fatalities and this study suggests that there is a *prima facie* case in 20 per cent of the deaths then that would mean, for example, on 1992–93 figures,[1] about 45 manslaughter cases (almost one a week) going unprosecuted. Such an omission would clearly be more significant than a discovery that there was a 10 per cent shortfall in prosecutions for, say, 'theft from shops' where there are already so many prosecutions: 61,016 in 1993.[2] The difference between no prosecutions (or one during 1994, *R v Kite and others*) and 43 prosecutions per year, in terms of the public consciousness of the crime and deterrent effects such prosecutions may have, is far greater than the difference that would be made to public consciousness and deterrence by a 10 per cent increase in prosecutions for 'theft from shops', which would simply push up the number from 61,016 to 67,118.

After a death at work has been reported, police officers visit the scene of the death and if the officer is satisfied that there is no apparent evidence suggesting that the deceased may have been killed by a fellow worker in circumstances that would amount to murder (i.e. death as the result of the defendant's conduct; which conduct the defendant performed intending that his victim should suffer death or serious bodily harm – *R v Hancock & Shankland* [1986]), then he will file a brief report and leave the matter to be dealt with by the HSE inspectorate.

In brief, one of the main procedural reasons why there are so few prosecutions for corporate manslaughter is that after a workplace death the police, usually, take only short statements from a company spokesperson and do not interview key personnel in the employing company because responsibility for investigating these deaths is seen to live with the HSE. The police are influenced by their training to regard work deaths as accidents. An entry from a training instructions (which also appears in the Computerised Help Desk for Operational Police Officers, a service which officers can tap into at police stations for quick current advice), reads:

> All inquiries into industrial fatal *accidents* should be conducted in liaison with the Health and Safety Inspectorate, who should be provided with copies of all witness statements [emphasis added].

Fatal incidents are thus officially labelled as accidents before they have been investigated.

Another legal obstacle in the way of a proper police investigation is an evidential difficulty. Evidence may lie in boardroom documents, but the police may encounter difficulty in getting a warrant to search for such documents unless they can show a serious crime has taken place;[3] showing that the death was the result of a serious crime (as opposed to a breach of regulation) may be impossible without access to the boardroom papers for which the warrant is sought. Chief Constable John Hoddinott made this observation:

> the offence of manslaughter turns on there being some gross negligence or recklessness. Unless you show the gross negligence or recklessness you haven't got an offence, and yet to go searching for evidence you need an offence that justifies your search. So, in a sense, it becomes circular – you might be in a

position where you can't go searching for the evidence because you haven't got an offence and you haven't got an offence until you can go searching for the evidence.

These deaths are alone in being regarded by the legal system as properly investigated by a body other than the police. Even other areas of non-conventional crime, for example Road Traffic Act offences, are regarded as sufficiently serious to be dealt with by the police. Yet the HSE is only concerned with violations of the Health and Safety at Work Etc. Act 1974, *not* with serious crimes like manslaughter.

In April, 1998 the HSE issued a statement in which it announced a change of policy whereby both the police and the HSE will attend the scene of a work-related death, and the police will conduct an investigation where there is an indication of manslaughter (or another serious criminal offence). The HSE will also investigate possible offences under the HSWA, but will not lay any information until the police and the CPS have reached a decision. Where the police decide that a charge of manslaughter or other serious offence outside the HSWA cannot be justified, the HSE will continue with its own investigation. If during the course of its investigation there is evidence indicating that an offence of manslaughter may have been committed, it will refer the matter to the police without delay. The protocol also deals with procedures where the CPS and HSE prosecute and the other wishes to retain an interest, joint prosecutions, and liaison at national and local level (Ecclestone, 1998).

How this works out in practice remains to be seen, although the observations made in this chapter (concerning operational methods), and in chapter 5 (concerning police perceptions) remain unaffected by the HSE announcement.

The incorporation of road traffic deaths into the jurisdiction of ordinary policing is instructive. One of the principal arguments advanced by those who support the 'negotiated compliance' approach to dealing with deaths and injuries at work (Bardach and Kagan, 1982; Hawkins, 1991) is that the conduct of employers which results in such harms is not intrinsically criminal. One senior officer of the HSE expressed the idea to the writer thus:

> when they go to work, employers don't go about their business in a way which shows they are up to no good. They don't set out to do anything wrong. They don't want any harm to happen to their employees. Most of the time it's wrong to start looking at them as criminals.

Similarly, John Rimington, former Director-General of the HSE, has said that offences against the safety of workers are not like ordinary criminal offences, even when they result in death:

> they are different from, let's say going out with intent to kill, murder [sic], rob or maim. They are usually, almost invariably negligence – sometimes just honest mistakes or errors; sometimes recklessness but that's the nature of the offence.[4]

This reasoning can be refuted in two respects: first, crimes are generally not defined by intention; and second, many crimes *do* arise from intrinsically lawful behaviour. We can examine each point more closely. The former Director-General of the HSE appears to demonstrate a remarkable misunderstanding of law in general and criminal law in particular. There are, in English law, over 7,200 separate offences (Seighart, 1980, p. 15). Most of these offences do not require the prosecution to prove that the defendant *intended* to produce the result that was produced; they are crimes involving the *mens rea* of recklessness or gross negligence, or they are strict liability crimes (e.g. violating licensing laws) which require no proof as to the defendant's state of mind. There are, in fact, about 3,750 such offences. It is, therefore, quite inappropriate to argue that injurious acts or omissions committed by employers are not crimes simply because they are not committed with intentional malice.

As to the other, related argument – that such injurious conduct is not really criminal because it flows from the performance of inherently legal conduct i.e. employment – this also is unsatisfactory. The same argument could be applied to death and injury caused by driving: the criminal law should not be used forcefully against those who make serious errors because the dangerous drivers did not set out to do something malicious, they were merely doing something legal very poorly. Such an argument, however, would be regarded as nonsensical by almost everyone with experience of criminal law and road traffic. The CPS prosecutes about 300 people annually for causing death by dangerous driving contrary to section 1 of the Road Traffic Act 1991. Most are given custodial sentences. Additionally, some drivers who kill in the course of dangerous driving are prosecuted for manslaughter.[5]

Let us consider these points in more detail. There is no legal reason why the police should not investigate a company and its directors after a workplace death. In none of the 40 case studies undertaken by the author did the police mount any kind of serious investigation, even where there was clear *prima facie* evidence that the deceased worker may have been the victim of organisational or managerial negligence. The police attended the death scene in every one of the 40 cases involved, as indeed, they are bound to do. Police officers attended the inquest in every case, again as they are bound to in order to give testimony as to identification, the general practice being that the deceased's next of kin identifies the body to a police officer who then identifies that body to the pathologist. In 38 of the 40 cases the police officer made no more than quick routine inquiries, as soon as he or she had noted that there were no 'suspicious circumstances'. In two cases the police indicated that they had made inquiries to ensure that there had been no foul play. The scenarios in question were those where the indices of suspicion used by police officers could reasonably have alerted the officer to the possibility of a crime: where the deceased had been working in the vicinity of others; where there may have been a motive from some vendetta between co-workers; where there would have been an opportunity for the crime to have been committed and yet give the appearance of an accident.[6]

One notable exception to the general reluctance of the police to initiate criminal investigations is the case of George Kenyon.[7] In May 1988 George Kenyon was working at Holt Plastics Ltd, a plastics crumbling firm in Lancashire. His job involved taking old or defective plastic bags and sheeting and putting them in to a 'crumbling machine'. This is a large metal vat about four feet high and four feet in diameter. Inside, a pair of rotating blades travel at 1,200 revolutions per minute with the force of a V12 Jaguar engine. The machine looked like a giant food processor. A safety device on the machine which prevented it from working while the lid was open had been deliberately re-wired so that the machine could work when the lid was open. This defeating of the safety system was to increase productivity, allowing a worker to collect the plastic bags, put them into the machine, turn around and repeat the operation (for hours at a time) without having to stop to put the lid up and down. Keeping the lid open and the huge blades spinning was especially hazardous as much of the plastic to be disposed of was in a continuous roll. One day, George Kenyon, near the end of a 12 hour shift, was putting a strip of the plastic roll into the machine. The end was caught by the blades and pulled very sharply in while the next part of the roll got caught around Mr Kenyon's upper body, probably his neck, and pulled him into the machine head first. Mr Kenyon was minced to death. As his father explained: 'they had to scrape George out of the machine and bury him in a coffin with almost nothing in it'.

Holt Bros. Ltd was a small family business which was, according to people who worked there, a very tough place to be employed. Employment, however, was very difficult to obtain in that area of Lancashire, so many workers endured more than they would have in other places or other circumstances. The company had been caught by the HSE five years before Mr Kenyon's death doing almost exactly the same thing – defeating a safety system on a potentially lethal machine in order to improve productivity.

Winifred Whitworth, George Kenyon's sister, gave evidence that her brother was often complaining to her about the appalling disregard for safety at Holt Bros. Asked why he did not make any formal complaint at work, she replied (inquest transcript): 'because he were frightened of saying anything, that he'd lose his job'.

The directors of the company, brothers David and Norman Holt, were tried for health and safety offences and manslaughter at Preston Crown Court in November 1989. For the first time in English legal history, a director, Norman Holt was found guilty of manslaughter in respect of a workplace death. The company was found guilty of health and safety offences and fined £500 for failing to register a factory (s.137 Factories Act 1961); failing to securely fence machinery (s.14(1) of the same Act) for which it was fined £25,000 – plus £10,000 costs – and, for breach of a prohibition notice (under s.33 of HSWA 1974), it was fined £1,000. David and Norman Holt were fined £15,000 and £5,000 under s. 37 of the HSWA 1974 for condoning the company breaches of the Factories Act, and David was fined another £500 under s.37(1) for the s.33 breaches.

The outcomes can be seen as unsatisfactory in several respects. First, the charge of manslaughter was dropped against David Holt, who was the leading director and the person at whose behest the machine's safety had been defeated. Norman was nominally a director but actually took no managerial role and worked on the shop floor. He said, when he discontinued instructing the same solicitor as his brother, he (Norman) was told: 'It's like an old Al Capone movie. You take the dive and you will be looked after.' The Crown said it dropped charges of manslaughter against David Holt through want of evidence against him, yet there were several witnesses in court on that day ready to testify against him. They could not understand the Crown's decision. Even the judge, Mr Justice Otten, expressed his dissatisfaction with counsel's decision. There appeared in this case to have been a breach of the Crown Prosecution Service's guidelines to Crown Prosecutors which states, under a heading of 'Accepting guilty pleas' (1994, p. 14):

> Crown Prosecutors should only accept the defendant's plea [to the prohibition notice breach, etc.] if they think the court is able to pass a sentence that matches the seriousness of the offending. Crown Prosecutors must never accept a guilty plea just because it is convenient.

The breach of the prohibition notice was in respect of an incident two days after the gruesome death of George Kenyon. When Mr Connor returned to the premises to continue writing his reports, he found that the machine, not long having had the minced remains of Mr Kenyon rinsed and hosed off it, was in operation again, *still with the lid up and the safety device defeated.*

Counsel in this case considered, but chose not to proceed with, a corporate manslaughter charge. It was felt that such a charge would not properly target the real human culprits.[8] The success of the police investigations and prosecution for manslaughter here seem to rest on the peculiar facts of the case: the terrible cause of death; the deliberate, easily-provable tampering with the safety mechanism; the firm's only having two directors; and the motivation for the tampering – to increase profit. The investigation was led by Detective Inspector Harry Hargreaves of the Lancashire police. Commenting on the oddity of a police investigation of this sort, Inspector Hargreaves said:

> It is very unusual for police to conduct an investigation like this but then this case was so different ... the evidence was far more, perhaps, than where people may consider manslaughter charges appropriate.[9]

Another case in which a police investigation led to manslaughter charges was in 1990 of P&O Ferries, arising from the capsize of *The Herald of Free Enterprise* in 1987 (Wells, 1993a, pp. 68–72, 111–13). On 7 March, 192 people were killed when the vessel capsized off Zeebrugge, having sailed with its bow doors open. There was, however, no automatic police investigation into the company's safety policy and attitude (Bergman, 1993, p. 4). The police did not launch a criminal investigation until November 1987, eight months after the disaster and three months after the publication of the public inquiry report. The police became involved only after the inquest jury in September returned verdicts of 'unlawful killing'. As will be noted (below) the coroner tried to avoid the unlawful killing verdict by telling the jury: (a) that, legally, companies could not commit manslaughter; and (b) that, even if he was wrong about that, P&O European Ferries (Dover) Ltd could not be found guilty of the recklessness [then] necessary for an 'unlawful killing' verdict as there was insufficient proof that the directors had been reckless. The High Court said that a company could be guilty of manslaughter (*R v HM Coroner for East Kent* [1989]) and the jury, in the teeth of the coroner's advice (he suggested accidental death would be most appropriate), returned a verdict of 'unlawful killing'. It was only after all this, and the threat of a private prosecution if the

Crown refused to act, that the DPP instructed Kent police to investigate the matter thoroughly.

On 8 December 1994, OLL Ltd became the first company in English legal history to be convicted of homicide. Peter Kite, 45, its managing director, also became the first director to be given an immediate custodial sentence for a manslaughter conviction arising from the operation of a business (Slapper, 1994f). Both defendants were found guilty on four counts of manslaughter arising from the death of four teenagers who drowned off Lyme Regis while on a canoe trip, on 22 March 1993, organised by the defendant leisure activity company. OLL Ltd was the company that ran the St Albans Centre. The same charges were brought against Joseph Stoddart, manager of the centre.

Mr Kite was sentenced to three years imprisonment; the company was fined £60,000. Mr Stoddart was acquitted on the direction of the judge when the jury at Winchester Crown Court failed to reach a verdict after deliberating for 92 hours.

An appalling catalogue of errors led to the deaths of the four teenagers, who drowned having been in the sea for over four hours after their canoes capsized. According to evidence given in court by people familiar with canoeing, the trip should never have taken place. Prior to the trip, the teenagers had received only one hour of tuition in a swimming pool by unqualified staff. The weather forecast on the day of the trip had not been checked properly, distress flares were not provided by the company, and the only safety equipment possessed by the instructors was a whistle. The students' canoes did not have 'spray decks' to keep out water. Nine months before the disaster two instructors had left the company because they were not satisfied with its safety policy. One wrote a letter to the managing director, Mr Kite, urging him to take a 'careful look' at safety otherwise he might find himself explaining 'why someone's son or daughter will not be coming home'.

Giving evidence, one witness, a former instructor at the company, testified that the safety standards were 'practically non-existent'. First aid kits, flares, hooded waterproofs, and tow ropes were not provided.

Saving on these costs, although endangering children, clearly benefited those who enjoyed the company's profits: OLL Ltd made a profit of £242,603 in the year ending October 1992 (20 weeks before the drownings), 13 per cent up on previous figures.

The activity centre did not alert the rescue services when the canoeists failed to arrive at their destination on time, as the centre was unaware of what time the students had departed. The planned trip – two miles on open sea – was alarmingly unsuitable for such novices, and the coastguard had not been alerted. The court was told that the instructors were barely competent to make the trip themselves, let alone supervise the eight children and their teacher.

When, very belatedly, Mr Stoddart did begin to worry about the safety of those on the trip, he tried to look for them himself by driving a car along coastal roads before he alerted the coastguards, and then, when he did alert the rescue services, he wrongly told them that the children had flares.

The Lyme Regis conviction may well have symbolic significance, and have a chastening effect on businesses which currently adopt a cavalier attitude to safety. How far it will affect the number of prosecutions in future is questionable. The case was arguably atypical of corporate homicide scenarios. The company, OLL Ltd, was small (Kite and Stoddart were the only people with directorial and managerial control over the company's affairs), so it was relatively easy to find the 'controlling minds'; the risks to which the students were exposed were serious and obvious and also, critically, they were not technical or esoteric in any way (anyone can see the dereliction of duty involved in not providing competent supervisors, flares, a lookout boat, in not notifying the harbour authority, etc.). For the prosecution there was also the serendipitous evidence of the letter from the former employees which indisputably made the managing director aware of the risks in question; risks which, as the prosecution was able to show, were not subsequently addressed with any seriousness.

Like the first successful prosecutions following the belated legal recognition that a husband can rape his wife (*R v R* [1992]), there is an appreciable significance in this historic conviction of a homicidal company. The effect of this may be, as Durkheim observed (1984, 1893, p. 63) to enhance social solidarity as the social foe is condemned: 'to heal the wounds inflicted upon the collective sentiments'. Any consequential instrumental effect of the verdict in the Lyme Regis case (such as a demonstrable improvement in national safety as erstwhile cavalier directors are jolted to review their policies; or an increase in the number of similar prosecutions) can only properly be judged in time by examining the annual tolls of commercially-related death and injury.

The most useful inference to be drawn from the 40 cases of workplace deaths in which there was no police investigation and the cases where there is, is that police investigations are likely to be mounted in the following circumstances: where (a) there are multiple deaths (like the Zeebrugge case); or (b) there is an unusually damning piece of evidence – such as the letter in the Lyme Regis tragedy; or (c) the facts are particularly horrific and present as similar to an ordinary crime (like the case of George Kenyon).

## The Crown Prosecution Service

The HSE has argued that the decisions by the CPS not to prosecute in many cases indicates that the crime of manslaughter is not applicable to workplace deaths (Bergman, 1994, p. 10). However, Bergman notes that the CPS's decisions were made in the majority of cases without requesting a CID investigation, i.e. it was made solely on the basis of the investigations by the enforcement agencies; and that particular cases that have been referred to the CPS have not *necessarily* been those where manslaughter is an appropriate charge, but because of attempts by solicitors and relatives to gain greater criminal accountability; and there appears to be a reluctance – perhaps political – on the part of the CPS to consider prosecution of company officers for manslaughter. Another reason, he conjectures, that might explain the CPS's limited involvement in manslaughter prosecutions after workplace deaths is its failure in 1989 to succeed in the prosecution of three directors for the Zeebrugge disaster.

There were only three other cases during the period 1991–94 where unlawful killing verdicts were returned by inquest juries in respect of work-related cases, resulting in the coroner's being forced to refer the case to the CPS; a period during which there were 1,425 deaths at work.

In the first, on 19 October 1993, an inquest jury in London returned a verdict that two men who died when a bridge they were demolishing collapsed on top of them were unlawfully killed. There was a starkly inadequate provision of a safe system of work and the incident was captured on video.[10]

The second took place on 28 February 1994, when a jury in West Yorkshire decided that six people who were killed when a lorry ran out of control, crashing into a car and a van before ploughing into shops, died as a result of 'involuntary unlawful killing'. The coroner said he had found a high standard of proof that the owners of the lorry were 'grossly negligent'. The brakes on the lorry were badly defective, as were the brakes on other lorries owned by the firm, and evidence was given to the inquest showing that the deaths could probably have been avoided if the brakes had been in a legal condition. The coroner said: 'That breach of duty arose from gross negligence to such a degree which should, in the opinion of this coroner's court, justify a conviction'.[11]

The third was on 5 May 1994, when an inquest jury in Kent found that nine American tourists and their driver (who was 'at work') had been killed unlawfully when the coach they were in crashed on the M2 in Kent. It was found that the company which owned the coach had detached speed limiters on the vehicle in question and on other vehicles in their fleet. The device, if untampered with, would prevent the coach travelling over 70 mph; in fact the vehicle was travelling at least 78 mph in wet conditions when it crashed.

In each of these three cases, the coroner sent the files to the CPS for consideration of manslaughter charges. In each of these cases the CPS decided not to prosecute, judging that it would be too difficult to satisfy the relevant evidential test set out in the *Code for Crown Prosecutors* (Crown Prosecution Service, 1994, p. 5) that

> there is enough evidence to provide a 'realistic prospect of conviction' ... a realistic prospect of conviction is an objective test. This test means that a jury or bench of magistrates, properly directed in accordance with the law, is more likely than not to convict the defendant of the charge alleged.[12]

Coroners can and do refer cases, prior to the inquest, to the CPS. In September 1990, three workers were asphyxiated by hydrogen sulphide whilst unblocking drains in Wateney Market, East London and in 1992, Tony Fishendon was electrocuted whilst working for a firm subcontracted to British Rail. The St Pancras coroner referred all these deaths to the CPS. The Southwark coroner also referred the deaths of Frank Warren, 42, and Nicholas Scott, 22, who were killed in the demolition of St John's Bridge, south London. No manslaughter prosecutions took place in any of these cases (Bergman, 1994, p. 10).

Two other workplace deaths referred to the Crown Prosecution Service, only happened after bereaved relatives of these workers had campaigned for many months and had written to the Attorney General. Again, no prosecutions took place (ibid.).

Similar findings resulted from my study of 40 workplace deaths. Only three were referred to the CPS, two by the HSE, the other by the police. Ultimately, in both instances, manslaughter prosecutions were rejected. In the first case, it was the difficulty of obtaining testimony which really defeated such a prosecution. A worker on board a large freight vessel docked in port was crushed by a load of timber he was helping to unload. The HSE inspector involved felt there was a sufficiently high level of blameworthiness in a least two of the firms involved to warrant such a charge. The problem for the CPS was identifying the locus of responsibility with sufficient confidence to put the case before a jury. The relevant evidential test (Crown Prosecution Service, 1994, p. 5) requires the CPS to weigh up, apart from the case against any prospective defendant, 'what the defence case may be and how that is likely to affect the prosecution case'. The complexity of organisational responsibility around the worker who was killed seemed to deter the Crown from proceeding. The deceased was placed in a highly dangerous situation, where he eventually received severe injuries which killed him. Who was responsible? The small firm of about 15 dock workers for which he worked; the contractor which engaged that firm; or the port authority? Each company exercised control over various aspects of the working practices which affected the victim in his work. In addition to this, the CPS had been informed that one of the key witnesses had left the city and could not be traced.

These issues are, however, related to resources and political will. If the hold being unloaded had happened to have been a much larger one and the number of people killed in the incident had been, say, 26; or one of the deceased was the President of the Board of Trade who was on a sightseeing tour of the docks, then perhaps the work it would have taken to (a) identify the locus of corporate responsibility, or (b) trace the missing witness, would have been carried out. These issues are further examined in chapter 5.

Manslaughter charges were considered by the CPS in the second of the two cases, but discounted for a more disturbing reason: incomprehension of the law.

The core of this case was that the deceased was being asked to work manoeuvring, at the top of a quarry, a very large, heavy lorry, with no effective brakes. The employer had no effective maintenance system. The person whose job it was to maintain vehicles had no qualifications and no relevant training. A worker was killed when his lorry crashed because the brakes failed to let him stop the vehicle. A letter obtained by the author from a senior CPS Prosecutor to a senior police officer dealing with the issues in the case revealed that: a) the prosecutor from the outset of his deliberations seemed to think that the expression 'unlawful killing' is synonymous with murder; an error excusable in a lay person but not in a second year law undergraduate and certainly not in a senior Crown Prosecutor. If the victim died through the gross negligence of anyone then that would be an unlawful killing, viz. the serious crime of manslaughter.

Such an error cannot, in these circumstances, be dismissed simply as mere logomachy. It evinces a fundamental misunderstanding of legal categories which are critical to the decision the prosecutor is being asked to make.

(b) The mechanic who knew the vehicle was to be manoeuvred at the tops of quarries was responsible for the maintenance of the vehicle which turned out to have no effective brakes, but had no qualifications for his job and had not been trained to service the type of vehicle in question. The deceased died from multiple injuries when his vehicle failed to stop at the top of a quarry. It may well have been that, in the context of earlier similar accidents or near-misses, the incident which killed the driver could be perceived as evidencing gross negligence on the part of the company. The prosecutor, however, did not seem to appreciate the significance of this, and made no attempt to solicit such information or to invite the police (perhaps in conjunction with the HSE) to investigate this matter.

There was no mention of the other vehicles in the fleet being checked to indicate how far the incompetence extended. One would need to know this in order to be able to decide whether the company operation of maintenance was, systemically, negligent.

(c) The prosecutor observed that 'whilst contributory negligence does not form part of Criminal Law, in this case, it goes to negate gross negligence on the part of any other party'. This is quite incorrect. The clearly established rule of causation in homicide is the defendant can be convicted if his acts or omissions were a 'significant cause' of the victim's death (*R v Cheshire* [1991]). If the maintenance system was as hopeless as it seemed to have been, such that there were no effective brakes on the vehicle, then the company's excuse that 'we did not know about it because the worker did not report the failure' cannot be countenanced. Even if it is true that the driver did not report the state of the vehicle, any reasonable system of maintenance should have detected the faults. If he did not report the faults, his omission may have been so as to avoid making a fuss (he was the only contract worker at the quarry, the others being employees, and so a renewed contract may have been seen by him as depending upon getting on with the work without complaining). Even so, in the context of the criminal law, if the conduct of the defendant is criminally negligent, the additional negligence of the victim is immaterial. In a case concerning defendants who had run over another man, Chief Baron Pollock directed the jury that it was immaterial that the victim was deaf or drunk or negligent and contributed to his own death (*R v Swindall and Osborn* [1846]).

(d) The best excuse given by the man responsible for the brakes was that the rear brakes – which were not at a setting to have any effect at all – *could have been contaminated with mud, thus giving the appearance of being in contact with the brake drum and needing no adjustment.* Mechanics are not usually employed to test brakes – probably the most critical part of any vehicle check – by just looking at them. Curiously, the prosecutor says in the letter that the mechanic's story was 'credible'.

There is now some evidence of a sea-change in attitude towards negligent employers (Slapper, 1997). Since legal history was made in 1994, when OLL Ltd became the first company to be convicted of homicide, another company,

Jackson Transport (Osset) Ltd, has been convicted of manslaughter, along with one of its directors, James Hodgson. This was a prosecution conducted in 1996 by special casework staff in CPS Yorkshire in cooperation with the HSE, who prosecuted certain breaches of health and safety law. Hodgson was imprisoned for 12 months and fined £1500, and the company fined £22,000. The case arose from the death of a 21 year-old employee who died after being sprayed in the face with the toxic chemical while cleaning chemical residues from a road tanker.

## The HSE/ECD Inspector's Involvement

Reckless corporate killings can be seen, in some aspects worse than murders. In orthodox morality intention to do wrong is regarded with greater abhorrence than recklessness as to whether or not harm occurs, but, as Reiman has argued (1979, p. 60), a reverse formula can be just as cogent: if a person intends doing *someone* harm there is no reason to assume that s/he poses a wider social threat or will manifest a contempt for the community at large, whereas if indifference or recklessness characterises the attitude a person has towards the consequences of his or her actions then s/he can be seen as having a serious contempt for society at large.

Murder is commonly regarded as the most heinous criminal wrong, although there is a good case for arguing that reckless killing is a socially more abhorrent and inimical offence. Most murders are committed by people who know or are related to their victims. They may, for example, have lived together for 20 years – the killer being a female partner who had been regularly beaten until she reacted with lethal force. Of the 297 female victims of homicide in 1991, 41 per cent were killed by partners, 20 per cent by their family (mainly parents) and only 14 per cent by strangers. In only 8 per cent was there no suspect. Of the 387 male homicide victims during the same year, 8 per cent were killed by partners, and 36 per cent were killed by 'friends [sic] or associates'.[13]

Most of these killers are, therefore, unlikely to re-offend in the same way, and are appreciably less of a social threat than the cavalier director whose work practices have killed but who is free to continue running the same company, or set up another one elsewhere.

The HSE deals only with offences under the HSWA 1974 and related legislation, and has generally not been referring serious cases of death at work to the CPS, although there is evidence that its policy is beginning to change on this issue. The police, who could initiate criminal inquiries and eventually pass the matter to the CPS, do not. They proceed on the basis that the inspector from the HSE or Environmental Health Department (EHD) will deal with the case. In these circumstances, therefore, consideration of manslaughter is systematically excluded. As Lacey et al. have explained (1990, p. 243), regulatory schemes are seen as quasi-criminal and tend to be couched in terms of failure to follow a prescribed process rather than being directed towards results, so that 'whereas conventional crime prohibits causing grievous bodily harm, safety regulations are concerned with failure to fence dangerous machinery'.

There is, thus, behind the annual figures for Health and Safety at Work Act convictions, a catalogue of injuries and deaths which do not feature as part of any official crime statistics.

The HSE has severely restricted resources (Foley, 1990, p. 8; Bergman, 1994, p. 99; Moore, 1991, p. 29) and has been mainly concerned, according to its former Director-General, John Rimington, to 'negotiate compliance' with employers. The 'primary effort' of the Executive was 'of assisting and advising the generality of well-conducted companies' (cited in Bergman, 1990a, p. 1108). For these reasons the HSE has not been as tenacious in pressing for a manslaughter charge as it might have been.

The HSE and CPS have responded to criticism by arguing that it is unnecessary for the police to be involved in the full investigation since the HSE will itself refer suitable cases to the CPS for its consideration. John Rimington stated that HSE inspectors receive thorough training in all aspects of criminal law which they need for their work, including guidance on when to refer a case to the police: 'Discussions between the HSE inspector and the police will take place if the most appropriate charge is one not available to an HSE inspector'.

Between 1974, when the HSE was established and 1990, there were over 9,050 deaths at work, yet the HSE had evidently not referred any case to the police or (1986–90) to the CPS. In 1991, investigations made by the author found little evidence of such a procedure being put into effect. Of the 40 cases examined in my study, at least eight (20 per cent) should, according to the facts of those cases, the evidence available (including testimony) and current legal definitions of manslaughter, have been further investigated with a view to testing whether there was, according to the CPS's important criterion (Crown Prosecution Service, 1994, p. 5.1), a 'realistic prospect of conviction'. Bergman (1994) has suggested that the percentage of cases prosecutable as manslaughter may be as high as 40 per cent.

There were parts of the eight cases warranting referral which did not appear to have been given sufficient weight by the HSE, or were not the subject of a thorough investigation. In these cases, the grief and loss suffered by the bereaved (often vented at the inquest) is just as intense and chronic as it is in conventional manslaughter cases, or those which stem from the causing of death by dangerous driving. Here, however, the state is conspicuously less interested. The HSE referred only two of the 40 cases to the CPS for consideration in relation to manslaughter charges, although there were eight which I considered should, on current law and prosecution criteria, have been at least the subject of referrals.[14]

It is not argued that rigorous prosecution of these cases, with swingeing fines against companies or custodial sentences for directors, would eradicate the problem of death at work (Slapper, 1994b). The principal interest is to examine how, and then why, there is an apparently casual attitude from the state in respect of workplace deaths when the level of blameworthiness in culprits, the loss to the bereaved and the general injury to society are equivalent to their correlatives in ordinary crime.

In none of these cases was there any evidence given concerning the previous safety record of the company or employer. This was, in each case, a serious omission. In order to be able to judge properly whether a certain incident arose from employer negligence, it would seem critical to know what, if any, warnings the employer had had about the danger which eventually materialised. The HSE inspector could take as evidence the company's accident book[15] and give the court a summary of any relevant entries. This procedure was used in none of the 40 cases. Sometimes a scrutiny of the company's history on accidents would exonerate it (especially if the inspector testified that the accident happened in an unforeseeable or inexplicable way). Sometimes, though, previous similar incidents could show that the risk which eventuated was demonstrably 'obvious and serious' to those who represented the 'controlling mind' (see chapter 2) of the company.

It is not argued here that these incidents *were* crimes. It is argued that there is strong *prima facie* evidence that they may have been, and that the question was not properly investigated by the criminal justice system.

The first successful prosecution for manslaughter for a workplace death which was taken against a director in 1990 (*R v Holt Bros.*) was referred to the CPS by the police not the HSE. The same is true of the *P&O European Ferries (Dover) Ltd* case and the Lyme Regis canoe case. A number of publications put the allegation on the public record (Bergman, 1992 and 1993; Wells, 1993a; Slapper, 1992a, 1993b).

The reluctance of the HSE officers to refer cases to the police or CPS becomes clear in the context of its self-avowed policy of negotiated compliance with the safety laws (HSE, 1989, pp. 4–5). This policy can be traced back from the 1974 legislation to the 1972 Robens Report which led to the Act. The report stated (p. 6) that:

> the traditional concepts of the criminal are not readily applicable to the majority of infringements which arise under this type of legislation. Relatively few cases are clear cut, few arise from reckless indifference to the possibility of causing injury, few can be laid at the door of a particular individual.

This thinking was drawn in turn from the ethos behind the 1833 Factory Act which set out to 'regulate the Labour of Children and Young Persons in the Mills and Factories of the United Kingdom'. In order not to constrain the economic development taking place in the nineteenth century, factory inspection, despite its operation under the criminal law, came, in Carson's words, 'to accept violation of the law as a conventional feature of industrial production, only meriting prosecution under the most unusual circumstances' (1979, p. 51). So, Alexander Redgrave, a Factory Inspector, could openly state in 1876,

> [i]n the inspection of factories it has been my view always that we are not acting as policemen, ... that in enforcing this Factory Act, we do not enforce it as policemen would check an offence which he is told to detect. We have endeavoured not to enforce the law, if I may use such an expression, but it has been my endeavour ... that we should simply be the advisers of all classes, that we should explain the law, and that we should do everything we possibly could to induce them to observe the law, and that a prosecution should be the very last thing we take up (ibid., p. 52).

It is because the HSE's understanding of its role is informed by this ethos that it is so manifestly indisposed to referring even the very serious cases of possible manslaughter to the police or CPS.

Since that time, a shift in policy, appeared. The matter was even raised for the first time in an HSE annual report (1991/2, p. 131) which states:

> HSE inspectors cannot themselves bring charges of manslaughter in connection with a workplace death. The responsibility for that rests with the Crown Prosecution Service in England and Wales and with the Procurator Fiscal in Scotland. However, when investigating work-related deaths inspectors have in mind the circumstances in which manslaughter charges might be appropriate. HSE liaises with the police and coroners' officials and, if they find evidence

suggesting manslaughter, pass it onto [sic] the police or in some cases the Crown Prosecution Service.

The beginnings of a new approach are to be found in the statement of the HSE issued in April 1998 (see p. 4). Here (Ecclestone, 1998), the HSE agreed a protocol was agreed with the CPS for dealing with work-related deaths with the intention of securing effective liaison between the enforcing and prosecuting authorities.

## Notes

1    There were 452 deaths at work during 1992–93, Health and Safety Executive, Statistical Services Unit (updated version of Annual report figure).
2    *Criminal Statistics*, Provisional Figure (1994). Courtesy of Home Office Research and Statistics Department, 5 October 1994. The figure for 1992 was 64,162 (Criminal Statistics for England and Wales, 1993).
3    Section 8 of the Police and Criminal Evidence Act, 1984 (PACE) provides for the issue of warrants by magistrates to enter and search premises for evidence of serious arrestable offences. This gives Justices of the Peace the power, on written application from a constable, to issue a search warrant where s/he is satisfied that there are reasonable grounds for believing that a 'serious arrestable offence' has been committed. A 'serious arrestable offence' (as distinct from an 'arrestable offence' defined by s.24) is defined by s.116 and Sched. 5 of PACE). The definition divides offences into two categories. One category comprise offences so serious that they are always 'serious arrestable offences'; they are listed in Schedule 5 and include manslaughter (along with, murder, treason, rape, kidnapping, incest and possession of firearms with intent to injure and attempts or conspiracies are treated as if they were completed).
     Police officers applying for warrants under this head may well encounter resistance from the Justices as there can sometimes be scant evidence of manslaughter without looking through the company records (exhibiting corporate knowledge of the risk in question), and they cannot look through the company records unless they can show evidence of manslaughter. This seems like a conundrum whose agonies Joseph Heller's Yossarian would appreciate.
     Any other arrestable offence is serious only if its commission has led or is likely to lead to any of the consequences specified in s.116(6), and these include: (a) serious harm to the security of the state or public order; (b) serious interference with the administration of justice or with the investigation of offences; (c) the death of anyone; and (d) serious injury to anyone.
4    *Panorama*, 'Risky Business', BBC1, 13 January 1992. See also the evidence given to the House of Commons Employment Committee in March 1990 under questioning from Greville Janner MP, cited in Bergman (1991, p. 36).
5    See for example *R v Pimm* [1994] RTR 391 and also *R v Seymour* [1983].
6    I am indebted to John Wain, HM Coroner for North Staffordshire, for all his thoughts on this matter; to his coroner's officers, and to the investigating officers in 18 of the 40 cases

who agreed to be interviewed about their opinions and working principles in relation to deaths at work. In 17 of these interviews the officer concerned had not previously dealt with a death at work.

7   I am indebted for much of my information here to Ian Connor, from the Health and Safety Executive, whom I interviewed at length in 1994. He was the inspector who investigated the case in 1988. He used all the reports he had made at the time, and his own notes to provide the detail here. I also note *The Health and Safety Information Bulletin* No. 169, January 1990 and Bergman, 1991.

8   Some of the penological arguments generated by violent corporate crime are considered in chapter 7.

9   During an interview with the author.

10   *The Independent*, 20 October 1993, p. 5.

11   *The Independent*, 1 March 1994, p. 5. The company has since been banned from operating. It was disqualified from operating its vehicles by the northeast traffic commissioner, who revoked indefinitely his licence for 30 vehicles and six trailers. Its managing director and transport manager were both disqualified from holding a goods vehicle operating licence for one year and three years respectively, *The Independent*, 22 December 1994, p. 3.

Sanders proposes a better test: whether, on the evidence, a jury or bench ought (on the balance of probabilities) to convict.

The expression 'the corporate account of events' is telling in relation to the issues of social psychology discussed in chapter 4. Such phrases identify the view of a tiny minority of personnel within an organisation – the directors – with the body itself. When news media announce 'Railtrack explained that …' or 'Ford said that the strike was the result of …', the views of 98 per cent of people who constitute the company are being excluded.

12   As Glanville Williams (1985, p. 115) and Andrew Sanders (1994, p. 946) have argued, this test favours people who are well-respected in society like police officers and businessmen – in whose favour juries and magistrates might be biased. It also disfavours the sort of victims who are unlikely to make good witnesses. Faced with opposing accounts of safety systems, precautions, etc. from well-groomed, articulate and self-confident company directors on the one hand and less articulate, less self-confident workers (often of the casual labourer type) on the other hand, prosecutors may take the view that, realistically, the 'corporate account of events' may be more credible to the bench.

13   *Information on the Criminal Justice System in England and Wales*, 1993, p. 15, Home Office, HMSO.

14   Cases 6, 8, 11, 13, 14, 31, 34 and 39.

15   An employer is under a duty to report certain accidents, diseases and dangerous occurrences (even if they have not resulted in injury) to the HSE. The accidents include all those which are fatal and a comprehensive list of serious injuries. All occurrences that are required to be reported must be recorded and details of the injuries must be kept in an accident book. The records must be kept for three years (this is the time limit on personal injury actions). The law is contained in the Reporting of Injuries, Diseases and Dangerous Regulations 1985 regs. 3, 4, 5 and 7 and Part 1 of Schedule 3.

# 4    The Legal Process (2): The Inquest

## The Coroner's Witness List

The Coroners Act, 1988, s.11 states that the coroner shall call as witnesses 'all persons who render evidence as to the facts of the death and all persons having knowledge of those facts whom he considers it expedient to examine'.

The real significance of inadequate investigation by official investigative bodies is that there will be very little evidence in the police report (which will be in the case file of the coroner) to prompt the coroner to summon as witnesses directors or senior managers from the employing company. Witness statement helps shape the coroner's perception of how the fatality occurred.

The actual order of calling the witnesses lies entirely within the discretion of the coroner (*R v Secretary of State, ex parte Devine*, unreported, 1988). This is important in practice because of the effect the coroner can create in the minds of jurors (and probably lawyers) by parading the *dramatis personae* in a particular sequence. There is a general pattern of bringing medical witnesses in near the beginning: (a) because this helps clear away the crucial medical cause of death; and (b) because this practice liberates the busy doctor so that he or she may go and attend to other matters. It was noted in the case studies undertaken by the author that if managers were summoned, they were often given an opportunity to give their accounts of systems and events before more critical eye witnesses. This had the effect of reducing the impact and real significance of the evidence of the deceased's fellow workers.

Many coroners, however, take an unwarrantedly narrow view of events leading to the death in question. Coroners' officers are drawn from the ranks of serving police officers. Indeed, when investigating a death, a police officer automatically becomes a coroner's officer. The professional outlook and assumptions of coroners are thus largely isomorphic with those of experienced police officers. There are sometimes attempts from coroners to justify their narrow view of what constitutes a proper inquest by reference to rule 36 and rule 42 of the Coroner's Rules 1984.

These rules state, respectively, that:

> The proceedings and evidence at an inquest shall be directed solely to ascertaining the following matters, namely (a) who the deceased was; (b) how, where, and when the deceased came by his death … Neither the coroner nor the jury shall express any opinion on any other matters.

> No verdict shall be framed in such a way as to appear to determine any question of (a) criminal liability on the part of a named person; (b) civil liability.

The rationale of these rules is to prevent the inquest, which is not an adversarial court, from pre-empting decisions which are constitutionally the province of criminal and civil courts. The diligence of many coroners to stop advocates for the deceased's relatives using the inquest to try to establish evidence or prove matters that might be helpful 'in another place' (i.e. a civil court), seems frequently to go too far. They stop counsel (many of whom seem unsure themselves on this point) from trying to elicit evidence which would, quite legally, go to an 'unlawful killing' verdict.

'How' someone died, coroners will often point out, is a different matter from 'why' he died, and the inquest is only concerned with the first question. This may be so, in one sense, but unlawful killing is a proper verdict and in order to establish it in some cases it may be necessary to take a wide view of the incident. If a worker is crushed to death when a huge steel tube falls on him because the slings by which it is being crane-lifted fail, then this unintentional killing may, apparently, be accurately described as an 'accidental death'. But suppose that the slings failed because they were too old and worn, and that similar accidents had occurred at the same workplace within recent years and that they had resulted in death or serious injury, or almost resulted in death or serious injury. If no new practices in respect of sling maintenance or purchase had since been adopted by the employer, then it could be shown that he was, thereafter, knowingly and wilfully exposing his employees to an obvious and serious risk of death or injury. Deaths resulting from such unjustified risk-taking may well be unlawful killings. It should be a matter for a jury to decide.

The following case study[1] provides a good example. If a warehouse employee is in a cage raised by a fork lift truck so that he may carry out a stock take on very high shelves, he is doing something perilous. If he falls and is fatally injured, then ostensibly this is a tragic and regrettable accident. The further one pursues inquiries about this, the wider the true culpability that comes to light. Call an eyewitness, like the warehouse cleaner, and she will describe the moment and aftermath of the fall. Call fellow workers and they will testify that what the deceased was doing was common practice. Call some shift managers and they will tell that the practice in question was the only way in which deadlines could be met. It came to light in this case that the equipment was defective, as all the four safety features were inoperative and at least one of them looked as if it had been deliberately defeated. It also came to light that there was no proper training system for people asked to drive forklift trucks. Calling in the national directors of the company in question and questioning them about their knowledge of how deadlines were set centrally and met at particular warehouses, what provision there was for site managers communicating up the company hierarchy that deadlines were unreasonable, if there had been any such communications, why there was no proper safety training, and why no proper maintenance of the cage and truck in question, would have elicited some helpful replies. Before that was done at the inquest into the *Herald of Free Enterprise* deaths, at the Winchester Crown court trial of OLL Ltd (Slapper, 1994f) and at Bradford Crown Court in *R v Jackson and Jackson Transport (Ossett) Ltd*, the public knowledge of just how culpable the companies were in respect of the deaths was very limited. There was no police investigation of the company policy or of its directors in the warehouse case, and the coroner did not summon any witnesses who might have been able to shed light on such a wider picture of how the fatality came about. The coroner took the view that such inquiries could not be justified according to the limitations of rules 36 and 42.

Nevertheless, one of the verdicts recommended as an option by the Home Office is 'unlawful killing', and in order to be able to establish this in relation to a corporate manslaughter scenario it is clearly necessary for a court to examine a concatenation of acts and omissions by company personnel that run back further than the immediate stages prior to death. The managerial context of the death needs to be examined. Although case law and the practitioner's manual, Jervis on Coroners, establish that an unlawful killing verdict is returnable in respect of a death at work, many coroners seem to be against the whole idea.[2] Matthews and Foreman (1993, p. 252) state that:

> since there is no rule that a corporate body cannot be guilty of corporate manslaughter, it is possible for an unlawful killing conclusion to be recorded where a corporate body would be so liable.

Judging by numerous previous cases (Bergman, 1991, 1993 and 1994) and the 40 cases studied here, many coroners seem to persist in the belief, advanced by the coroner Mr Richard Sturt (below), that companies cannot be responsible for killing anyone, even though the High Court has ruled that his view was legally incorrect. None of eight coroners interviewed could recall a case in which they had felt obliged to suggest an unlawful killing conclusion where the facts had involved a death at work. Most indicated that such a conclusion would only really be appropriate in the most extraordinary circumstances. One of the coroners was invited to put an unlawful killing option to the jury by the advocate appearing for the bereaved family (case 31). He acceded to the request only begrudgingly.

This disposition against offering this conclusion to the jury, extends to even the clearest *prima facie* cases. In the BR electric arcing case (Anthony Fishenden, see below), for example, the highly experienced lawyer Louise Christian took a year to gather evidence for an unlawful killing conclusion, and a very powerful case was put to the coroner, but he refused to even let the jury consider such a conclusion. There is a way in which this appears legally wrong, as the coroner is personally deciding something critical in a jury inquest, something which it seems should be left to them. Matthews and Foreman note, in *Jervis on the Office and Duties of Coroners* (1994, p. 39), that 'it should not appear that coroners are seeking to erode the jury's function'. It is telling that the headline to a newspaper report on the Fishenden inquest read: 'Coroner clears BR over electrocution' (*The Guardian*, 8 September 1994, p. 8). The decision caused an uproar and disorder in the courtroom. It is later contended that this decision was, legally, highly questionable. Notably, the best defence, legally, for such a decision is that a coroner is not bound to offer to the jury a conclusion which he will speak against, as this could be confusing to jurors. He may speak against it if the evidence, taken at its highest, is such that a jury, properly directed, could not properly reach that conclusion.[3] It is very difficult to imagine how that formula, applied to the evidence in Fishenden, could have lead to the unlawful verdict being excluded.

The coroner has the sole right to summon witnesses to an inquest, so s/he must bear the main responsibility for their absence from these proceedings, but it should be noted that, in deciding who should be called to give evidence, the coroner relies on the statements collected by the police and the HSE inspector who visited the scene of the death. However, neither the police nor the HSE inspectors are disposed to take statements from such senior people. There are some alarming cases of the coroner's declining to summon key witnesses even where he has been prevailed upon to do so by interested parties.

Tim Owen, a barrister who has represented many bereaved families at inquests has made the following observations:

Using a restricted notion of what 'how' [in rule 36] means, coroners often rule out questions which seek to cover ground over several weeks before the death. In law, as an interested party, a family has the right to request certain witnesses but the coroner decides whether they are relevant in determining *how* someone died, and they often refuse requests.

Jan Leadbetter was killed on 16 July 1990 on a construction site, managed by Bovis plc, in central London. He fell down an unlit shaft. His sister, Yasmin Zimnowodski, wrote a letter to the coroner asking him to summon as witnesses Jan's foreman, a union (UCATT) officer and a director of the company. They would, she said, be able to explain matters of site safety to the inquest. The coroner did not reply to her letter. She persisted with her request and eventually the coroner did reply, but said he saw no point in inviting a director. He said that Mrs Zimnowodski was probably confusing the inquest with the Crown Court. His letter said *'we are not looking for any criminal negligence or blame. We are, at an inquest, only concerned to ascertain facts'*[4] [emphasis added]. This is simply incorrect. In order to establish whether the proper verdict in this case was the perfectly well established one of 'killed unlawfully' it would be legal, proper and essential to examine the broader context of the death to see whether there had been criminal negligence on the part of the company. For deaths at work, the decision as to 'how' the deceased met his death is for the jury. It is not for the coroner. It is, therefore, not for the coroner to arrogate to himself the task of deciding that there was no unlawful killing. Unless the *prima facie* case of unlawful killing is 'incredible or worthless' he is legally obliged to put that option to the jury. If the coroner does not summon and examine company directors and listen to the arguments of union and safety representatives, then he cannot judge the quality of their opinions. In many death at work cases, like those involving the self-employed, cases where a director of a small firm dies, etc., there will clearly be no need for the coroner to call company directors with a view to testing the evidence of unlawful killing.[5]

There is no right of advanced disclosure of evidence for lawyers representing interested parties at an inquest. The contents of witness statements, reports prepared by the police, HSE inspectors, and other experts, will not usually be disclosed to lawyers. At the outset of the inquest, only the coroner will have a detailed picture of the events leading to death. This means that diligent and inquisitive lawyers at the inquest will have to go on 'fishing expeditions' when examining some of the witnesses in order to build up an idea of what happened, and how it came to happen. In 1971, the Brodrick

Report[6] recommended, that there should be advanced disclosure at inquests, but this recommendation has since been ignored. The common coronial justification of this secrecy is that, were it otherwise, the press would get to deal with sensitive materials (like suicide notes) in an insensitive way. Such an argument, however, entails acceptance of the assumption that lawyers furnished with such information (to help arrive at the most appropriate conclusion to the inquest) would pass such sensitive data to the press.

In this study into 40 workplace-related deaths, it was found that 32 of the cases had the potential to be seen as adversarial, or to become so in a civil court. There was, at first sight, an identifiable culprit in the form of an employer whose negligence might have been responsible for the deceased's death. The remaining eight cases[7] involved situations like the death of the owner of a small firm, the death of a self-employed man in circumstances where the occupier of land (a domestic house) had not broken any civil law duty of care,[8] the death of a son working for his father, etc.

From the above 32 cases, key senior figures were not summoned to the inquest in 21 of them (i.e. 66 per cent of cases where it would have been possible); cases in which the managerial and corporate framework around the worker who was killed should have prompted the coroner to summon directors. It is arguable that these omissions may be attributable to earlier omissions by the police to take statements from such company officials, but it is important to remember that the coroner could nevertheless summon whom he felt appropriate to shed light on the events in question. The following example illustrates this deficiency. The inquest concerned the death of a worker, crushed to death by a fall of heavy pipes on a British Gas site. At the end of the evidence, the coroner, when summing up for the jury, offered them 'accidental death' or 'misadventure'[9] as possible verdicts. They retired. The jury came back and told the coroner they were having trouble because they had not heard any evidence from a British Gas manager, someone on site when the incident occurred. In a most surprising turn of events, the coroner acceded to the request and it transpired that the site manager had been in court all the time. He appeared to have been summoned but not called. After hearing his evidence the jury retired again, and then returned 20 minutes later. They reached the verdict that the deceased had died due to the breakdown of safety procedures and lack of supervision.

It was only the curiosity of the jury in complaining about a gap in the evidence that brought the manager to the witness stand; the coroner had been happy to let the jury reach their verdict without this crucial witness.

From the 32 cases, key senior figures were not summoned in 21 cases, i.e.

66 per cent of cases where it would have been possible. Of the 21 cases where there was no examination of company directors or senior managers, I consider (assuming the legal examination was effective and well prepared) that, it *may* have made a significant difference to the way the fatality was perceived by the jury in 12 cases.[10]

Broadly, the aim of the rigorous examination of such witnesses would be to elucidate the company's safety policy, system and historical record. The fatality would need to be set in this context to properly determine *how* it occurred. One of the established verdicts at an inquest is unlawful killing. It is established that this may be against a company (Matthews and Foreman, 1994, p. 252). The purpose of the inquest is to ascertain how the deceased came to meet his death. Thus, the historical background (in the form of the firm's safety record) is required in order for the jury to be able to properly decide whether the deceased died an 'accidental death' or whether gross negligence was a causal factor in which case the most apposite verdict would be 'unlawfully killed'.

*Adjourning the Inquest When a Case Looks Like it Might Involve Manslaughter*

There is no reason, legally, why this should not happen more often. The coroners' manual, *Jervis on Coroners*, states that an inquest should be adjourned 'where the coroner himself considers from evidence given at the inquest itself that a person might be charged with one of the offences set out … above' (ibid., p. 210). These offences include manslaughter (ibid., p. 206). Jervis says that in such circumstances, the coroner should refer the case to the DPP or the CPS. An example is given of how this discretion to adjourn might be exercised. It is where, in a case of homicide, no sufficient evidence to charge anyone emerges until part of the way through the inquest. This was, no doubt, written with an individual culprit in mind, but the same mechanism could be used in respect of a company. It may well be that until senior managers are examined in court by counsel for the family, it is not clear who, if anyone, was culpable for the death.

At the inquest into the death of the worker who died from a major head injury when he fell from a forklift truck whilst working on a platform at a cash and carry warehouse (case 14), there was evidence that the deceased was killed as the result of engaging in a highly hazardous activity (as part of his work duties) which had been necessitated by the pace of work demanded by the company at a very high level, and condoned by senior managers. The faults could not be located simply with site managers and attributed to momentary disorganisation or personal deficiency. The deceased, like many other employees, was instructed to work with forklift trucks without having been given proper training. The company, a large national concern, would be well aware of the dangers posed by forklift trucks and the need for operators to be given proper training and for the vehicles to be effectively maintained. There was evidence that the warehouse in question had been sent materials on this very issue a year before the fatality. Yet the vehicle in question was in an appalling condition, with none of its safety features working, and even evidence that at least one feature had been deliberately defeated in order to allow the machine to be used more quickly.

The testimony of people who worked at the warehouse suggested that the hazardous practice which was responsible for the death had been condoned by senior site managers as the only way in which the work in question could be done within time limits set managerially. There is a comparison to be made here between this case and the Lyme Regis canoe case (p. 78 above and see Slapper, 1994f). In the latter case, the jury eventually convicted the managing director Peter Kite, and the company, OLL Ltd, of manslaughter of the four children who drowned off Lyme Bay, but they did not convict the site manager, Joseph Stoddart. The evidence suggested that however bad the decisions taken locally by the leisure centre manager, they had been taken in the context of a policy about resources and spending set higher up in the company. Because anyone can make an honest and perhaps pardonable mistake once, it is critical in an investigation looking to discover whether there has been gross negligence; to ask historical questions: has this sort of thing happened before? Did the people who made this decision or countenanced that terrible policy, have any reason to know what they were doing entailed a serious and obvious risk? In the canoe case there was strong, arguably incontrovertible, evidence that Mr Kite and his company *did* know the dangers of the policies they were operating because of a letter sent to Mr Kite by former employees who had left because of the atrocious safety standards at the centre. The letter (read out in court) said: 'we think you should have a very careful look at standards of safety otherwise you might find yourself explaining why someone's son or daughter is not coming home'.

Did the company that employed the forklift driver have knowledge of the particular practices which led to his death? To gain a reliable answer to this question one would need a proper investigation with access to company accident books and records and testimony from safety representatives and trade union personnel. It would have been possible and desirable for the coroner, having heard the evidence unfold at the inquest, to adjourn it and ask the police to investigate the matter, possibly in collaboration with the EHD inspector whose spirited investigation had exposed all the indicators of serious crime. As it was, the inquest quietly plodded on to register on the public record that the deceased had died from a 'misadventure'.

## The Unlawful Killing Verdict and Gross Negligence

There are other procedural obstacles and caveats that lie on the path to a prosecution for corporate manslaughter. The almost invariable pattern of events at the inquest following a workplace death is for the coroner to direct the jury to a verdict of 'accidental death'. In the 40 cases studied here, the verdict of 'accidental death' was returned by the jury in 33; the verdict of 'misadventure', which is generally regarded as legally indistinguishable (Matthews and Foreman, 1994, p. 250) – and most members of the public would be challenged to explain what, if anything, is the significance of the dichotomy – was returned in a further five cases. Taking these as one category (they are categorised together in the annual Home Office *Statistics of Death Reported to Coroners in England and Wales*), therefore, the same conclusion was returned in respect of 38 of the 40 deaths, that is in 95 per cent of cases.[11] This is notably higher than the level of such a verdict when all inquests (concerning all suspicious deaths, deaths in police or prison custody, etc.) are taken. Inquests were held on just over 20,000 of the deaths reported to coroners in 1993; of these verdicts of death by 'accident or misadventure' were returned in 48 per cent of these inquests.[12] The figures do not distinguish between inquests that return verdicts of accidental death and those which decide the death was due to misadventure.

A 1994 case, affording considerable news coverage, raised this issue, although nowhere in the broadcasting or print media, nor in journals which give commentary on such developments, was the legal propriety of the coroner's conduct questioned. The case concerned the death of a scaffolder, electrocuted as he worked in a London garden near overhead British Rail cables. Anthony Fishenden, aged 25, had been on this job for two weeks. He suffered a 25,000 volt shock when current arced through a 21 foot metal pole he was carrying. He was erecting the scaffolding on a four-storey house in West Hampstead on 6 August 1992. His brother-in-law told the inquest that he heard a bang and a buzzing sound followed by a scream. He said:

> I ran round to the front of the building and saw Tony lying on his back in the garden. His feet were still on fire when I got there. I tried to lift him up but his

skin was coming off and he slipped back on to the floor. I sat with his head in my lap I thought I was picking leaves off him but it wasn't leaves – it was the skin off his chest coming away in my hands.

The inquest had been adjourned for over a year at the request of the lawyer for Mr Fishenden's family, as she was collecting evidence to support an unlawful killing verdict.

When the inquest was eventually held on 7 September 1994, there was uproar in court when the coroner, Dr Douglas Chambers, refused to allow the jury to consider the unlawful killing verdict. The deceased's mother screamed at the coroner:

> Why are the jury here? You are telling them what verdict to return. You are saying my son killed himself. He took his own life. This is just a sham. My son was killed by British Rail.

Two points entirely justify the uproar at this inquest. First, as noted above, a coroner may legally not withhold an 'unlawful killing' verdict from the jury 'where there is evidence which could not be rejected as incredible or worthless'. There was also substantial evidence that Mr Fishenden's employer was highly culpable. He had provided no instruction about safety, no warnings about the need for special care when working near electric cables, and no proper system of supervision. The coroner in this case should have been well aware of the law on this matter, as it was *his* decision to withdraw an unlawful killing verdict from a jury in an earlier case (see *Diesa Koto*, chapter 1, p. 45, n. 43) that was overturned in 1993 by the High Court as legally wrong.

Second, the facts in the awful case of Mr Fishenden show that there was substantial evidence that BR were grossly negligent in respect of life and limb, i.e. there was evidence that the deceased had been killed as a result of the crime of manslaughter by gross negligence committed by a corporation; evidence which 'could not be rejected as incredible or worthless'.

Prior to Mr Fishenden's death, three people were killed and 13 seriously injured by arcing electric shocks from BR overhead cables. Before Mr Fishenden was electrocuted, several children had been badly injured in north London, but BR ignored or openly rejected the requests of the victim's relatives to improve safety. The grandmother of one of the earlier victims campaigned to persuade British Rail to improve its safety in relation to cables and the dangers of arcing. The case was eventually referred to the Chairman of British Rail by the grandmother's MP. With alarmingly insensitive bluntness the chairman, Sir Bob Reid, replied:

... No additional danger signs have been placed in the area because this tends to be counter-productive. A whiff of danger acts as a magnet for a mindless minority and encourages them to trespass. There have been instances where vandals or trespassers have endeavoured to emulate this arcing phenomenon, perhaps by holding a metal bar toward the power source. It works – spectacularly, too. But I hardly need add that perpetrators of such outrages only do it once!

The applicable formula for determining whether there was gross negligence manslaughter, is that expounded by the House of Lords in *R v Adomako* [1994]. In essence the test is rather circular. It states that in order to convict a defendant of gross negligence manslaughter, a death must have resulted from conduct of the defendant that was criminally lacking in care, and 'criminal' is a standard to be set by the jury. Lord Mackay, the Lord Chancellor, said that how far conduct must depart from acceptable standards to be characterised as criminal was necessarily a question of degree. Any attempt to specify that degree more closely was likely to achieve only a spurious precision. He said the jury must decide whether the negligence in question is criminal, and that (p. 87a)

> this will depend on the seriousness of the breach of duty committed by the defendant in all the circumstances in which the defendant was placed when it occurred. The jury will have to consider whether the extent to which the defendant's conduct departed from the proper standard of care incumbent upon him ... was such that it should be judged criminal.

Because British Rail had long been aware of the potentially lethal danger their cables presented, and, further, because that awareness must have been sharpened by the deaths and serious injuries suffered as a result of the same dangerous cables, there was thus clear evidence that in respect of Mr Fishenden's death, British Rail had taken an unjustifiable, obvious and serious risk with life.

The significance of the 'unlawful killing' verdict is its symbolic recognition (often very important for bereaved relatives) that it was a criminal wrong that killed their loved one, not simply an 'accident' or 'misadventure'.

Only if a verdict of 'unlawful killing' is returned would the case be referred to the DPP for her consideration as a possible case of manslaughter. In order, though, for a jury to be able to decide that there had been an 'unlawful killing' by a company, it would be necessary to initially recognise the *mens rea* in at least one director or someone who was a 'controlling mind' of the company (see chapter 2). Yet directors and senior managers are almost never called to give evidence at these inquests. There may be considerable evidential difficulty in satisfying the doctrine of identification in many of these cases (Slapper, 1993; Wells, 1993a; Gobert, 1994a, 1994b) and proving that the negligence was 'gross', but if juries are not given the opportunity to deliberate on these points then we cannot be sure how hard the tests are to satisfy. It should be remembered that Lord Mackay confirms in *Adomako* that matter of whether negligence is 'gross' (i.e. criminal') is pre-eminently a question for the jury.

## The Unlawful Killing Verdict and Unlawful Act Manslaughter

Most strikingly, coroners decline to offer the jury the verdict of 'unlawful killing' even where it has already been found in a criminal court (the Magistrates' Court or the Crown Court) that a company was guilty of a health and safety offence in respect of the very incident which killed the deceased. In such circumstances, the guilty company will have been fined for a crime; the wrong in question, although a so-called regulatory offence, is indisputably a crime because it results in a fine. As Lord Atkin once observed, a crime is simply anything that the state has chosen to criminalise:

> The domain of criminal jurisprudence can only be ascertained by examining what acts at any particular period are declared by the State to be crimes, and the only common nature they will be found to possess is that they are prohibited by the State and that those who commit them are punished (*Proprietary Articles Trade Association v Att-Gen for Canada* [1931], p. 324).

One of the current categories of manslaughter is 'constructive' or 'unlawful act manslaughter'. This occurs where the defendant has killed by an unlawful and dangerous act. The only *mens rea* required is an intention to do that act and any fault required to render it unlawful (Smith and Hogan, 1992, p. 366). It is irrelevant that the defendant is unaware that the act is unlawful or that it is dangerous (*DPP v Newbury* [1977]). It is also irrelevant that he is unaware of the circumstances which make it dangerous, if a reasonable person in his position would have been aware of them (*R v Watson* [1989]). A rather awkward gloss was put on this formula by Lord Atkin, delivering his opinion in a case in 1937 involving a road traffic death. The upshot of this was that the unlawfulness of the act must arise other than through negligence, i.e. it must be unlawful for some other reason (*Andrews v DPP* [1937]). Additionally, the formula insists on there being an 'unlawful act', an omission will not suffice.[13] (These matters are examined in detail in chapter 1.)

Thus, there is the possibility in theory that some of the annual deaths at work are in this category (Reville, 1989; Wells, 1989). In the case studies undertaken by the author, it was found there was clear and ample evidence on which a jury *could* return a verdict of 'unlawful killing'. Of the 40 cases investigated, five had already resulted in convictions at the time of the inquest. A criminal court (either the Magistrates or the Crown Court) had decided that the company had broken the criminal law: the Health and Safety at Work Etc. Act 1974. That satisfies the requirement that the act be unlawful. As the prosecution was brought following a death, there is a good *prima facie* case that the breach of the HSW Act was also dangerous. Provided it can be shown that the employer committed an 'act' (and this may be a sticking point: would an instruction be an 'act'? See chapter 1) then there is at least a case that the death resulted from the crime of unlawful act (or 'constructive') manslaughter, so that the jury should consider 'unlawful killing' as a conclusion. Unlawful killing covers 'all cases of homicide' (Matthews and Foreman, 1994, p. 251). In this study, the option was only left open to the jury in one case (case 31); a case, ironically, where no HSE action had yet been taken against the employer. A bold lawyer for the deceased's family sought to persuade the coroner that the verdict of unlawful killing should be put to the jury. The coroner sent out the jury and initially argued against such action. He eventually, and somewhat begrudgingly, acceded to the advocate's request, but later confided that he had not really been persuaded that unlawful killing was appropriate but wanted to avoid the trouble of having his summing up to the jury judicially reviewed.

The law here is clear. On appeal the High Court has ruled that:

> a verdict of unlawful killing should be left to the jury at an inquest where there is evidence which could not be rejected as incredible or worthless on which the jury could return such a verdict (*R v Greater London Coroner, ex parte Diesa Koto* [1993]).

## The Involvement of Lawyers

It is also important to appreciate the role of lawyers at inquests. Because of the difficulties, outlined above, in relying on coroners to call directors as witnesses so that the jury may properly consider a verdict of 'unlawful killing', the availability at the inquests of lawyers who have the aim of guiding the court in that direction becomes imperative if there is to be a proper hearing of all matters. There are, however, very few attempts by lawyers to intervene at inquests with the aim of encouraging an 'unlawful killing' verdict. There is no legal aid awardable for proceedings in a coroner's court,[14] thus bereaved families either have to pay for these services themselves or rely on the support of the victim's Trade Union if he[15] belonged to one. In fact, many families are not in a position to pay for representation at the inquest. Even many of those who could pay must fail to see any point in taking such action. They may wish to try and pursue civil litigation to receive compensation, but often the solicitor they consult about that matter will not wish to tackle the 'controlling minds' of the employing company at the inquest because to do so would be seen as hostile and adversarial (part of the criminal law process) and not conducive to a negotiated settlement (the civil law process).

Even when lawyers are present they are reluctant to request the coroner to summon company directors or follow argument designed to produce an 'unlawful killing' verdict. The lawyers who are provided by unions to attend the inquest are generally content that the story and evidence uncovered in the coroner's court are consistent with employer negligence to ensure that any dependants are successful in claiming compensation. As Labour Research has concluded, referring to these lawyers:

> Generally they are not instructed by unions to push for a verdict of unlawful killing by emphasising the criminal nature of the death. This effectively rules out a successful manslaughter case being pursued, as the sort of evidence needed for this is not brought out at the inquest (Labour Research, 1990, p. 13).

Peter Jordan, a solicitor, and former Deputy Director of a major regional Legal Aid Board, stated in an interview that lawyers instructed in a civil matter would rarely regard it as appropriate to use the inquest to try and establish evidence useful for a prosecution. This could upset the delicate process of negotiation leading to a civil settlement:

> The style of interaction in criminal and civil cases is fundamentally different. In a civil claim your purpose is to obtain compensation without running unnecessary risks which may be attendant on a court trial. This can involve delicate negotiation on the way to a settlement. The combatant, adversarial style associated with criminal cases reduces the dispute to a more all-or-nothing contest: guilty or not guilty? In that atmosphere those who act for prospective defendants in a criminal case are likely to 'close down the shutters' and contest every point prejudicial to the outcome of a prosecution. So, frequently, lawyers instructed on a civil matter will not see much point in pressing any point at an inquest.

Trade unions can pay for legal representation at an inquest but, by the nature of the work in which many of the victims have been engaged, there is low union membership and relatively few such sponsorships are made. Between 31 March 1989 and 1 April 1990, 427 people were killed at work, of whom 139 (over one-third) were working in the construction industry. Most of these victims were not trade union members but were working 'on the lump'. According to Foley (1990, p. 6):

> By 1990, over 1.5 million people were employed in the building industry; six per cent of the country's total work force ... In London and the South East ... lump workers accounted for 80 per cent of the labour force on many sites.

In this study of 40 workplace deaths, the level of legal representation was found to be quite high in spite of the present restriction on legal aid for the inquest procedure. Taking the 32 potentially adversarial cases from the corpus of 40 investigated, there was representation for the relatives at 26 of the inquests, i.e. in 81 per cent of cases in which it would have been important to the verdict. It was also noted that companies represented at the inquest ensured their solicitors engaged barristers in 65 per cent of cases whereas families did so in only 23 per cent and that lawyers acting for firms, in contrast to those who acted for families, were generally more competent and self-assured. There were two instances of very accomplished and dedicated advocacy. The lawyers in these cases (13 and 31) were well prepared, clearly experienced in the coroner's court, and quick to identify the significance of and to respond to emerging facts and opinions. The lawyer in case 13 was a barrister, and in case 31, a solicitor who specialised in personal injury litigation and had dealt with several work fatalities. In the former case, for example, it was sharp witness examination by counsel for the widow that established: 1) that the company's safety officer was ineffective and unfamiliar with the company rule book even in fairly rudimentary respects and even though he must have known what sort of thing he would be quizzed about at the inquest; and 2) that the company's main 'excuse' – the deceased could and should have been wearing a safety harness secured to an external fixture before he descended into the highly dangerous hopper – was nonsense because there was no such fixture to which the harness could possibly have been attached. The company witness had been either disingenuous or was alarmingly dull-witted about his safety responsibilities, but either way his exposure as such in court was very professionally achieved.

The solicitor who specialised in personal injury litigation was the only lawyer to invite the coroner to put the option of an unlawful killing conclusion before the jury. All his witness examinations were purposeful and directed to exposing the full culpability of the company. He had done most of his information-gathering *before* the inquest. He knew what he was going to be asking and what sort of answers he would elicit (despite the impediment of ignorance of the contents of the files the coroner had in front of him).

The overall quality of the lawyers' performances in the above study, however, suggested that the proper function of advocacy at inquests is not being met in practice.

The inquisition is not an adversarial hearing, it is not gladiatorial. But advocates are bound to represent their clients' interests in helping the court to discover 'the facts' (*R v South London Coroner ex parte Thompson* [1982]). But facts do not exist independently from assumptions about what is relevant, significant and so forth. What one would elevate to the status of fact all depends upon one's assumptions and fundamental premises. At inquests it all depends on which side a lawyer represents. As the historian E.H. Carr observed (1961, p. 18) about historical facts:

> The facts are not at all like fish on a fishmongers slab [that historians or students just walk up to and take]. They are like fish in a vast and sometimes inaccessible ocean; and what the historian catches will depend, partly on chance, but mainly on what part of the ocean he chooses to fish in and what tackle he chooses to use ... History means interpretation.

Much the same is true of the lawyer at the inquest. By piecing together certain pieces of experience pertaining (at different levels of abstraction) to the death, the advocate can 'construct' the facts that best suit his client.

The indefensible way in which many coroners jealously guard the documents and letters in their file and the consequential need for lawyers to embark on 'fishing expedition' examination of witnesses in order to ascertain facts was noted earlier. The coroner can see in his file all that the witness has said (and not said) in his written statement to the police or the HSE inspector. He may also have letters from experts and company officials. The lawyer does not necessarily have these, nor does he have the legal right to see them. Witnesses are frequently asked questions to which advocates clearly had not the slightest clue as to what the answer would be, contravening a fundamental rule of witness examination. The result is that it becomes very difficult for advocates to be seen to establish an interpretation of events that the death resulted from an unlawful killing. Lawyers cannot argue to the jury for a particular result. The hearing is inquisitorial so the jury must decide simply on the evidence uncovered at the inquest. Lawyers can, however, argue to the coroner (who must first send out the jury) that he should offer a certain conclusion to the jury (*R v East Berkshire Coroner ex parte* [1992]). The danger is that in asking questions of witnesses in such circumstances, advocates can devastate the picture of events that they had wished to emerge.[16] It is true, of course, that there is no such thing as cross-examination at inquests because the proceedings are nonpartisan. It follows from this that it should not matter where answers lead the court; provided they are honest they will help achieve a true verdict. In practice, however, inquests arising from deaths at work can often be *de facto* adversarial, with representation for the bereaved family and the company and its insurers. In such a context witnesses will have a vested interest in perceiving the arguments of, and keeping to, a partisan interpretation of events.

Apart from the evidential difficulties faced by lawyers in the coroners' courts, there are other factors which, taken together, tend to produce a quality of advocacy at the lower end of the scale. If the immediate concern following a death is to arrange legal representation, the family of the deceased often depend on their family lawyer or turn to the local high street solicitor. It has been observed that to the lawyer unversed in the ways of coroners, a request for legal advice about inquest procedures leads to a sequence of culture shocks (Owen, 1991). Coroner's courts are on the periphery of the legal system and so most lawyers have very little experience of how they operate. They are unfamiliar with the rights they have as lawyers, the significance of some of the evidence and the application of the verdicts. This can lead to a deficient performance by the legal profession (Bergman, 1991, pp. 61–5). In my study, it was sometimes apparent that the advocates had not understood the significance of some of the evidence. In case 30, for example, there were many curiosities that emerged from testimony which could and should have been rigorously dealt with by the man there to represent the interests of the deceased's family, such as details of the employer's safety policy and safety record, the availability and use of breathing apparatus and why, quite unlawfully, there was no jury at this inquest? The advocate did not entirely justify his claim to that title: he said nothing throughout the entire hearing except the phrase 'No thank you, Sir' which he delivered promptly eight times when the coroner inquired whether he wished to ask any questions of the successive witnesses.

There is no reason to believe that any of these lawyers are simply lazy or indifferent. Poor performance is more likely a response to highly-pressured work which does not leave sufficient time to devote to proper pre-trial preparation, let alone pre-inquest preparation.

Furthermore, because the outcome of the inquest cannot be used in evidence in a civil or criminal case, and because the outcome is limited to a few options, none of which will be fatal to any side in any forthcoming litigation, these courts are a good place for firms of solicitors to send freshly qualified lawyers to gain experience. This study found that in many instances the lawyer for the family was very young, apparently inexperienced, and using a delivery which was variously too halting and nervous, or over-dramatic and pompous, or too conversational. Their 'main aim' in appearing is to benefit from the information-gathering exercise that the inquest presents so that he or she would be in a good position to litigate or negotiate a settlement. This dress rehearsal for the civil court is the ulterior purpose of most advocates involved in the process. Even the eminent coroner and author of an influential text on coronership, Dr Gavin Thurston, acknowledged the role of the inquest in settling matters related to civil litigation, and stated that it would be 'affectation' to deny this function (1976, p. 17). Why use lots of time corresponding with doctors and consultants about medical matters when these issues can be expeditiously clarified by an expert summoned to court and paid for from public funds, especially when a lawyer can examine such a witness? It is obviously much more difficult getting supplementary answers in a correspondence.

Conversely, the experience and consummate skill of the highest-paid corporate lawyers has been cited as a deterrent against the state bringing a prosecution for corporate manslaughter (Cullen, Maakestad and Cavender, 1987; Dowie, 1977). Braithwaite (1983, p. 241) has argued that there are various ways in which corporate lawyers are able to utilise their resources and expertise. They can, for example, focus on the complexity of company structures and records usually to the disadvantage of those who act for the prosecution.

## Costs, Resources, and Awkward Law

Another factor which appears to play some part in having shaped the prosecutorial policy over the last few decades, is the matter of costs and resources. The costs of the investigation and prosecution in a case of corporate manslaughter are very high. The great resources and high-powered legal departments of many companies which might have come under suspicion at one time or another are enough to make those who act for the state, at the expense of the public purse, reluctant to start a very expensive case that they may lose.

After the collapse of the Zeebrugge prosecution on 19 October 1990, *The Times* stated that this failure had 'cost the taxpayer more than £1 million' (20 October 1990) and the estimated costs of the whole proceedings have been put at about £10 million (Bergman, 1990b, p. 1496).

Two developments witnessed in recent times lend additional significance to issue of costs: first, the increasing complexity of corporate structures and the prevalence of multifarious companies engaged in work on a single enterprise, and second the Court of Appeal's rejection of the principle of 'aggregation' by which a company could be incriminated from the combined failures of several of its directors.

Addressing the first point, Foley has noted (1990, p. 16) that the system of subcontracting and the multiplicity of firms working on a single site enables employers to hide behind each other, shifting the responsibility for safety from contractor to contractor to diminish the consequences of their own negligence.

Deaths in multiple employer work sites make up a considerable proportion of the annual toll of workplace deaths. In this study of 40 workplace deaths, 11 (27.5) per cent of the deaths involved those who were working on sites where two or more contractors were undertaking work. Comparable studies in Australia by Haines and Polk (1989), and Haines (1993) have made similar findings. Haines and Polk (1989) found that in Victoria, 30 per cent of all work deaths in 1987 involved more than one company. In her 1993 study Haines states that multiple employer work sites were present in between one-third and one-quarter of cases.

The resulting complexity of debate concerning boundaries of responsibility, and the number of parties will significantly aggravate the challenge to prosecutors considering criminal liability. The increase in esoteric technology's endangerment of the population in Beck (1992) has been accompanied by a growing diffusion of managerial responsibility within large corporations. As there is also a discernible tendency for fewer companies to dominate large parts of the economy (chapter 6) every legal entity is not *de facto* equal before the law. In practice it will be much more difficult to secure a conviction against a large organisation or a small one working on a multiple-employer site than against other employers because of the evidential problems of proving the legal demarcations of responsibility.

The second point, on aggregation, was argued in the judicial review brought by members of the Herald Families Association. They sought to establish that the instances of fault amongst several people acting for P&O could be combined so as to show that the company itself had been reckless. John Alcindor was deputy chief superintendent of P&O's marine department. He had received a suggestion that indicator lights showing the state of the loading doors be fitted to the bridge. He did nothing to implement that suggestion. Jeffrey Develin, chief superintendent of the marine department and a director of the company, bore a major responsibility for the safety of the fleet and the systems in operation on board vessels. It was Mr Develin's department which failed to install the indicator lights and instead passed the matter on to the technical department. Wallace Ayres, a director and head of the technical department, failed to respond to two requests for indicator lights to be fitted to the bridges of vessels.

On this matter, Bingham LJ ruled that:

> Whether the defendant is a corporation or a personal defendant, the ingredients of manslaughter must be established by proving the necessary *mens rea* and *actus reus* against it or him by evidence properly to be relied on against it or him. A case against a personal defendant cannot be fortified by evidence against another defendant. The case against a corporation can only be made by evidence properly addressed to showing guilt on the part of the corporation as such (*R v HM Coroner for East Kent ex parte Spooner* [1989]).

This principle here has been endorsed elsewhere. It is adopted, for example, in Clause 30(2) of the Law Commission's Draft Criminal Code Bill (Law Commission, 1989, p. 76) and David Willcox, a solicitor with Partner, Beaumont & Son, who act for a range of airline companies, has argued (Law Society Lecture, 'Corporate Manslaughter', Chancery Lane, London, 20 March 1991) that this position is necessary to prevent a company being convicted on too low a threshold of evidence. Wells has shown (1988, 1993b) how notions of personal responsibility in criminal law are unsuitable when applied to corporations.

The Bingham LJ ruling appears to make it virtually impossible for a company to be convicted for manslaughter because the way that responsibilities are distributed through a corporate body makes it extremely unlikely that the necessary fault will ever reside entirely in a single identifiable individual. The analogy with a personal defendant used by Bingham LJ seems inappropriate. Companies gain many benefits from the principle of aggregation. Indeed, the very notion of a separate legal personality being accorded to a group of people *qua* a company is founded upon the principle of aggregation. With benefit comes responsibility. *Qui sensit commodum debet sentire et onus* (he who has obtained an advantage ought to bear the disadvantage as well). It is perverse to dispense with the principle of aggregation just at the point when its application would implicate the company in a serious crime. This apparent perversity, however, becomes more intelligible in the context of a political economy which accords priority to the commercial goal of profit and which is thus loath to render seriously criminal conduct which can be seen simply as commercial impetuosity.

An allied difficulty is where company directors manage to distance themselves from the dangerous decisions taken by their managers. The board of directors encourages senior managers to behave in ways that are most profitable to the company. They give no illegal instructions to the managers, nor do they publicly acquiesce in or condone wrongdoing; far from it, they condemn such 'unacceptable behaviour'. Nonetheless, the system is geared to reward decisions which boost profitability even if those decisions are illegal (Geiss, 1967; Boisjoly et al., 1989; Tonry and Reiss, 1993). The key is whether the manager is caught. The political economy is criminogenic, the culture of industry encourages companies to break the law, and companies encourage executives to do the business which actually involves getting hands dirtied with illegal money or blood. The culpability can thus be tracked back from the offender to the company, from the company to the commercial culture, and from the commercial culture to the political economy. Such an analysis has been used in other studies covering a wide range of organisational crime (Tonry and Reiss, 1993; Ermann and Lundman, 1992; Croall, 1992). Jamieson has noted (1994, p. 14) how executives in top corporate positions can purposely design control systems so that their own liability is protected should illegalities occur.

She cites as a most brazen example of this the Congressional testimony exposing the Iran-Contra government scandal in 1988. The concept of 'plausible -deniability' was presented to the public as a threshold for carrying out a secret agenda that if exposed, would be untraceable to top officials. Where members of the National Security Agency were able to deny knowledge of illegal activities, clandestine pursuits proceeded unfettered.

There were several cases among the 40 studies here which raised suspicions of a similar phenomenon. In case 14, for example, one of the difficulties the CPS may have encountered, had the case been referred to it, would be applying the doctrine of identification, by which it must be shown, for a prosecution to succeed, that at least one director representing the 'controlling mind' of the company had the full *mens rea* (mental element) of the offence. The deceased died from a major head injury when he fell from a forklift truck whilst working on a platform at a cash and carry warehouse. There was evidence that people as senior as the shift manager were aware of and condoned the unlawfully dangerous practice of 'travelling' the forklift trucks with the cage high in the air. There was strong witness evidence that the managers were also aware that the safety mechanisms on the trucks did not work. To exacerbate this state of affairs there was additional evidence that these decisions had been taken in order to facilitate work targets; it would be impossible for the targets to have been met if all the safety regulations were adhered to – and it would, no doubt, be a bothersome expense to have to pay for many more workers to be trained to drive the trucks, particularly if that qualification would have been the grounds for the workers claiming higher pay.

The directors of the company (which operated scores of outlets nationally) may plausibly be able to say that they knew nothing of this deplorable practice at this rogue store. The driver of the truck in the fatal incident said the workers had to do dangerous things otherwise 'we wouldn't be able to complete all the jobs we were expected to do over the shift because of the deadlines set by the managers'. In the same way, it is probably the case that the managers were only setting daily, nightly (the victim was killed on the night shift) and weekly deadlines in order to meet the quarterly targets set by their regional managers, who in turn were trying to accommodate or impress the board of directors.

The three preceding chapters have looked at how, through the *mechanics* of the criminal justice system there are intrinsic obstacles to a conviction for corporate manslaughter: the cursory investigations by the police and HSE inspectors; company directors being left uninvestigated; the unwillingness of coroners to facilitate proper consideration of unlawful killing verdicts; the CPS's misguided reliance on the HSE to refer suitable cases of suspected manslaughter; and the latter's self-image of an advisory adjunct to industry. The operation of much of this system is perpetuated because of the social perceptions of the people who operate it. It is appropriate to look at this in some detail, and I turn to make such an examination in the following chapter.

## Notes

1 Case 14.
2 Note (4) to the prescribed form of inquisition (the standard form on which the results of all inquests must be entered [Coroners Rules 1984, Sched. 4, Form 22] gives a comprehensive

list of suggested, though not compulsory, conclusions to the 'how' question that the inquest is bound to answer by virtue of Rule 36. The list includes 'natural causes'; industrial disease; ... want of attention at birth; suicide; ... lawful killing; ... open verdict; unlawful killing ...'. The object of this list is to standardise conclusions over the whole country and make the statistics based on the annual return more reliable by avoiding, as far as possible, any overlap or gaps between the different conclusions.

3    See *Ex parte Diesa Koto*, applying *R v Galbraith* [1981].

4    I am grateful to the London Hazards Centre for sight of this correspondence.

5    See for example, cases 2, 4, 12, 24, 25 and 27.

6    Report on the Committee on Death Certification and Coroners (22 September 1971), Cmnd. 4810. Chaired by Norman Brodrick.

7    Cases 2, 4, 12, 15, 24, 25, and 28.

8    The duty is to take such care as is reasonable in all the circumstances. It arises from *Donoghue v Stevenson* [1932], and statute but is restricted (under the statute) by the provision that the occupier can expect a worker to appreciate and guard against any special risks 'ordinarily incident [sic]' to his job; s.2 Occupier's Liability Act, 1957.

9    No distinction is drawn between these two in the conclusion and for statistical purposes. It is sometimes suggested that 'accident' connotes something over which there is no human control, or an unintended act, while 'misadventure' indicates something deliberate (but lawful) human act which has unexpectedly taken a turn that leads to death: Jervis (1993, p. 250); Burton, Chambers and Gill (1985, p. 84). This distinction, if valid philosophically, is not used consistently. Thus the results of one coach crash was accidental death (*Re Dalicia Moss* [unreported], *The Times*, 14 October 1983 (Exeter Coroner)); whilst the verdict of another coach crash with very similar facts was misadventure (*Re M4 coach crash* [unreported], *The Times*, 9 November 1983). In this research, the coroner in case 39 put the difference to the jury thus:

> Now what are the verdicts that are available? Well it seems to me it is one of two: either it is misadventure or it is accidental. Now again I am afraid it is a matter of considering matters which seem to have almost the same meaning. Accidental death is appropriate for circumstances where the act which would give rise to a death was an unintended one usually, in my view, that is connected or used where there is an outside agency and the common example of that is a road traffic accident. Now misadventure is where someone engages on a course of activity which in itself goes wrong in other words it is an intentional act attended by an unintended misfortune. It is for you to decide which of these two you feel most appropriate.

In case 40, a different coroner only put the 'accidental' option to the jury with these words:

> An 'accident' is an unforeseen event or course of events i.e. whatever happened here was unforeseen by Mr Morton ... It can also mean 'the unexpected result of a deliberate act'.

Some coroners only rely on one of the two phrases in respect of work deaths, e.g. Mr Christie, from Buthorpe put only the 'misadventure' option to his juries.

I would argue that both phrases are equally unsuitable as descriptions of many deaths at work. Many fatal incidents are accidents in the sense that they were unintended by both employer and employee, but they are sometimes highly foreseeable from the employers

point of view and would thus be better explained as 'delinquent deaths' ('delinquency ...
2. Failure or negligence in duty or obligation', *Collins Concise English Dictionary*).

10  See cases 3, 6, 9, 10, 11, 13, 14, 16, 29, 31, 32 and 36.

11  Of the remaining two cases, the jury in one case (case 1) returned an 'open verdict' (used
as a last resort where there is insufficient evidence to come to any other of the established
conclusions), and in the other case (case 3) gave a description: ' Mr White died of injuries
due to the breakdown of safety procedures and lack of supervision'.

12  *Statistics of Deaths Reported to Coroners: England and Wales 1993*, Home Office Statistical
Bulletin 7/94, 21 April 1994.

13  This is especially odd, since it has been decided, probably correctly, that it is legally possible
to commit murder by omission: *R v Gibbons and Proctor* [1918].

14  Legal Aid Act, 1988, Part 1 Schedule 2 (by omission). Legal Aid by way of representation
at proceedings before coroners was approved in principle by parliament in 1949 (Legal
Aid and Advice Act 1949) and again in 1974 (Legal Aid Act 1974, s.7, schedule 1, Part 1,
para. 4), but this provision was not to come into force until a day appointed by the Lord
Chancellor. No such day has since been appointed.

15  Statistics on death at work are not classified according to sex. However, females represent
a very small proportion of those killed at work. None of the 40 cases in my study involved
a female fatality, and one figure produced by the HSE shows that of 227 fatalities at work
reported to its Field Operations Division, all but eight were male (1993, p. 86).

16  A good example is given by Du Cann (1980, p. 116). A young man was once charged with
having unlawful sexual intercourse with a girl under 16. The corroborative evidence
supporting the girl's story came from a farmer who said he had seen the pair lying together
in a field. He was cross-examined thus:

COUNSEL: When you were a young man did you never take a girl for a walk in the
evening?
FARMER: Aye that I did.
COUNSEL: Did you never sit and cuddle her on the grass?
FARMER: Aye that I did.
COUNSEL: And did you never lean over and kiss her while she was lying back?
FARMER: Aye that I did.
COUNSEL: Anybody in the next field, seeing that, might easily have thought you were
having sexual intercourse with her?
FARMER: Aye and they'd have been right too.

# 5 Social Perceptions of the *Dramatis Personae*

Previous chapters have examined the consistency of decisions made by police officers, HSE inspectors, coroners, lawyers and Crown Prosecutors in their official responses to deaths at work; consistency both within their own occupations and between their occupations.

Much of this consistency is, at first sight, attributable to the rules which govern these people. Nevertheless, rules very rarely have clear, unambiguous application to any given situation. They are always subject to an element of discretion at the moment when they are applied or not applied to a given situation (Cross and Harris, 1991; Twining and Miers, 1976) and when they *are* applied, this also can produce alternative results. A coroner, for example, must legally hold an inquest where there has been a suspicious or unnatural death. A case could present itself, referred by a hospital, where there is no obvious reason for the death of a middle-aged person. The first question is whether there can be found any reason, medically, to explain the death and thus avoid the need for an inquest. The coroner has to decide whether to bring the deceased into the category of having died an 'unnatural or suspicious death'. He will study the case notes and consult medical experts. Even if, however, the deceased is brought into the category and an inquest is held, the conclusion, after more evidence is acquired, might still be 'natural causes'.

The daily operation of the legal machinery illustrates this point. Each week hundreds of lawyers up and down the country are on their feet in law courts arguing to the judge, in effect, that they fully accept the validity of a particular binding case authority, or the validity of apparently relevant legislation but that those provisions do not apply to their clients' situations for certain reasons. The doctrine of *stare decisis* (binding precedent) applies, but the material facts are distinguishable from the earlier authority; or, the scope of the Act does not extend to the facts in issue. Rules, in other words, do not automatically determine the outcome of any given situation (Lloyd, 1979, p. 270; Hart, 1961, p. 124).

When judges make decisions in hard cases (Dworkin, 1977) they are often influenced by public policy considerations (Griffith, 1997; Lloyd, 1979; Lacey, Wells and Meure, 1990; Slapper, 1994c). When the personnel involved in the official response to death make decisions they are influenced by social axioms, often directly deducible from the same precepts from which judges extract their tenets of public policy. It can sometimes be difficult to separate out the distinct elements which connect, progressively, as social axiom – precept – point of view – perceived fact, because '… fact, value, role and vantage point are all intimately bound up in the process of perception' (Twining and Miers, 1976, p. 76).

Owing to various factors of social and historical development it is very common for deaths at work to be perceived as 'accidents' or, in any event, if they are wrongs, they are seen as wrongs which are suitably dealt with as infringements of regulatory legislation.

Popular ideas and implicit assumptions play a part in determining how the criminal justice system operates. In discussing the law which prevents sleeping in public transport facilities in many states of the USA, Chambliss and Seidman point out (1971, p. 82) that the conduct at which the law is aimed is clearly defined, but in practice certain types of people sleeping in the stations will be treated differently from others. A homeless, unwashed vagrant will be treated differently from a neat executive who has nodded off whilst waiting for a commuter train, even though both people are asleep in a station.

Quite often, decisions of police officers which stem from factual interpretations are presented as legal and lapidary. Police officers who, without properly investigating the background to the death, deem a work site death 'accidental', are making a factual, personal, subjective, evaluation. They are likely, however, if especially challenged, to defend their judgement as legal. Coroners who arrogate to themselves the decision as to whether a death *could be regarded as* an unlawful killing are doing the same thing in cases where there is evidence that could 'not be rejected as worthless or incredible' (*R v Greater London Coroner ex parte Diesa Koto* [1993]). The reason for this, arguably arrogant, stance which dresses opinion in a little brief authority is that the question whether a particular matter is one of law or fact is a question of *law*.

The reasons why HSE inspectors have not always investigated directors after someone has been killed at work is partly because of limited time and resources (James, 1992, p. 98)[1] but also because of commonly held notions about the nature of serious crime. As Quinney (1970, p. 16) has observed, 'crime is not inherent in behaviour but it is a judgement made by someone about the actions and characteristics of others'. Coroners may be seen to share the same sort of assumptions as police officers and HSE inspectors. Such an outlook is the product of the axioms arising from the society we inhabit.

When interviewing coroners, HSE inspectors, police officers, lawyers and CPS counsel in the cases which informed this project, I found one fairly common perception which is appropriate to adumbrate before looking in closer detail at the views of the separate occupational groupings.

Put in its simplest form it is this. The type of employers' risk-taking that results in death is not really criminal, it is a legitimate and proper cost-benefit calculation process gone wrong. This is very different from the youth who drops a brick from a supermarket roof believing it may or may not hit someone. The employer has a legitimate ulterior purpose in taking a risk with his employee: the creation of goods, services and employment. The youth with the brick has no such justification.

The essence of 'gross negligence' as it applies in criminal law is the taking of 'an unjustifiable risk'. Not all risk-taking constitutes recklessness. Leading authors on criminal law put it this way (Smith and Hogan, 1996, p. 64):

> Sometimes it is justifiable to take a risk of causing harm to another's property or his person or even causing his death. The operator of an aircraft, the surgeon performing the operation and the promoter of a tightrope act in a circus must all know that their acts might cause death but none of them would properly be described as reckless unless the risk he took was an unreasonable one ... *whether it is justifiable to take a risk depends on the social value of the activity involved* relative to the probability and gravity of the harm involved [emphasis added].

If someone pushes a piece of concrete off a bridge on to an oncoming train, sincerely hoping it will hit only the roof of the train and frighten passengers, he will be guilty of manslaughter if it goes through the driver's window and kills him. The risk cannot be justified as there is no social value in throwing concrete at trains.

This issue of 'social value' being capable of offsetting risk becomes critically important in the context of employment (Pearce and Tombs, 1990; Tombs, 1995). There are case precedents which address this point squarely and conclude that in order for industry to work it is necessary for people to be exposed to a certain degree of risk – the world would be a safer place without railways and roads but there would be a high price in comfort and convenience to pay. The level of risk an employer may expose his workers (and the public) to is a question whose answer depends not just on ideal safety but also on economic questions. In one case (*Stokes v Guest* [1968]) the plaintiff's husband was frequently required by the defendants, in the course of his employment as a tool setter, to lean over oily machines; he died of scrotal cancer. The plaintiff alleged that the defendant company ought to have known of the risks of this disease and were negligent in not warning her husband and in not giving periodical examinations. The question arose whether the company, through their full-time doctor, Dr Lloyd, had been negligent. In the course of his judgement, Swanwick J, said:

> ... a factory doctor, however, as emerged from the evidence, when advising his employers on questions of safety precautions is subject to pressures and has to give weight to considerations which do not apply as between a doctor and his patient and is expected to give and in this case regularly gave to his employers advice *based partly on medical and partly on economic and administrative considerations.* For instance, he may consider some precaution medically desirable but hesitate to recommend expanding his department to cope with it, having been refused such an expansion before; *or there may be questions of frightening workers off the job or of interfering with production* [emphasis added].

There was in this case an example of the last type of consideration. In a memorandum to the defendant's labour manager, Mr Powis, on the subject of a worker called Aldridge who had been advised by his GP and a Dr Senter to cease working in oil or risk getting scrotal cancer, Dr Lloyd disagreed with what the court had heard was 'high-powered medical opinion' and urged the man to stay on at work and keep up his earnings. The memorandum finishes: 'If we all took the medical advice given in this case, we might as well close the works and much of British industry'.

The alarmingly callous cost-benefit calculation made by Ford in the Pinto case (below), which measured the cost of prospective deaths from burning against the cost of recalling and refitting an unsafe car, is really one which is regularly made in industry and commerce. The real difference here may just have been the company getting caught with an internal memo which showed the cost-benefit calculation (Dowie, 1977).

The point here is that when death results from unsafe work practices, the context of employment presents a *prima facie* excuse of a wrong, but not a criminal wrong, it is a calculation of a 'justifiable risk'. The social perceptions of the actors in the criminal justice system[2] (police officers, HSE inspectors, coroners, lawyers and CPS officers) can help to explain why the system works in the way that it does.

The mechanics of the criminal justice system have worked to preclude prosecutions for corporate manslaughter. Nonetheless, there are ways in which the system could have been made to work so as to allow for such indictments to have been made. It is largely due to the interpretations of circumstances made by the *dramatis personae* that the system is not made to operate in a way which would indict companies for manslaughter. It thus becomes necessary to ask why and how these people come to acquire these precepts.

## The Police

When a police officer is summoned to a death at work, he or she will usually have formed many assumptions before arriving at the scene. The officer may be bracing him or herself to view the body, and may very well be mentally running through the procedures that should be followed. This, of course, is a common and understandable operational phenomenon, often very useful because it avoids the risk of being thrown from the proper procedures by the shock of witnessing the aftermath of a terrible incident.

From the investigating officers in this study of 40 workplace deaths, 18 agreed to be interviewed. The evidence presented here results from these interviews.[3] Of these officers, 17 had not investigated a death at work before the incident in question. The officers were also junior and generally quite young. Taking the corpus of 40 cases, no incident was attended or investigated by any officer above the rank of sergeant.

The most striking aspect of the ensuing aggregate of information and viewpoints was the extent to which the officers prejudged the nature and cause of the incident. Being aware of the circumstances of some deaths, the investigating officers went to the scene aware that they should explore certain possibilities with a view to excluding foul play or suicide as the cause of death. The officers were all aware that what was reported as death at work may not have resulted from an 'accident'; all 18 mentioned that they would check to see that the death (or serious injury[4]) was not the result of a crime. Three officers mentioned the possibility of suicide, but none demonstrated an awareness that the crime of gross negligence corporate manslaughter could have been to blame for the death and should thus prompt a certain type of inquiry. The police perception is partly explicable on the basis of the training (chapter 3). Police trainees are instructed about how to proceed when faced with 'industrial fatal *accidents*' [emphasis added].[5]

There appear to be two further reasons for the police officer's limited perception of his or her duties. One is that as the HSE would be investigating the death and its surrounding circumstances, that organisation would prosecute for an appropriate offence in the local Magistrates' or Crown Court if necessary. The other reason is concerned with perceptions of the nature of real crime and what is proper police business.

Regarding the role of the HSE, although officers generally knew that it was not empowered to prosecute for manslaughter (12 officers, 67 per cent knew the law on this point), its significance was not, perhaps, fully appreciated. They would rely on being brought back on the case by the HSE or CPS even though this almost never happened.

There is another element to this problem. There is a common view amongst police officers that they and their organisation are not best equipped to unravel matters concerned with work practices and the interrogation of managers about safety practices. This appears to be an unnecessarily modest view. With their legal powers to question in the investigation of a serious crime, the police could have clearly established whether any director was likely to have known of a 'serious and obvious risk' to the life or limb of his employees in the cases in question. In the case of George Kenyon (chapter 3) who was minced to death in a machine like an enormous food processor, there was a police investigation for manslaughter in the same way as there is in other cases of conventional crime even if the facts are unusual.[6] The machine had been deliberately interfered with so that it operated with the safety lid up. This was a decision taken to improve the productivity of the firm even though it quite obviously exposed the machine operator to a serious risk of horrible injury and death.

The George Kenyon case can be compared with one from this study (case 6). An assistant manager was electrocuted when he went into the roof space of a leisure centre to investigate a leak in the roof. The leisure centre had been wired by utterly incompetent electricians (anyone can call him- or herself an 'electrician'; the title is not contingent on having passed particular examinations or served a particular apprenticeship). The centre then failed to have the system checked and maintained according to regulations. There was even evidence that management had been made aware that the system was faulty. It was argued in chapter 3 that the reason the police took up the challenge in Kenyon whilst they were indifferent to scores of workplace fatalities which present comparable level of company culpability, may be discovered on three facets of the Kenyon case namely, easily identifiable 'controlling minds'; damning physical evidence; and gruesome facts.[7]

In contrast to the Kenyon scenario, the scale of the leisure centre operation was very large. The centre was owned and controlled by a large local authority. The fault in not ensuring that the centre was shut until its electrical circuitry had been corrected would have been comparatively difficult to locate with the managerial structure. This would have called for interviews with many personnel who worked at the leisure centre and many who worked at the civic centre. Such an investigation would require persistent and efficiently coordinated interviewing. This would take up many hours of police time.

Regarding 'damning evidence', the facts in the leisure centre were less obvious. There was a piece of metal plate in the roof which had become live. That sort of thing, however, is not such a rare event. Such dangers do occur in commercial and domestic settings through mistakes which are not the result of criminal negligence. Unlike the defeated safety mechanism in the Kenyon case, the physical evidence here – the live plate – may only assume a criminal character when juxtaposed with other facts obscured in the history and the management of the centre. A report commissioned by the police from the local electricity board might, though, have produced the evidence that the centre had been wired with criminal negligence. In any event, by having had the centre wired by incompetents and then having failed to have arranged for proper maintenance (so that the grave errors remained undetected) those responsible for the building appear to have been guilty of one of the four forms of gross negligence outlined by the Court of Appeal (and later affirmed by the House of Lords) in *R v Adomako* [1994].

Finally, according to the pathologist who gave evidence at the inquest, unlike George Kenyon, the victim in the leisure centre died an instantaneous death, and, apart from burn patches on two parts of his body where he had connected with the current, was unmarked.

Whilst the level of blameworthiness is probably very similar in both cases, there are reasons why the police would be less likely to perceive the death in the leisure centre as something warranting an investigation by them. Other than the rudimentary investigations made at the scene of the death, no police enquiry was set up in this case. In brief, it did not present with any of the characteristics of normal crime. At the back of the police perception are implicit considerations of public policy.

The considerations may be characterised as follows. With a great deal of effort, occupying perhaps three or four officers for many days, the police might be able to piece together how this fatal incident was allowed to happen, but the expense would not really be justified as it was, after all, a death at work. The resources of the police would be better used catching real criminals (a similar argument applies to HSE inspectors (Harris, 1992). There are, in police work, just as in any other occupation, those who will, for convenience or gain, produce all sorts of justifications for misconduct. One former

Metropolitan Police Inspector has told (Graef, 1989, p. 324) of practice by which some officers were always keen to attend 'sudden deaths' so that they could – in suitable cases – take money from the deceased's house. They said it was 'just a way of making a few bob'. The officer recounting this story was sick after one incident when £40 (the only money she had) was taken from the flat of an elderly deceased person.

> The guys would be looking over your shoulder saying, 'Is there much here guv? Is there much?' They say it's no big deal because a lot of the time what you find goes to the Exchequer – that's their logic.

This example is not cited to suggest that this sort of view is rampant in modern policing. It is cited as an illustration of how perception of 'facts', and the ideational context in which they are set, can be strongly influenced by factors like convenience. Often a person sees in a scene what it best suits him or her to see. Personal interest operates not just to put blinkers on us sometimes (whereby vision is limited but not distorted) but can, as in the extreme cases of stealing from the dead, operate as a pair of distorting lenses on reality. A much more modest version of this seems to operate in the police procedure after a work death. Assuming that the officer has found no evidence to suggest the deceased was the victim of a conventional crime (albeit one disguised to look like an accident) then events can rule as follows. If, while the ambulance crew mop up the body, and the HSE inspectors mop up the investigation and take care of a prosecution when appropriate, the busy, pressured police officer can attend to business other than interrogating company directors about technical safety arrangements, he or she most probably will.

The fact that the police recognise some types of conduct as properly attracting their attention while other types are treated, if at all, with less rigour has been examined before (Reiner, 1978, 1985 and 1991, pp. 200–4). The phenomenon can be illustrated by comparing the lack of police investigation in the leisure centre case with one, this time with comparable facts, when a police investigation did take place. In *R v Holloway* [1994] the Crown prosecuted for manslaughter an electrician whose criminal negligence had resulted in a father's being electrocuted in his kitchen in front of his one year-old son. Stephen Holloway was an unqualified electrician who had wired the central heating system at the house of Nicholas French. Mr Holloway had connected a live wire in the programmer to an earth lead in the junction box. The error meant that, at certain times, anything connected to metal pipe work in the house was live. After members of the family had repeatedly suffered shocks from the system and a delivery driver had been knocked from the top of an oil tank by the jolt he received, the electrician had twice checked his work and declared it sound. Mr French was standing in stocking feet on the damp floor when he touched the sink – which was live – and caught the massive shock which killed him. Ashford CID took up the investigation after two South-Eastern Electricity officials called to the scene of the incident and said that the error was an appallingly elementary one. Holloway was found guilty of manslaughter at Maidstone Crown court on 30 January 1990 and sentenced to nine months imprisonment, suspended for two years.[8]

For his bereaved family and friends, the loss of the 29 year-old assistant manager of the leisure centre, electrocuted as the result of lethal wiring performed by an incompetent electrician, has caused terrible suffering. For his bereaved family and friends, the loss of Nicholas French (aged 23) by being electrocuted as the result of the lethal wiring performed by an incompetent electrician has also caused terrible suffering. In the case of Nicholas French, however, the police decided to investigate, prepare a file and send it to the CPS – action that resulted in a manslaughter conviction. In the leisure centre case, the police never returned to the scene of death after the initial interviewing on the day of the death. The local authority was later prosecuted for an HSWA offence and fined. In some ways these different responses mean little to the people affected by the loss: neither a serious prosecution nor amnesty will bring back the deceased or ameliorate the suffering of the bereaved. Some of the merits and demerits of different prosecutorial and penological policies are examined in chapter 7. Here the question is concerned with perceptions. In the police view of the world and their proper function in it, the decision to act in cases of individual or gang crime, or even organised crime, but not in organisational crime, results from cultural assumptions and the practicalities of the job.

From the evidence collected in this study, the issue hinges on two perceptions. The first is that fatal incidents at work are seen as 'accidents' unless there are any suspicious circumstances or obvious evidence of gross negligence. The second is the perceived role demarcation as between the police and the HSE inspectors.

Much of the police *modus operandi* emanates from perceptional problems. Like others, the police use 'schemata' to help understand the relation of old and new information. They are thus predisposed by past experience to behave in certain ways (Vernon, 1952). Bartlett (1932) defined a schema as 'an active organisation of past reactions or of past experience ...'. Vernon (1955) has described schemata as 'persistent deep-rooted and well-organised classifications of ways of perceiving, thinking and behaving'. These schemata, of course, do not only assist us to quickly see the sort of things we are looking for, but also *not* to see certain things. The schemata into which the observer fits the new experience may be an inappropriate one.[9] It is such a phenomenon which seems to influence police perception when they are called to a work fatality.

The incident will perhaps have been reported to the investigating officer as an 'accident'. This word, and its grammatical variants, abounds in the literature of official reports and academic commentary. It is, though, highly prejudicial to a balanced assessment of how the death occurred (Carson, 1979; Wells, 1993a, p. 12). No one would think of describing a sudden death in a hospital as 'manslaughter' unless and until such a legal cause had been firmly established, but it seems permissible to refer to work deaths as 'accidents' (as opposed to 'incidents') as a default classification. These deaths are accidents in the very limited sense that they were 'unintended'. But the word 'accident' also carries another, quite distinct, connotation, listed first in some dictionaries: 'an *unforeseen* event or one without apparent cause' [emphasis added] (*Collins Concise English Dictionary*, 1992). Applied to many workplace fatalities, the term 'accident' is thus a misnomer as they have been foreseen (by worried employees, if not by cavalier employers or diligent HSE inspectors). The police perception, based on past social and legal experience, will thus simply perpetuate existing practice even if, as it is here, the case for past practice is unsustainable. The data which go to construct the relevant schemata used by police officers include: (a) the fact that all detailed inquiries are normally undertaken by HSE inspectors; (b) the fact these incidents do not involve proper 'police business' because they do not result from wrongdoing in the way that notion is understood in police culture; and (c) that many fatalities at work are accidents that have not involved any gross negligence from an employer.

Addressing the idea that we treat new experience according to our established experience, G.H. Lewes (1879; Abercrombie, 1969, p. 58) stated that:

> the new object presented to Sense, or the new idea presented to Thought, must also be *soluble in old experience,* to be recognised as like them, otherwise it will be unperceived, uncomprehended.

Deaths at work are not new experiences to the police as an institution (as opposed to individual police officers who may meet such incidents rarely if at all). There is an established police experience on how to deal with deaths in general (Joyce, 1989; M. Young, 1994) and certain types of death in particular. Assumptions about deaths at work are thus passed down the generations and amongst officers. What is emphasised here is not that a police officer arriving on the scene of a work site death will mentally process the data from that case according to his previous experiences of such things.[10] Rather, it is emphasised that even before arriving at the scene, the police officer will, through the received wisdom of police schemata, be likely to have adopted certain views about the fatality. He or she, for example, will almost certainly not be contemplating the possibility of taking statements from senior personnel with responsibility for safety. In many cases this omission will be vindicated, *ex post facto,* but the approach means that there will be systematic exclusion of criminal investigations in the 20 per cent of deaths that this study indicates warrant being carefully screened by the police.

There have been attempts to change this police perception. On 14 October 1991, a deputation from the builders union UCATT went to Scotland Yard to try and persuade the Metropolitan Police to take a more concerned, investigative approach to deaths on construction sites. The number of deaths was rising (then, to over 150 a year) even though the industry had been suffering a recession so there were fewer projects. Peter Lenehan, the executive director of UCATT, said after the meeting that he had been encouraged by the police response. He said:

> We have maintained for some time that where building site deaths are caused by gross recklessness, there must be a police investigation to see if a crime has been committed.

The union was encouraged by the response of the police, which included an undertaking to issue all Metropolitan Police officers instructing them to investigate whenever there was an allegation that a death had been the result of criminal negligence.

It remains to be seen how far this will change the police perception. Three years on from the meeting, in an interview with the author about deaths at work in general and the change, if any, in police practice in particular, Mr Lenehan said that there had been no detectable change in general policy, either in the Metropolitan Police area or in the provinces. He identified the real problem as the techniques used by the construction companies in the aftermath of the incident:

When the officer turns up, the first person he sees is the agent [i.e. the construction company's contracts manager or site manager], and the agent will have seen to it that any witnesses to the incident are removed to a different location. I've worked in this industry for 30 years and I've seen all the tricks. The police officer will not get any real evidence but not because he doesn't want to, but because the agent has sorted out that there are no witnesses. There might be people who could say a few things about the firm and the way it does things but they're not going to do that. They could be put on the black list.

An officer can only perceive what is evident to him (or angles of it). To the extent, then, that site managers are able to ensure that there are no witnesses to the incident, the investigation is effectively frustrated. It will often be pointless to go to directors and try to establish some failing in the system of safety operated by the firm if the death in question cannot be satisfactorily explained in a way which shows that it was *caused* by the systemic failure. To achieve this the prosecution will require reliable witnesses to the incident. The danger of the fuel tank position in the Ford Pinto, and the callous contempt for human life evidenced by the motor company's actuarially-based decision not to recall the defective cars and refit them, were not in doubt when the company was prosecuted for manslaughter in the United States in 1978. The case failed, however, because the three deaths in question could not be shown, beyond reasonable doubt, to have resulted from the defective car as opposed to careless driving on their part (see chapter 7).

If the police fail to get the necessary witness evidence during the initial investigation then the matter is very often effectively closed. The report that the coroner reads when deciding who to summon as witnesses will, even if the death looks suspiciously as if it resulted from employer gross negligence, not present enough hard evidence in the form of witnesses to support an unlawful killing verdict.

Abercrombie notes (1960, p. 600) that successful detectives differ from less successful ones in their ability to perceive as relevant to the solution of their problem pieces of information which others ignore, regard as irrelevant or do not see. She refers to G.K. Chesterton's story *The Invisible Man*. This is the story where it was known that a man intended to commit murder, and four men were set to watch the house in which his victim lived. When questioned to what persons had entered the house, they said no one. In fact, the murder been committed by a postman, who had been 'mentally invisible' because ad seen his visit as relevant to the customary delivery of mail and t to the unusual event of crime. In some deaths at work the invisible ompany director. To many police officers, the director's behind-the-scene role in the events which culminated in death will not be appreciated as significant. This tendency to fail to identify directorial fault is conducted by a particular facet of that fault: it is nearly always an omission rather than an act; it is what directors have not done rather than what they have done that is possibly criminal. Thus, both the possible offender and the possible offence are invisible.

There are philosophical and jurisprudential arguments about whether particular types of *actus reus* (the physical element of a crime) are acts or omissions (Smith and Hogan, 1996, pp. 52–4). Ultimately, however, such conundrums are not important in this context because, as Smith and Hogan observe (1996, p. 48),' the courts have long accepted without debate that murder and manslaughter are capable of commission by omission'. A vivid illustration of this type of case can be found in *Stone v Dobinson* [1977] (see chapter 1, pp. 23–4).

From the 40 case studies undertaken by the author, in each of the eight cases which were suggested warranted serious investigation for manslaughter, the *actus reus* of the possible crime was an omission. For example in the leisure centre case (case 6), the local authority and/or the leisure centre management failed to have the centre wired by competent electricians, then failed to have the wiring checked in accordance with the regulations – a check which would have revealed the seriousness of the faults. In the other seven cases which all resulted in a death: a mining company failed to raise an arch which overhung a conveyor belt, and, failed to mend a broken safety gate; a construction company failed to provide chaffers to cushion slings against the sharp concrete edges of the beams which were to be lifted; a company making bitumen, tarmac and concrete materials failed to provide scaffolding or pipes to which safety harnesses could be attached by men who had to go inside hoppers to clean them; a cash and carry warehouse failed to train forklift truck drivers, failed to service and repair its lifting cages, and failed to prohibit their misuse; one company failed to have repaired the guard box on a potentially lethal swing grinder; another failed to operate a suitable system of work by which heavy tanks could be lifted safely; and a quarry failed to provide a proper system of truck maintenance by a suitably qualified person.

McCabe and Sutcliffe (1978) studied police procedures for recording crimes, based on participant observation in two police districts (two stations in Oxford and one in Salford). The purpose of the research was to understand how police decide whether to record alleged crimes that are reported to them What the study suggests about police perception and exercise of discretion relevant here. It was found that the way police perceive certain conduc!

very important, and in some cases can override regulation. Despite a (short-lived) Home Office instruction to ignore, for statistical purposes, thefts under £5, the researchers say it was their observation (1978, p. 81): 'that most police officers accepted without much questioning that offences of dishonesty are crimes and should be recorded as such'.

Overall, the researchers found that one of the main reasons why the police exercised their discretion not to prosecute was a perception that the case would be difficult to get to court and would be unlikely to result in a conviction. They may perceive problems in getting the defendant to court, or getting witnesses to testify. Such reasoning meant they were reluctant to prosecute vagrants, alcoholics, gypsies and those involved in 'domestics' (violent family rows).

From 18 police officers interviewed, three officers alluded to the difficulty, in general, of convicting white-collar criminals. None articulated this directly as a reason for not pursuing directors when examining the basic facts of a death at work, but it seemed to be a significant part of the schema that would be used by some officers when assessing the situation and deciding how to proceed. Conscious of the need to use police resources well on behalf of the public, or with a thought to how superior officers would regard such conduct, a junior officer may be unlikely to go after senior personnel in a company (especially if it is a reasonably prosperous one) if they think such action will ultimately be fruitless. In this way the role of the police as, in Young's term (1971), 'negotiators of reality' can be seen very clearly. It illustrates the principle that a situation defined as real by society will be real in its consequences. Police have a view of their typical 'customer' and the sort of misdeeds within their proper jurisdiction. A variety of historical and sociological reasons account for these outlooks (Reiner, 1978 and 1985). More by way of following as a negative corollary from this first proposition than by a separate genesis, police view other types of conduct (such as negligent management) as outside their job remit. The more these assumptions are acted upon, the more they create a reality for others to adopt. The police do not perceive the invisible omissions of care made by pinstriped directors, away from the incident (in time and place), as being real crime. They are regarded as accidents. Officers thus do not investigate with any rigour. There are thus almost no prosecutions for manslaughter. The public record therefore discloses that companies do not commit manslaughter. Police, therefore, are reluctant to devote resources to dealing with the alleged problem. The problem has been designed out of reality by police practice.

One factor above others seems to be implicated in promoting the perception, common amongst police officers, that fatal incidents at work are regrettable accidents rather than events suitably investigated by police for evidence of homicide. The factor is the consensual nature of employment relations. From many conversations with officers, both in interview and in less formal conversation, standard thinking can be characterised this way. The employee goes to work voluntarily and in exchange for pay. He is not legally obliged to take risks with his life or limb. If he chooses to expose himself to known perils then, although his dependants may be able to sue for negligence, and although the HSE may prosecute for a regulatory offence, the fatality is not really a crime. Deaths in a work setting are just habitually seen in this way – and by habitually it is meant the institutional habituation of police practice. This can be compared to psychological phenomena of perception.[11] We have all had to learn how to see ordinary things, generally as a natural part of infant development. Studies of adults congenitally blind because of cataract who have been able to see after an operation have shown just how difficult the process of learning to see really is. Perceptual schemata are built up very gradually. It can take up to a month for people to learn to distinguish even a small number of objects (Abercrombie, 1969, p. 47). After 13 days of training, a patient could not say what the difference was between a square and a triangle without counting the corners. In another case (Senden, 1932) although a cube of sugar could be correctly named when seen on the table it was not recognised when suspended by a thread against a different background. Sudden deaths where the body, with blood pouring from the head or mouth, is found on the pavement outside a pub late at night will, similarly, be recognised more easily as possible manslaughter cases than almost identical objects lying on the factory floor.

## HSE Inspectors

Without interviewing the actors in any given situation, a researcher is in danger of imputing motives to them that are, in fact, not those which really motivate (Cicourel, 1968).

Evidence-gathering from discussions with HSE inspectors and interviews undertaken for this study would characterise the primary aim of the inspectorate as one of wishing to ensure compliance with the law. The approach of inspectors is to use education before an improvement notice, an improvement notice before a prohibition notice, a prohibition notice before an s.2 or s.3 (HSWA 1974) prosecution. Inspectors are thus habituated to an outlook on their work, and the human subjects of their work, which is inconsistent with an adversarial mode of 'policing' industry.

There are many factors which affect the perception of law enforcers. The status, reputation, past record, degree of cooperation and the appearance of suspects (even when the suspect may be a company) being dealt with are all significant (Carson, 1970a, 1970b and 1979; Reiner, 1985; Nelken, 1983; Cain, 1973; Hutter, 1986). Hutter, for example, notes (1986, p. 125) that:

> During their inspection of premises, officials will assess both their physical condition and the character and abilities of the personnel who manage and work within them. The physical appearance of property will offer clues about the financial state of a business and the character of those who work there ... the *degree of luxury and comfort in the offices and canteens of a workplace are indicators of financial position* ... the physical condition and maintenance of property are also taken as clues to the character of those in charge [emphasis added].

This is a narrow and dangerously misleading supposition for officials to make. It is probably true that in general, larger, wealthier firms spend more on safety training, equipment and procedures than smaller firms desperate to save on costs. As Marx and Engels charted, there was support for the Factory Acts by the larger capitalist concerns as such law on hours and conditions would put out of business some of the smaller competition (Marx, 1954, 1887, chapter 10; ibid., chapter 15, sections 8e, 9; Engels, 1969, 1845, pp. 23, 197ff). Nonetheless, one cannot generally gauge corporate criminality by the quality of carpets in its head office foyer. Ford's cruel and clinical cost-benefit analysis allowed officials to watch coolly while hundreds of the company's customers suffered unimaginable agonies in car fires. The company was indicted for homicide. Up to 900 people were estimated to have been killed as a result of this company's policy, yet it probably had a well-decorated head office.

Quite how contentious is the *modus operandi* of gauging legal trustworthiness and making safety assessments by crude external signs can be judged by comparing it with the same method being used in a different context. In *The Signs of Crime: A Field Manual For Police* (1977), David Powis, then Deputy Assistant Commissioner to the Metropolitan Police, gave detailed information, based on his many years of experience as an officer in the field, on how to spot crime and criminals (cited in Roshier and Teff, 1980, p. 189). The book is endorsed in a Foreword by Sir Robert Mark as virtually the only good book written on police work. The text contains indicators of suspicious characters who should attract police attention. The indices of suspiciousness include: young people in general but particularly if they are in cars; people in badly-maintained cars, especially if they have a tatty, dog-eared licence; people of untidy, dirty appearance, especially if they have dirty shoes (even manual workers, if honest, are clean and tidy); and people who are unduly nervous, confident or servile in police presence, unless they are doctors who are naturally confident. People of smart, conventional appearance (which commands natural authority and respect) are generally law-abiding, especially if they smoke a pipe.

At one level this advice is risible nonsense. Yet, in principle, it relies on the same criterion for sorting the good from the bad as the HSE's rule of thumb about the quality of a firm's interior décor. It is not uncommon for the HSE inspector to show an unhealthy respect, even occasionally deference, for those whose cavalier attitudes result in human suffering. This point came across, tangentially, several times in interviews with HSE personnel conducted for this study, but one observed moment in a coroner's court articulated this point much more poetically.

The courtroom was quite small, poorly served by windows and with a dull illumination. This was at the end of another harrowing inquest. The desperate, grieving relatives were still sitting, weighted with despair to the hard wooden benches. Lawyers were collecting their papers together and jurors and members of the public were shuffling out of the courtroom. The mother of the deceased could be heard keening in the small corridor outside. Snatches of conversation from around the court were occasionally audible as the noise of the exiting scuffle faded. Then two people who were gradually moving out separately made eye-contact and moved together in a friendly way; they shook hands and exchanged warm greetings directly in front of the bench where the bereaved were sitting. One of the hand-shakers was a self-confident man with an expensive appearance. 'Hello David,' he said 'Nice to see you. Is everything well? I hope that material on Torrington is okay. If not just let me know, okay?' The friend being greeted was just as warm, but not just as well-dressed or, according to popular prejudice, as well-spoken. This was the HSE inspector. Many inspectors like this one, who see their principal role as one of fostering a 'negotiated compliance' with safety law, are on surprisingly friendly terms with their counterparts – the managers of directors responsible for safety. This prejudices any instance of serious (criminal) negligence being perceived accurately and recognised for what it is. The deferential attitude of HSE inspectors to some company senior personnel is, occasionally, like the warm hand-shaking in court, explicable using the rudimentary principles of Sutherland (1949).

More often, however, the interaction is more subtle and complicated. The HSE inspectors do not go gently on business because, as inspectors within capitalism, they are merely reflexes of capital, restricted regulators, hypnotised by the pendulum of profit; they are real, conscious, critical people whose actions can and do affect the world in which they work. Whilst being mould-breaking, refreshingly imaginative and marvellously generative of new criminological research, Sutherland's main theorising was weak in some respects (Nelken, 1994) and rather reliant on a crude structuralist approach (Nelken, 1983, p. 210). Showing how the development of modern policing was neither automatically determined by the economic dictates of capitalism nor woven capriciously by the idiosyncratic concerns of a few pioneers, Reiner (1985, p. 33) notes that the personal views and qualities of certain people arguably did affect the course of history. The inspectors whose outlooks and actions I came to know quite well were not unsympathetic to workers' best interests (being an HSE inspector would have been a perverse choice of occupation for anyone with antipathy towards employees and their safety). Most of them, on the other hand, had an appreciation of the needs of the owners of industry (often characterised as the 'needs of industry'). This was generally seen not as serving the interests of shareholders but serving the collective interest whereby levels and conditions of employment were as high as possible. One inspector put it this way:

> You are not going to go in there and just be bloody-minded about the rules. You have to be realistic. If it seems as if a firm is having a very hard time in the recession, and it is hanging on by the fingernails, then you won't necessarily require it to spend thousands on repainting all the walls, even if there might be a technical violation.

Carson adverts to the same perspective when he notes (1970a, p. 396) that although in modern capitalism 'the dangers of collision between divergent interests' have survived largely undiminished, the inspectorate's task comprises the implementation of 'dominant values' in these situations without stifling progress on the one hand or leaving the conflict to resolve itself in social disarray on the other.

In chapter 3 there was evidence that many HSE inspectors are not inclined to investigate cases in a way which seeks proof of manslaughter. They do not, as a matter of standard practice after a fatality, look at the safety record of the company concerned to put the death in its historical context. What might be a foolishly perilous system of work resulting in death quickly becomes a criminally grave matter if a similar thing has happened before at the company and nothing or little has been done to prevent such a recurrence.

The HSE has only begun to refer cases to the CPS for consideration of manslaughter charges since 1990 and the number of annual referrals seems very low. Between April 1992 and March 1998, 59 cases investigated by the HSE have been referred to the CPS where there was a possibility of a manslaughter charge. In 18 of these, the CPS decided to bring prosecutions and four have led to conviction. Seven cases are still under consideration (Ecclestone, 1998).

These omissions are, at one level, easily explicable. As the primary task of the inspector is to enforce the HSWA, he or she will be more concerned with the provisions of that legislation than the common law. Inspectors are trained, primarily, in the evidential and legal requirements of the HWSA, and in particular sections 2–9. Unlike the police, the HSE inspectors do not have a feel for the sort of criminal investigations, collecting of evidence and witness statements which are required to satisfy the burden of proof for manslaughter. Since 1993 there has been some training given to new inspectors and its effect remains to be seen. In those cases where the circumstances of death indicate a particular atrocious culpability on the part of the employer and, where a coroner has referred the case to the CPS, Bergman (1991) has attributed the failure to prosecute to the fact that the HSE file on a case has not been researched or framed in the best way to convince Crown Prosecutors that there would be a 'realistic prospect of conviction' – the necessary evidential test.

The police attending the scenes of deaths at work are disposed, procedurally and by their working schemata, to regard such incidents as accidents which are properly dealt with by the HSE inspectors who attend. This outlook is understandable from officers whose principal and rudimentary task is dealing with conventional street crime. Similarly, the working culture, perspective and procedures of the HSE inspectorate have historically been such as to put manslaughter considerations outside of their standard thinking.

Many HSE personnel are on friendly terms with the safety personnel from companies 'monitored' or 'policed' by the inspectors. Pearce and Tombs (1990 and 1991) have argued that the proponents of 'compliance' modes of regulation have an incorrect view of the determinants of business conduct, misunderstand how the police deal with conventional crime and order maintenance and contribute to the climate where business is increasingly trusted to regulate itself. This argument has been opposed by Hawkins (1990 and 1991) who has argued for the need to refine theories of organisational compliance and for discretion in the use of harsher penal options available to be requested by the regulatory authorities. Here, other observations can be made. According to one of its officers, the HSE sees

> ... a large number of employers struggling with a difficult economic situation but willing or anxious to fulfil their health and safety obligations and often looking to us for help and advice. We see some who are ignorant or indifferent and needing a jolt; and we see employers who would in any world rank top for health and safety.[12]

A good illustration of problems resulting from an over-sympathetic inspector arose at an inquest into the death of a mine worker who died after suffering a severe head injury while travelling on a conveyor belt out of a mine at the end of a shift (case 8). The HSE Inspector of Mines had worked for 16 years for mining companies. Clearly, this must have coloured his view about acceptable/unacceptable standards of conduct. He would be more 'defendant minded' in the way that, conversely, many judges are 'prosecution minded'. This supposition was borne out by two things: (a) he was alarmingly complacent about breaches of regulation which he reported in his evidence, e.g. the tunnel arch through which the deceased was travelling on the belt and on which he might have knocked himself out turned out to be below regulatory height but the Inspector only disclosed this upon being pressed by counsel. Even then he made no particular comment about it. It was *his* evidence which seemed to influence the coroner to eagerly pursue what the company had done *since* the death rather than look at what it had omitted to do before the death; and (b) he spent the recess engaging in good humoured badinage with the mine manager and his lawyer while the mine workers were left a few metres away to contemplate how rigorously their own safety was being guarded by the inspector.

In her study of 'proactive enforcement strategies' in the regulation of business and industry in England and Wales, Hutter (1986) charts the importance of discretion in the way the inspectors enforce the law. Accepting the analysis of Richardson et al. (1982, p. 123), she argues that:

> whereas proactive strategies take account of the preferences of agency personnel, reactive strategies are generally shaped by public priorities. Proactive work is in many respects hidden from the public eye, but the agency's performance in response to complaints and major incidents and serious accidents is more visible and agencies are aware that their work is more likely to be directly judged by a third party (Hutter, 1986, p. 117).

The problem here is identifying the origin and nature of 'public priorities'. Is the expression used here with a similar connotation to the phrase 'public policy', as it is understood by the judiciary?[13] If so, then in the same way that judges have more of a say in what is *public* policy than members of the public, senior personnel in the HSE will have a great deal of influence over determining the criteria by which a third party (like a journalist) judges the regulatory response. Rather awkwardly, this means that the preferences of senior agency personnel are actually determining the way inspectors deal with both minor *and* major breaches of law.

In a footnote, Hutter argues that she has focused on 'major accidents' in recognition of a point made by Sally Lloyd-Bostock, namely that health and safety agencies do exercise a great deal of discretion in their response to many minor accidents which come to their attention. By contrast, it is argued here that there is a very important discretion exercised by HSE/EHD inspectors investigating fatal incidents at work; a discretion which is constantly exercised against bringing in the police and the CPS.

## The Coroners

Looking at the role of coroners' definitions in societal reactions to suicide, Maxwell Atkinson noted (1971, p. 166) that:

> There has ... been a readiness to see suicide rates as being somehow related to various social processes, yet until relatively recently experts have ignored the fact that the rates themselves are also a product of complex social processes.

This technique of examining the social processes involved in the production of statistics has been looked at elsewhere (Kitsuse and Cicourel, 1963; Wiles, 1971; Bottomley, 1973). It was argued (detailed in chapter 2) that there were annually about 200 deaths 'at work' which are not recorded as such because they are caused on the roads and are classified with other road traffic deaths. That people can be 'at work' whilst in a vehicle on the roads is not recognised by current systems of classification. Realistically, therefore, the true figure of deaths at work is probably nearer 600 than the officially recorded 400. Other than that serious statistical error, there is very little hard evidence that the annual statistics for deaths at work omit other times or instances of death.[14]

Coroners' definitions, as in cases of possible suicide, significantly affect the way that deaths at work are classified and registered. Coroners' perceptions help to keep all of the annual work-related deaths (302 according to the latest HSC Annual Report 1996/97), out of the statistical tables of annual homicide figures.

In the previous chapter it was argued that coroners could, legally, carry out their duties in a way which shifted possible cases of manslaughter back to the police for further investigation, or to the CPS for consideration of charges. They could do this at any stage before opening the inquest if the statements they read suggested this might be a prudent option. They could also, if the evidence as they heard it develop during an inquest suggested a prima facie case of manslaughter, adjourn the inquest and send the file to the police or CPS. Another option would be to let the inquest run and then put to the jury the possible conclusion of 'unlawful killing'. Such courses of action however, are almost never taken by coroners.

Insofar as these decisions ever have to be justified or explained by coroners, the reasons given are, as one would expect, of a legal nature. Justifying his decision not to put to the jury the unlawful killing option in the case of Tony Fishenden (in chapter 2), the coroner Dr Douglas Chambers explained that he was not bound to put to the jury any conclusion 'if the evidence presented, taken at its highest, is such that a jury properly directed could not properly reach that conclusion' (Matthews and Foreman, 1993, p. 241). This is supported by the case law: *R v Inner North London Coroner, ex parte Diesa Koto* [1993]; *R v Galbraith* [1981].

It is important, nonetheless, to go behind these legal reasons to examine the schemata coroners are using to come to these uniform decisions.

Perhaps because of their predominantly legal background, the sensitive nature of their work and an understandable wariness of journalism, many coroners are very guarded about their work. Under the Coroners' Rules (1984, rule 57) anyone who, in the opinion of the coroner, is 'a properly interested person' is entitled to inspect documents and notes given in evidence. This has been given some very narrow interpretations. Rule 57 gives no guidance as to who is a 'properly interested person' but the practitioners' manual *Jervis* suggests that it is anyone who is entitled to be represented at the inquest. Rule 20, covering representation, is clearer than rule 57. It lists the people entitled to be represented as including, parent, child, spouse or personal representative of the deceased, the beneficiary of a life insurance policy, the insurance company, someone who may have contributed to the death, a trade union representative (if the death occurred at work), an enforcement officer under the Health and Safety Etc. Act 1974, and a chief police officer. Additionally it includes anyone else who in the opinion of the coroner is a properly interested person. In one case into a possible naval suicide, the coroner refused to allow the deceased's brother to be represented even though he was the only member of the family who wished to be represented. The coroner said 'brother' was not on the list in rule 20 (*R v HM Coroner for Portsmouth ex parte John Keane* [1989]). In another High Court case it was held that a coroner inquiring into the death of a black person in a London police station was entitled to rule that a local organisation concerned with police/black community relations was not a 'properly interested person' and therefore not entitled to representation (*Times Law Review*, 30 April 1983).

A Campaign for Freedom of Information Report (1991) states that some coroners are using this power in 'an arbitrary and extraordinarily illogical way'. One coroner denied access for a study of platform safety funded by London Underground and carried out by the Department of Community Medicine at Charing Cross and Westminster Medical School. A Home Office spokesman is quoted in one report (*The Guardian*, 2 January 1991) as saying that there was a long-standing tradition of independence for the coroner. 'The coroner has to have discretion otherwise he or she would not be independent of the state.'

Of eight coroners interviewed, there was a remarkable similarity of outlook among these men on the theme of deaths at work. The consistency of approach seems to stem from a similarity of previous and ongoing experience, and their social and political opinions. The body of coroners is quite small: there are approximately 144 coroners in England and Wales, of whom 24 are 'full-time' coroners in cities and populous counties; additionally there are approximately 243 part-time deputies and assistant deputies. As a group, coroners are, sociologically, rather homogeneous. There is no official data published about the sociological features of England and Wales.

HM coroners of England and Wales are predominantly male, white, middle-class lawyers (mostly solicitors). On average about 90 per cent of the incumbents are lawyers, mostly solicitors (approximately 80 per cent); the remainder are doctors, a few of whom hold duel qualifications in law and medicine. They are members of the Coroners' Society of England and Wales, and most convene several times a year for updating and professional training sessions run by the Society.

Maxwell Atkinson (1971) takes up a theme first addressed by Jack D. Douglas (1967): that it is not valid to use coroners' records as a source of data because they just reflect the views of coroners about what constitutes suicide. Douglas (cited in Maxwell Atkinson, 1971, p. 172) observed that: 'regardless

of the effect of formal definitions, it is clear that coroners do in fact use different *operational* decisions of suicide'.

Not only do coroners' views sometimes not exactly match official definitions but, as Maxwell Atkinson's research shows, those coronial perceptions tend to clarify and strengthen the social picture of what is meant by 'suicide' (ibid., p. 86).

The same phenomenon was distinctly evident in relation to coroners' thinking about the appropriateness of the 'unlawful killing' conclusion for deaths at work. Their 'operational decisions' about which witnesses to summon, what lines of questioning are permissible from advocates, and which conclusions to put to the jury, are based on an interpretation of what is 'proper' that is not in accordance with the letter of the law (as shown in chapter 2).

Coroners are instructed by their professional manual to return conclusions of suicide only where there is 'positive evidence of intent' (i.e. that the deceased intended to kill him- or herself). Suicide notes are clearly helpful to the coroner in determining this issue and, provided foul play being covered up with such a note is ruled out, the coroner will rely on them. The trouble is that such notes only appear in about 30 per cent of suspected suicides. Maxwell Atkinson shows that in the other 70 per cent of cases, the coroner relies on certain 'cues'. Under modes of death, for example, taking over 10 barbiturates is a good indicator of suicidal intent, whereas death by drowning is too vague to be, on its own, much of a pointer. Location can also be a good pointer, so several barbiturates taken 'in the middle of a wood would be more likely to lead to a suicide verdict than one taken in bed'. Coroners are also interested in performing 'psychological autopsies' on the deceased to look for cues. Maxwell Atkinson recounts an example of a coroner going through a file with him and identifying the cues as they accumulated (ibid., p. 181):

> There is a classic pattern for you – broken home, escape to the services, nervous breakdown, switching from one job to another, no family ties – what could be clearer.

In the context of deaths at work there is evidence to suggest that the same operating principle is being used. Coroners have an idea about what an 'unlawful killing' looks like. This idea is the product of an almost instinctual, impressionistic appraisal, rather like the police officer who smells a rat or the examiner who considers that the script reads like a first class answer.

Maxwell Atkinson notes that the coroner's practical starting point is the general circumstances of the death. In the case of a death resulting from a car

crash, for example, it is highly unlikely that much will be made of the deceased's family history, whether or not the dead man had experienced a broken home in childhood or details about his current financial situation. Conversely, if a man dies by hanging it would be considered appropriate to look for such evidence.

The schemata used are not especially subtle. They provide a useful template with which to conduct investigations expeditiously, and they are founded upon some simple commonsense propositions. Largely this seems to be a matter of resources. Both full- and part-time coroners are busy people with an unending series of clients to interview, console or appease (by telephone call, letter, or in an office visit). Some of HM Coroners are remarkably diligent and thorough in leaving no stone unturned in the process of investigating any death whose causes look remotely suspicious or problematic: the sort that could result in verdicts of suicide, natural causes aggravated by neglect, or unlawful killings. Much coronial work, however, is not so conscientious and fastidious. Coroners could treat each case like a new Sherlock Holmes mystery. They could utilise lateral-thinking techniques, and leave no stone unturned in each case. As soon as any of them did such a thing, they would most likely be overwhelmed by a growing mountain of other, disregarded work. Their administrative staff resources are not such to allow each death inquiry to be treated with the organisation of a police murder investigation (albeit with the purpose of examining other possibilities like suicide, accidental death, etc.) The schemata, like the ones used in suicide cases, serve a useful practical purpose of facilitating the inquiry by making use of accumulated social experience. The trouble is that any errors in this scheme will usually be perpetuated.

To say that coroners' perceptions of social affairs influence the way they apply the rules in work death cases is a view indirectly supported by reference to another aspect of their treatment of the suicide case: that a wide-angle social lens is used by the coroners when trying to determine 'how' the deceased died in a suspected suicide case, whereas when viewing events around a workplace death, coroners decline to pick up the same lens, preferring to look at the incident through a drinking straw. They appear not to mind breaking from a strict interpretation of the word 'how' to get to the bottom of a possible suicide, but they will steadfastly refuse to be as relaxed in their interpretation of the word 'how' in cases of death at work.

The reason for this inconsistency appears to be associated with the fact that an 'unlawful killing' verdict causes a lot more 'upset' in other parts of the legal system. The police and CPS become involved, the local press leap on the case, and, a little later, the national press and sometimes broadcasting

media. In ordinary cases of homicide where a man has been found with a knife in his back, I found no objection to the conclusion from coroners. With work fatalities, the general thinking was summed up by a comment from one coroner:

> It's all nonsense. I mean what is the point? A company can't really kill people. The reason they [lawyers] will argue for that verdict is to assist in the claim. That's all they're really interested in.

It is not just in cases of possible suicide where in order to get the 'correct conclusion' the coroner will be prepared to roam with his inquiries over a wider compass. As Scratton and Gordon have shown (1984), in controversial cases like that of the death of Blair Peach, the coroner will take evidence from a general context. The coroner in that case directed the jury that the conclusion depended upon the interpretation of 'reasonable force' as it applied to 'overall police action in Southall'.[15]

As shown in the previous chapter, coroners in work-related deaths will often, citing rules 36 and 42 of the Coroners' Rules 1984, refuse to summon witnesses or allow summoned witnesses to be questioned if it appears that lawyers are trying to get evidence to assist in a civil action. Coroners will often just obstinately not accept the point that although the advocate could be asking the contentious questions for the illegitimate ulterior purpose of preparing for the civil case, the very same questions could be, and in fact sometimes are, asked to establish that there is enough evidence of unlawful killing for that conclusion to be put to the jury.

From interviews with coroners, the point which seemed to weigh heaviest with them in framing a perception of deaths at work as nothing more than dreadful accidents, was the legal, consensual nature of the setting in which the fatality occurred. The point was adverted to by all of the coroners interviewed and emphasised by seven of the eight. Extracts from two of these interviews can illustrate the point:

> *Coroner 1*: ... But of course these [workplace deaths] aren't killings in any real or legal sense. When Joe Bloggs goes to work and something awful happens, well then, this is some dreadful mistake, something no-one foresaw would occur. There might have been a breach of regulations by the employer, or, and I have seen it often enough, the worker taking risks and just getting on with it, but that's not criminal. Remember, this conclusion requires satisfaction of the criminal burden [i.e. jurors need to be satisfied beyond reasonable doubt that the death resulted from gross negligence].

*Coroner 2*: ... I know what the P&O Ferries case says [*Herald of Free Enterprise* capsizing off Zeebrugge – corporate killing possible] but those circumstances were exceptional. Where there have been serious errors, it's the fellow who's supervising on the site, the foreman, or a junior manager who may have been responsible. They might make very poor decisions which have tragic results, and of course, these may be the subject of litigation but they are not normally criminal deeds, and these decisions aren't taken at the board [of directors] so you cannot bring the company, the company as a legal person, into the picture.

These views both rest on a premise that companies do not acquiesce in levels of risk-taking comparable to those which are sufficient to convict doctors, dentists, rugby players, drivers and football fans of manslaughter. There is no hard evidence adduced to support the premise, only further prejudice and speculation.

Thus coroners use unsupported supposition to wean a presentiment, and then they use the resulting phantom body of evidence to support the legal decisions they make in work death cases (not remitting cases to the CPS, withholding the 'unlawful killing' from the jury, etc.) These legal decisions create precedents which then crystallise into a hard legal and social conception that wherever manslaughter can be committed – on a rugby field or in a doctor's surgery when s/he writes a prescription – it cannot occur at work. There is ample evidence to substantiate Maxwell Atkinson's view (1971, p. 186) that: 'deaths are actually defined in the social contexts in which they take place'.

The inquest into the death of the mine worker (case 8) provides a good illustration of a set of basic facts which, rigorously investigated by an experienced team of police officers, taking advice perhaps from mine safety officials, could well have produced a *prima facie* case of manslaughter. The deceased had been killed in a mine. He died from a serious head injury which he had sustained either by banging his head on an overhead arch as he was travelling out of the mine on a conveyor belt, or (being asleep or unconscious) having been carried, through safety gates, to the end of the conveyor belt and then dropped precipitously over the edge on to a concrete and metal surface below. The facts were such that whichever way the death had occurred, it was the result of serious and chronic breaches of safety which be could tracked back to corporate responsibility: the arch was too low and in breach of the relevant guidelines, and the safety gates were (a) set too high above the belt, and (b) not working, i.e. they did not, as they were supposed to, stop the belt if something large pushed through them. The danger of the arch and the danger presented by the defective gate were both known to the mining company. The colliery manager reluctantly confirmed this in answer to an advocate's question.

Nevertheless, the coroner could not see there being any possibility of this death's being classified as an unlawful killing, or, if he could, he was intent on that conclusion's being kept out of the inquest's deliberations.

Within two minutes of the colliery manager's having admitted that the company was aware of the faults in the arch and the safety gate, the coroner pursued a line of questions with him which sought to establish that the mine had since been made safer in all but one of the ways recommended by the HSE inspector in a report *after* the fatality. This narrative excursion was perhaps reassuring, and within the coronial jurisdiction insofar as it sought to examine the circumstances which, if not remedied, might lead to further deaths.[16] It is noteworthy that coronial discretion can be used like this (here to show the company in a good light) but is often not used, notwithstanding requests to do so, to help create a wide picture of how a person came to be killed. The coroner was keen to go into detail about what the manager of the colliery had done *since* the death but there was virtually no discussion about the nature of the defective safety gate. How long had the gate been in that condition? Had any worker reported it as being unsafe? The coroner did not examine the manager on such points. He evidently took the view that it was more important to ask about events subsequent to the death.

The manager testified about the aspect of the HSE's recommendations which he had not yet been able to successfully install at the pit. This concerned a use of electronic safety tags (like the Marks & Spencer store security tags, he said) to be worn by all men and which would stop the conveyor belt automatically if anyone wearing one travelled passed the safety gate (e.g. because they were asleep, unconscious, etc.). Work was being done in a research and development department to get a tag which was capable of withstanding the heat, sweat and knocks which it would have to endure in the ordinary course of work. The coroner enthusiastically went into all of this in some detail although it was not pertinent to the primary purpose of the hearing – determining 'how' the deceased met his death.

In a second case study (case 38), a close scrutiny of the facts shows that someone either failed to communicate, or failed to read and disseminate to staff, a critically important safety information sheet. The deceased, aged 20, was bending over a large tank containing chemicals. He had been instructed to help with repairs to the tank's gauge. There was a huge explosion and he was thrown over 100 feet. When his workmates found him, the victim was still alive but his right arm was missing and the skin from his face was gone. The rest of his body was severely damaged by the explosion. There was an extrusion of internal organs. At the inquest a workmate wept and shook recalling these facts. He said, 'he was alive but there was just nothing we could do for him'. The circumstances of death were horrific and more disturbing than the basic facts of many murder and manslaughter cases.

At the centre of the story were the following facts. The tank contained a chemical, toluene, which is potentially very dangerous because it is volatile and flammable. The chemical supply firm stated that they had sent, by fax, information about the chemical to the firm for which the victim worked. At the inquest the coroner requested evidence of this. None could be produced. All the supplier could show was evidence that all the financial aspects of the deal had been examined fastidiously by the parties. They were evidently less fastidious when it came to communicating about crucial safety aspects of the product. This aspect of the case was not pursued by the coroner. In this sense the inquest was a shambolic mess whose outcome the coroner must have prejudged – this is the only reasonable explanation for how such important evidence (relating to possible criminal negligence) was treated with such lack of interest by the coroner and his witnesses. If the person killed by the exploding chemical had been the Secretary of State for Employment, who happened to have been visiting the company, then it is unlikely the coroner would have been as evidently indifferent to the evidence as he was in this case.

At the close of the hearing, the coroner asked the representative from the HSE whether he had heard anything in the course of the inquest which would prompt him to request an adjournment of the inquest for the Executive to commence proceedings. The Inspector said that he had not any such evidence. Then, summing up for the jury the coroner said: 'I do not believe you have heard anything which implies gross negligence or which should lead you to consider a verdict of unlawful killing'.

Taking the view that, in fact, the only reasonable verdict was 'accidental death', the coroner then invited the jury to remain where they were (in court) to decide their verdict.[17]

The coroner was correct in believing that there had been no incriminating evidence, but that absence could well have been the result of the lack of rigorous investigation into the business communications between supplier and purchaser. If a company is making money from selling chemicals that can, when ignited by the smallest spark (from a hand-held torch being switched on, or from the static of a plastic jacket) explode, then it clearly has an obligation to inform buyers properly about the risks. This is not a petty point – failure to give proper warnings can result in serious injury and death. If the message was received by the purchasing firm but ignored or not properly acted upon then this may constitute an equally grave omission. It is not to say that either party *was* blameworthy, it is to say that the necessary information and testimony on which to make such a judgement was not given. There is the possibility that there was criminal negligence in this case, every bit as inimical as in 'conventional' manslaughter cases where culprits have been convicted and given custodial sentences. If there was, then it managed to disguise itself successfully behind the pinstriped suits, faxed messages and the educated tones of the company managers. In any event, the disguises kept away any unwelcome interrogations in court, whether or not there was anything to hide.

The facts of a further case (case 39) involving another appalling death showed it was entirely preventable. The victim involved need not have been smashed to death in the tipper truck his employer had provided. It failed to stop at the ridge of a deep quarry not because it was struck by lightening or subjected to an unexpected seismic shake but because all the brakes were defective. The man employed to carry out the maintenance on the company's large fleet of vehicles was unqualified as a mechanic and untrained in maintaining the particular make of vehicle in question. The coroner's perception of this case and the general setting of work-related deaths are evident from his summing up which is quoted at length below. It is followed with a fictional summing up which could have been given on the same facts, but which proceeds from a different perspective.

*Extract from the summing-up given*:

> ... All we do know is that he was an experienced truck driver and he was self-employed but was under contract to this firm A & V Centrals, he had been working for some time on this site and was therefore considered by one of his companions well known and obviously a very experienced man with it [sic] and though his contract employer thought very highly of him and gave a very good account of the sort of person he was, but all his companions did as well they say he was an experienced man who didn't take risks [sic]. What we do know of course is that the braking system was defective and there was a moment obviously when he needed to employ those brakes and they didn't work and with that huge weight it's not surprising that he careered down the bank, overturned in the way that he did and he suffered those injuries that Dr Crenthorne referred to in his post-mortem report – that the ruptured spleen if you remember which gave rise to the haemorrhage and then that was the medical cause of his death.
>
> Now what are the verdicts that are available? Well, it seems to me it's one of two: either it is misadventure or it is accidental. Now again I am afraid it's a matter of considering matters which seem to have almost the same meaning. Accidental death is appropriate for circumstances where the act which could

give rise to a death was an unintended one usually, in my view, that is connected or used where there is an outside agency and the common example of that is a road traffic accident. Now, misadventure is where someone engages on a course of activity which in itself goes wrong in other words it is an intentional act attended by an unintended misfortune. It is for you to decide which of these two you feel most appropriate. I see things here from one way but my view of that is only a matter of interest as far as you're concerned because you are the jury, you are the people who have got to come to a conclusion because it is your verdict not mine. Would you now go away and consider these matters very carefully and then come to a decision, but as I indicated earlier you have to do not only that but set out in a succinct form the facts upon which you base your verdicts and I would suggest something like this (and I am not trying to tell you what to do but just give you an indication). Just say that John Holley on the 8 May 1992 was working on the site when, and then describe how you find what happened as a result of which he received severe injuries which proved fatal or which he received fatal injuries. That is the way to frame it but again it must be your words but bear it in mind I have to write it into a very small space and my writing leaves a lot to be desired. The fewer the words the better as long as they succinctly set out those facts upon which you base your verdict. Now if you do have any questions that you need to have guidance upon, if you would let Mr Jordan [coroner's officer] know he will tell me then I will reassemble the Court and you can address the questions to me and I will endeavour to answer.

*Part of a summing up that could have been given*:

We know that Mr Holley was an experienced truck driver and that he was self-employed. He was under contract to this firm A & V Centrals where he had been working for four weeks. You may decide, therefore, that it was unlikely to be ignorance of the truck or its capabilities which was the real cause of the disaster that led to his death. We have been told that he was an experienced man who did not take risks. What we also know is that the braking system on this truck was disastrously defective. From the expert testimony you have heard, it is fair to characterise the vehicle as having virtually no effective brakes. That is, of course, especially dangerous for a very heavy vehicle that the company knows will be repeatedly manoeuvred at the top of a dangerous precipice – the edge of a quarry.

You have been told that the man employed by this company to maintain this and other vehicles, Mr Potter, was not a qualified mechanic and he had, furthermore, no training in how to service or repair this make and model of vehicle. This is a very responsible position, and it is not clear why this man was given the job in preference to many able individuals who were qualified and who had been trained by the vehicle company to carry out servicing and repairs.

You have heard that Mr Potter did keep a diary of the servicing of the 20 vehicles under his charge but only minimal entries were made. No service or other manuals for the dump trucks are kept by A & V Centrals. Mr Potter had a service check list for the type of vehicle in question, which he obtained from someone at his previous employment, but that list is kept in his office and rarely consulted. As far as the rear axle is concerned, the brake *linings* were in very good condition – they were hardly worn at all. They had been adjusted to a minimum setting whereby the brakes do not operate at all – this was only the appropriate setting *to facilitate removal of the brake drums*. Mr Potter, should, of course, have noticed this. He told you he did not notice it, perhaps because the brakes 'could have been contaminated with mud thus giving the appearance of being in contact with the brake drum'. It that a satisfactory way to test brakes? Would you be happy if your vehicle or the brakes on an aeroplane you were on had had its brakes tested in such a way; where the sole test involved a mechanic saying, 'well, they look alright'? Remember, of course, that the tipper truck was a very large, heavy vehicle used to manoeuvre at the rim of a precipitous quarry.

It is relevant for you to remember that according to safety law, maintenance is to be judged by outcome rather than the way any individual works. If something ill-maintained causes injury or harm, it is not open to those responsible for its maintenance to try to persuade the court that, in fact, their system of maintenance was acceptably efficient. The outcome of Mr Potter's maintenance programme was that three out of four rear brakes did not work. Following Mr Holley's death and an HSE investigation, the company was prosecuted in a criminal law court and was convicted (after pleading guilty) to the offence of failing to provide proper protection against risks to people affected by the company's work. There was a moment when Mr Holley needed to employ the brakes and they didn't work and with that huge weight it's not surprising that he careered down the bank, overturned the way that it did and he suffered those injuries that Dr Crenthorne referred to in his post-mortem report – the ruptured spleen which gave rise to the haemorrhage and then that was the medical cause of his death

Now, what are the verdicts available? It seems to me there is one of three. I think that you should consider unlawful killing, accidental death and death through misadventure. Unlawful killing is a conclusion you may return if you are sure, not on the balance of probabilities, but beyond reasonable doubt, that this sad death resulted from gross negligence. You must first find that there was a duty owed to the deceased by some other party (like an employer). You must be sure that the deceased died as a result of that duty being broken, and that there was gross negligence. What is gross negligence? Let me quote to you from a judgement which the House of Lords has recently approved as being the best way to characterise what in law is meant by this term 'gross negligence'.

> In order to establish criminal liability the facts must be such that, in the opinion of the jury, the negligence of the accused went beyond a mere matter of compensation

between subjects and showed such disregard for the life and safety of others as to amount to a crime against the state and conduct deserving of punishment (Lord Hewart CJ in *R v Bateman* [1925], p. 11).

Gross negligence can manifest itself in different ways. It might be 'indifference to an obvious risk of injury to health' or 'an appreciation of the risk coupled with an intention to avoid it but also coupled with such a high degree of negligence in the attempted avoidance' as you think would justify a conviction. Was the system of maintenance so bad, that, in your view, it allowed Mr Holley to die. Was the level of negligence, in your view, such that it should be left for the bereaved to take any necessary civil action, or did it go beyond that? Did it reach a level of indifference to life and limb which, in your view, requires the state to intervene and prosecute for a very serious offence?'

This fictitious summing up is presented with a limited purpose. It illustrates how someone with a perspective on events different from that of the real coroner in the case could slant the summing up in a very different way but still only using evidence from the inquest. It has had to be deliberately vague as to whom (which legal person) may have committed the unlawful killing. It would probably be wholly inappropriate for Mr Potter to be prosecuted. He was merely an instrument of the company, albeit one not fit for its intended purpose. For the company to be guilty of manslaughter, however, the doctrine of identification would have to be satisfied (chapter 2) and it would have to be shown that at least one 'controlling mind' of the company knew of the risks posed by the sloppy maintenance system but acquiesced in that risk. The alternative summing up would have been better composed in a way which included the possibility of corporate responsibility.[18] This was not possible, however, because the HSE, as is its customary method of investigation and case presentation, did not produce a case history profile of the company A & V Centrals. It might well be that from previous accidents logged in the accident book,[19] or even past offences there was ample evidence that the company director (there were three – father, mother and son, but only the son ran the company) *was* aware of the dangers.

## Crown Prosecutors

There is no published figure for how many referrals for consideration of manslaughter are made to the Crown Prosecution Service in respect of workplace deaths each year. Even at the highest estimate (Bergman, 1994, p.

8) it seems to be fewer than 10. Nevertheless, the CPS has acted consistently to reject taking criminal action even where juries at inquests have been convinced to the criminal standard (i.e. beyond reasonable doubt) that the death(s) in question were the result of an unlawful killing. This can often seem perverse. Consider two cases.

A verdict of unlawful killing was given at the end of a seven day inquest into the deaths of two demolition workers at British Rail's St John's Vale Bridge station in South London. Frank Warren and Nicholas Scott died when the south span of the 140 year-old, three span bridge fell on top of them in an uncontrolled collapse during demolition. The work was being carried out by Tilbury Douglas Ltd of Ipswich on behalf of British Rail and was recorded on videotape. The members of the jury were all quite aware that in order to return the verdict of 'unlawful killing' they had to be satisfied the death resulted, beyond a reasonable doubt, from gross negligence. During the inquest, expert witnesses told the court that the method chosen for demolition by first taking out the centre arch of the bridge 'made an accident inevitable'. Under hostile questioning this was amended to a '98 per cent of probability'. The lack of a safe method statement was compounded when the workers were directed not to even follow such statement as existed. The CPS had here what they would not have in ordinary homicide cases; they had substantial proof that a jury believed beyond a reasonable doubt that the deaths had resulted from manslaughter.[20] They also had the incident on film. In what way was there an insufficiency of evidence? The difficulty came in proving who knew what and who was responsible for what. The inquest heard contradictory accounts from various managers of who said what and to whom. The inquest was also challenged by several witnesses who exercised their right not to incriminate themselves.[21] They did not reply to any questions put to them.

Crown Court cases are expensive – an average case runs at about £8,800 per day.[22] The CPS has come under criticism for a high number of cases dropped before trial and for the quality of its performance in general.[23] It has also been criticised for bringing unnecessary prosecutions. The charge was best illustrated by a case in 1996 where costs of £100,000 were incurred after a case of the alleged robbery of 20p was brought to court (*Daily Telegraph*, 2 June 1998).

The proofs required to satisfy the doctrine of identification (see chapter 2) are challenging enough when there are just the personnel of one large company to examine, but the problem is greatly compounded when there are, as there were in this case, several subcontractors. It is also helpful to remember that the CPS appeared to be very chastened by the failure of the Zeebrugge case even though, as Bergman has shown (1991, 1992 and 1994) the reasons that the case fell were peculiar to its facts and should not be regarded as fatal to the chances of other cases.

In interviews with Crown Prosecutors from different regions and with different levels of experience the above case was discussed. The preponderant opinion as to why this case would not have been perceived as one presenting a 'realistic prospect of conviction' was the real challenge in persuading a jury that at least one person who could be identified as the 'controlling mind' of the company had made a grossly negligent decision which exposed workers to an obvious and serious risk. This though, like the problem of reducing crime, is, at root, a problem of political will, political priorities, and resources. With enough good lawyers and investigators it would be possible to find out precisely who was responsible for what, who knew what, when they knew it and how, if at all, they acted on that data. Where unravelling the complexities of events regarded as politically important, great lengths are gone to, in order to obtain the most reliable interpretation of events. Lord Justice Scott and the eminent counsel Prisley Baxendale spent 400 hours examining witnesses in order to unravel the mystery of the 'arms to Iraq' sales scandal. They collected 200,000 pages of oral and written testimony.[24] Technically, it would be possible for the CPS to remit the case back to the police for further investigation on a series of identified points, and to keep sending it back until a satisfactory clarity and cogency of evidence was obtained. This, of course, would not be done in the ordinary course of events, as it would be difficult to justify the necessary public expenditure to discover whether there was manslaughter of two unknown workmen who, in any event were engaged in dangerous demolition work.

Similar considerations apply to the case of Jasbir Singh, another instance of a referral made to the CPS for consideration of manslaughter charges. The CPS rejected the case for proceeding with a manslaughter charge. It stated that there was 'insufficient evidence' to prosecute Bradford chip manufacturer Idwal Fisher despite the verdict of 'unlawful killing' returned at the inquest. Mr Singh suffered fatal head injuries in April 1991 when he fell 12 feet to the ground from a box on a forklift truck. He had been recladding the inside wall of the firm's warehouse when the incident occurred. The practice of raising people in an unstable box on a lift truck is highly dangerous. The technical director of the firm admitted that the deceased had been instructed to clad high places on the walls but had not been told how to do it other than to make use of the truck and box. It was revealed at the inquest that the firm did, however, have two hydraulic lifting cradles but these were being used elsewhere at the time of the incident. There was a sign on the side of the forklift truck which said 'Do Not Carry Passengers', but this warning was overridden by managerial instruction. As one technical expert said at the inquest: 'No-one should be carried on it whatsoever since the lack of hand-holds means the slightest imbalance would result in the person falling out'.

This was a case where the CPS asked the police (West Yorkshire CID) to re-investigate the matter, but the resultant file still did not contain sufficient evidence to proceed. The Crown Prosecutors were not disposed against a case being made here but, again, the matter tacitly hinges on resource questions. The time, expense and exertion required to marshal the necessary evidence need to be off-set against the likelihood of a conviction and the public interest in bringing a prosecution. Securing a conviction against the ordinary person is challenging enough – according to the *Judicial Statistics* 1994, the chances of being acquitted in the Crown Court following a 'not guilty' plea are quite high: statistically, a defendant has three chances out of five of being acquitted if he/she pleads 'not guilty' (Smith, 1994, p. 1088). Burdened with the responsibilities of not just proving gross negligence and causation, but also satisfying the doctrine of identification puts a considerable obstacle before any crown prosecutor contemplating a corporate manslaughter prosecution.

In 1951, Lord Shawcross, the Attorney-General, made the classic statement on public interest in this context. He said: 'it has never been the rule in this country – I hope it never will be – that suspected criminal offences must automatically be the subject of prosecution'.[25]

The perceptions of Crown prosecutors which are relevant here are those concerned with looking at what the real chances are of a jury convicting a company, or a director, for manslaughter at the Crown Court. The prosecutor, when deciding whether to proceed, is not concerned with what a reasonable jury, properly directed, *ought* to decide. As Williams (1985) and Sanders (1994) have argued, this test favours people who are held in high esteem socially – like financially successful business people. In the instances of the CPS rejecting cases of possible workplace manslaughter, the decisive perception is that of the prosecutor's evaluation of an imagined jury's judgement of the case. The problem is that, rather like the equation of a Fleet Street editorial writer's opinion with 'public opinion',[26] the prosecutor's purportedly objective assessment of what a reasonable jury would think about the case is almost inextricably bound up with his or her own subjective viewpoint as a member of the public. If it is right that the CPS litmus test of case credibility is one which, in fact, superimposes a lawyer's-eye view over that of the man or woman on the Clapham bus (en route to be empanelled as a juror), then cases are really being screened by a ghost grand jury to see if they should get to trial. The jural spectres haunting the system are all off-duty lawyers – they are CPS lawyers asking themselves the question 'what would a reasonable juror think of this evidence' and, in order to answer that question, they take off their legal hats and see what they as individuals would make of it. How far it is possible for a trained practising lawyer to divest him- or herself of a legal outlook is a matter of debate.

It is, of course generally prudent not to judge people solely on the basis of what they say about themselves. The CPS lawyers claim not to be disposed against working to convict companies or directors whose recklessness results in death; and their main explanation for the conspicuous lack of proceedings is an evidential one. But, other cases show that, when they regard it as appropriate, they can overcome quite considerable evidential challenges and use law in an unobvious way to put the public seal of disapproval on injurious conduct. A bank clerk who made a woman physically ill through a campaign of obscene telephone calls was prosecuted by the CPS for grievous bodily harm and convicted at Chester Crown Court. The woman had suffered vomiting and diarrhoea brought on by severe psychological trauma. In a public statement, the CPS said it had decided to charge the culprit with inflicting GBH with intent (a charge which carries a sentence of up to life imprisonment) 'to reflect the seriousness of the offence'.[27] The CPS said that the defendant had earlier pleaded guilty to the charge normally pressed in such cases – the offence of making obscene phone calls under the Telecommunications Act. Although this carries a maximum sentence of £1,000 fine and three months imprisonment this was thought unsuitable. A CPS spokeswoman said: 'we felt that was not enough. It did not adequately reflect the seriousness of what he had done'.

These cases can be contrasted with the Lyme Regis canoe tragedy in which four schoolchildren died off the south coast in 1993 (Slapper, 1994f). This was not a standard death at work case where an employee is killed in a factory. Nevertheless, the deaths happened in the context of a company's operation (the leisure company which ran adventure courses including the canoe trip on which the victims perished) and the deaths were attributable to the work practices of the company. The company would be open to prosecution by the HSE under s.3, Health and Safety at Work Etc. Act 1974.[28] Here the official response to the deaths was very different. There was a very prompt and thorough police investigation followed by a CPS reference and then indictments were brought against the manager of the adventure centre, the managing director of its operator company and that company itself (see chapter 1, pp 23–4).

The level of blameworthiness here, although atrocious, is not, it seems, significantly worse (if it is worse at all) than the gross negligence shown by the employers in at least four of the 40 death at work cases I studied and the St John's bridge and Bradford warehouse cases above. Whereas the latter were not even referred to the CPS, the Lyme Regis case swiftly resulted in a Crown Court trial. Various facets of the Lyme Regis case could distinguish it – the fact that the victims were children, that it was not just one or two deaths but four, the fact that it was not all over in a second like some accidents but the victims took over four hours to die in ghastly circumstances while their friends were holding on to them in the freezing open sea trying to give them mouth-to-mouth resuscitation, and the fact that the company was small so it was relatively easy to satisfy the doctrine of identification. Each of these features may have played some part in the minds of those prosecutors who decided to proceed with the case (a decision which was approved by senior personnel). If the approach by the five prosecutors interviewed by the author is indicative then there is, in fact, a real adherence to the published code. One of them spoke thus:

> I won't say that you never let the social aspect of a case intrude into your thinking. Sometimes you do have a gut feeling about a case but really the thing is going to stand or fall on the evidence. The evidential test is hard to satisfy because a good defence lawyer can discredit even quite a convincing prosecution case ... in cases like those [corporate manslaughter] you would have to be very confident about witnesses.

This, and other replies, were reminiscent of Nelken's findings (1983, p. 191) in examining the enforcement of the Rent Act 1965. Some harassment officers told him that they deliberately tried to exclude from consideration the effect of their decisions on the state of their council's housing stock. These decisions were affected by more down to earth organisation and career matters.

## Lawyers and Workers

There is a small percentage of lawyers who are dedicated in principle, emotionally and socially to the protection and furtherance of the interests of workers *vis-à-vis* employers.[29] In the 40 cases in this study, there was representation for the family of the deceased in 26.[30] Of the 29 lawyers it would be fair to describe only one as being sympathetic to the particular type of case in question, a judgement made on the performance of the advocates in court, and having discussed this area of law, and their views on it, with 26 of them.

Many lawyers, quite understandably, would contend that in the same way that 'justice is blind', so a good lawyer is someone who is prepared to put the best case for anyone regardless of their class, race, political ideas, sexual orientation or previous encounters with the legal system. They argue that not being dedicated to a cause is a virtue not a weakness. No judgement is made about such a view here. The purpose in raising this point is to help the reader to begin to position him- or herself in the legal edifice, to know the perspective of most lawyers who, at inquests concerned with work deaths, represent clients related to the deceased. As argued in the previous chapter, the principal use of the inquest for most litigation lawyers is to harvest evidence, test its strength, seek clarification on technical points from pathologists and specialist HSE inspectors and gauge the credibility of witnesses. Most will be happier with an 'accidental death' verdict than an 'open verdict' because although both are consistent with the civil law notion of negligence, the former evinces a greater level of proof that there was negligence – the open verdict means that the jury would need further and better detail in order to be able to say, even on the balance of probabilities, that the death was an accident (as opposed, perhaps, to suicide or homicide).

Most of the lawyers with whom I discussed this matter (20 from the 26 above; 77 per cent) said they could not see any advantage in any case in arguing for the coroner to leave the 'unlawful killing' verdict to the jury. The scenario put to them was deliberately imprecise: it referred to a very bad case of employer negligence. The 'unlawful killing' verdict could not, *per se*, be used to assist argument in a civil court. They were evidently not concerned with the emotional satisfaction that the verdict, in appropriate cases, could bring to the bereaved relatives whom they represented, neither were they concerned with the simple, juridical justice of the matter – if it looks like an 'unlawful killing' it should go down on the record as one. The main aim of the lawyers was to be successful in achieving the best settlement for the relatives or to win the litigation in the civil court. The inquest was generally seen as only of interest to the extent that it facilitated the litigation process and enhanced their litigants' chances in that battle.

There is evidence that many workers, particularly in types of work with disproportionately high death rates (like construction, agriculture, quarrying and mining), are afraid to give testimony about how a workmate died, or the unsafe practices of their employer, because to do so would jeopardise their future prospects of employment.

Peter Lenehan worked on construction sites for 30 years. He was a safety representative for the last 10 of those years. As executive chairman of the union UCATT (Union of Construction, Allied Trades, and Technicians), remarks he made to the author in an interview refer to the ways in which site agents try to ensure that any witnesses that there were to a workplace fatality are not around when the police and HSE inspectors arrive. He explained that employment terms for almost everyone working in construction are either casual or short-term.[31] Employers and their agents (site managers) thus have an enormous power over the conduct of the workers.

The following is a case in point (case 36). At the inquest into the death of the driver of a mechanical digger, one of the first witnesses called had been operating a machine similar to the one being used by the deceased. Critical to the proper determination of the cause of death in this case was the 'work plan' that had been set by the firm. The witness's manager was in court with him. The witness in question was asked by the coroner and by counsel: 'were you aware of a work plan? Did you ever see the plan? Did you see the plan being shown by the manager to the deceased?' There was an obvious pressure on the witness to not give answers that would be uncomfortable to his manager. His answers sometimes sounded apprehensive. He often looked over to his manager – a few feet away in the court – as if to see whether what he was saying was discomfiting. At times he appeared not to know whether he should give the real answer or prevaricate. According to Lenehan and Foley (1990) the employers' blacklist does operate effectively in the construction industry.

A similar awkwardness arose in another case (case 31). At the inquest, a workmate of the deceased often faltered at points of pivotal importance to the story of what happened. The impression given was that the colleague did not wish to say anything which was untrue and which would betray his late workmate. On the other hand, he did not wish to be voluntarily hostile to his employer. The distinct impression given was that it was the perceived risk to his employment that kept the testimony of the witness guarded and laconic. A report on the first six months of the charity Public Concern at Work (which offers free legal advice to members of the public or employees who phone in to reveal malpractice in financial and safety matters) shows substantial evidence to support the contention that workers are dismissed or disciplined for acting against their employer, even where the employee's interference is legal.[32]

The rights protecting a worker in relation to both safety and giving evidence against an employer are clear and established. It would amount to the crime of contempt of court for an employer to demote or dismiss an employee for having testified against him in a law court. The dismissal would also (assuming other conditions are satisfied, like the employee having to have been in the employment for two years) amount to unfair dismissal.[33]

At one level then, the problem is one of perception. Employees perceive a risk to their livelihood if they come forward to testify against their employer. The construction union UCATT has estimated[34] that 40 per cent of construction sites fail to register with the HSE. During a visit to one such site with a television crew (for a BBC programme),[35] a union representative pointed to many serious hazards around the work area: ladders not attached to scaffolding, heavy concrete blocks on precarious piles above work areas, inoperative safety mechanisms on lifts, etc. The latest HSE figures in the annual report for the period 1996/97 show that there were 89 fatal injuries to workers in the construction industry. One worker, speaking incognito (he wore a full-face balaclava), said to the interviewer:

> I've been out of work, and, now I've come back into work again here, you know, and I've got children and that to feed so I have to do it. And if I was to say something about it, I'd get thrown off and they'd get someone else to do it, there's so many people out of work, they'd get someone straight away see.

Asked by the interviewer if he had complained about work conditions he replied: 'Well no, not yet but I have been on other sites where I've been thrown off for complaining, they just get someone new and that's it'.

Legally, however, one argument runs, the risk of being dismissed is more apparent than real because any employer who did act to sack or demote an employee who gave evidence against the company would be brought to book by law. Nonetheless, it is not clear that the legal protections afforded to workers, do offer real protection in most cases. Where employees have full-time contracts of employment with local authorities, public sector bodies or banks and are members of a union, then the legal rights in issue have a real significance. There are though, virtually no deaths in these areas of employment. Of the 32 cases where the basic facts presented the possibility of a manslaughter investigation, the people who have testified about the incident and/or the company practice, would have been employed on a short-term contractual or casual labouring basis in 14 cases (44 per cent). They *would* thus be subject to the unprotected hostility of the employer.[36]

Overall, the perceptions here combine to filter these cases out of the system. I found next to nothing to suggest that any decisions are taken with the premeditated purpose of acting to the detriment of labour or the advantage of capital. People are acting on social axioms as they perceive them. Altogether there is a 'coherence without conspiracy' (Nelken, 1983, p. 212). This finding is also in line with Sutherland's argument (1949) that the common tide of criminality excluded crime committed by people in the higher socioeconomic classes, and this prejudice was perpetuated by the legislature, although not in a conspiratorial way.

## The Social View

The views and assumptions of the *dramatis personae* involved in the official response to deaths at work are evolved mainly within their respective work cultures. What has been looked at is what these views are and how they affect the decision-making processes. It is also important to comment briefly upon what could be called the wider social culture in which members of these various occupations live and work; the way we 'culturally absorb' (Kinney et al., 1990, p. 27) death and injury at work 'as if they are part of life itself'.

The most striking aspect of the official response to deaths at work (see chapters 1 and 2) is that they are not treated as seriously and as culpably caused as deaths in other circumstances (Wells, 1993a; Bergman, 1991, 1992 and 1994; Slapper, 1993b and 1998). In the context of corporate conduct, an indisposition to perceive reprehensible behaviour as criminal arose partly due to accepted versions of what the results of a crime look like.

Carson (1979) has shown how factory crime came, historically, to be 'conventionalized'. He notes that the significance of the history of the regulation of factory crime is its legacy in today's perceptions. Once a 'low profile' approach to legal proceedings has been institutionalised within an enforcement agency, the approach becomes circular and self-perpetuating (Becker, 1971, p. 336; Carson, 1979, p. 55).

Traditionally, the illegal activities of corporations and those of conventional criminals have been defined as involving very different consequences. Corporate misbehaviour has been viewed as entailing a diffuse, impersonal cost to society. The harms, for example, produced by price fixing, false advertising, or mislabelling, have been perceived as increased financial burdens on the consumer (Swiggert and Farrell, 1980).

The authors note, in their detailed study of the media coverage of the Ford Pinto case (see chapter 6 for a detailed analysis) that: (a) the indictment against Ford marked a significant definitional shift, expanding the scope of the criminal law; and (b) that, in the course of events leading to the indictment, the greatest shift in public opinion and public perception was accomplished through a 'personalization of harm', i.e. a transformation of the problem from one of mechanical defect to one of personal harm.[37]

There is today a greater public awareness of the nature of violent white-collar crime. Consider a popular film (staring Gene Hackman and Mary Elizabeth Mastrantonio) shown in cinemas throughout the USA and the UK, and now a popular video in both countries. It has also been broadcast on commercial television in the UK.

The film, *Class Action* (1990), is closely based on the Ford Pinto, and concerns a legal action arising from deaths caused by a defective car. The weighty legal and political matters are given relief by emotional aspects of the story; the legal opponents in the case are father and daughter. The car suffered from a faulty design which meant that when the left-side direction indicator was turned on, circuitry around the petrol tank became very dangerous; a slight rear-end collision at such a moment would cause the petrol tank to explode into flames.

This conversation between a lawyer and the Chief Executive Officer (CEO) of the motor company goes to the heart of the matter.

*Lawyer*:   ... Why didn't you just change the blinker-circuit?

*CEO*:   I told Flannery to tell him about the problem about a month or so before he died. He called in his chief bean counter.

*Lawyer*:   What's a bean counter?

*Lawyer II*:   A risk management expert? Right George?

*CEO*:   Yeah. So Flannery shows him the data and asks him how much it would cost to retrofit.

*Lawyer*:   You mean recall?

*CEO*:   You get it; to retrofit 175,000 units. You multiply that times 300 bucks a car give or take, you're looking right around $50 million. So the bean counter, he crunches the numbers some more and he figures that you have one of these fireball collisions about every 3,000 cars, that's 158 explosions ...

*Lawyer*:   Which is almost exactly how many plaintiffs there are.

*Lawyer II*:   These guys know their numbers.

*CEO*:         So you multiply that times $200,000 per lawsuit, that's assuming everyone sues and wins. See, it's cheaper to deal with the lawsuits than it is to fix the blinker. It's what the bean counters call a 'simple actuarial analysis'.

The film centred round the civil actions, but the idea of corporate crime was an abiding part of the theme. There is thus evidence that the social perception of how companies commit violent crime is improving in the sense that more people are acquiring a clearer, wider picture of corporate operations which cause physical injury and death, and do so with very high levels of blameworthiness. It is not suggested that identifying homicidal behaviour in companies is new – the family and fellow workers of the deceased in the *Cory Bros Ltd* case in 1926 would have seen the deceased as a victim of a crime (the firm was prosecuted for manslaughter); and generations who know Upton Sinclair's *The Jungle* would be familiar with how companies can kill. What is suggested is that in recent times (since the Ford prosecution in the USA, and the Zeebrugge case here) there has been a distinct development. The change has been such that there is a wider social awareness and people are not simply seeing the results of commercial carnage as *equivalent* to the sort of crime prosecuted in the courts, they are seeing it as something which can and should be prosecuted. The centre of gravity in this public debate has now effectively moved from the areas of criminal jurisprudence (can companies commit manslaughter) to formulaic and penological ones (how shall we determine corporate culpability, and how shall we sanction guilty defendants).

Examining the social assumptions and perceptions of those who act officially in the response to deaths at work can assist in understanding why the system works in the way that it does. Up until 1995, the mechanical operation of the system brought only four prosecutions for manslaughter arising from commerce during this time. An ethnomethodological exploration of each of the various occupational groupings provides evidence of why these people, like the HSE inspectors or coroners, interpret the rules as they do. This chapter has sought to unveil some of their precepts. We can thus be more enlightened than when we simply watched the operation of the rules, but there are still important inquiries to satisfy. Chief among these is the question: how does the political economy generate and cultivate these occupational precepts? It is therefore appropriate to consider the historical and economic factors that have engendered certain ideas.

## Notes

1   The former Director-General of the HSE, John Rimington, gave evidence to the House of Commons Employment Committee in March 1990. He admitted that budgetary constraints prevented the HSE from being as stringent in its enforcement policy as some of its inspectors would like it to be. He said that this is the reason why, where it does prosecute, it often does not press for the magistrate to refer cases to the crown court. He said:

> We have often in the past hesitated to make representations because of the very considerable extra resources ... involved in doing it. You double the amount of time or very nearly ... It occupies the inspector who is in charge of the case ... for as long as 24 or 30 weeks instead of 10 or 12 weeks ... it is very frequently necessary to appoint a Queen's Counsel so a new briefing has to start: so that it is very much more expensive for us to go to the Crown court, very easy for us to go to a magistrates' court (p. 6 minutes, cited in WEA, Bergman, 1991).

2   Strictly speaking, coroners, HSE inspectors and lawyers are not a part of the criminal justice system. They operate within it some of the time; nevertheless, for convenience, I use the phrase to incorporate these occupations in this chapter.

3   I am also grateful to coroners' officers from Staffordshire, Liverpool, London, Essex and Norwich for their time and patience and, at times, in the grim context of unnatural death, their tension-releasing black humour, in discussing these issues with me. These officers were all former police officers.

4   Sometimes the victims were gravely injured but not yet dead at the time a police investigation began. Of the 40 cases, this was so in seven (18 per cent). Of these cases some were taken away by ambulance at about the time the police officer arrived.

5   This is taken from the training programme of a Midlands police force and the Computerised Help Desk for Operational Police.

6   See, for example, *R v Still and McAlister.* Kerry Still and Andrew McAlister attended a World Cup qualifying match between Wales and Romania in 1993. After the match they discharged a powerful marine distress rocket into a section of the stadium full of spectators. The rocket struck and killed John Hill. They were charged with murder and pleaded guilty to gross negligence manslaughter. The defendants had said they believed the rocket was simply a hand-held flare and would just give off smoke. They had not intended to injure anyone (*The Guardian*, 12 May 1994).

   The police have, similarly, found no difficulty in identifying criminal negligence when it occurs in otherwise peaceful, legal, recreational contexts. William Hardy was, after a police investigation, prosecuted for the manslaughter of Seamus Lavelle, a member of an opposing team, during a rugby match (*The Independent*, 27 July 1994).

   Other jurisdictions have also seen some unusual prosecutions for manslaughter. Jean Fournet-Fayard, President of the French Football Association, was charged with manslaughter in connection with the collapse of a stadium in Corsica in January 1992 (*The Independent*, 2 June 1992).

   Strangest, though, of all the unusual manslaughter cases which I have found was the one reported in *The Straits Times* of 25 April 1992, under the headline 'ELEPHANT SLAPPED WITH MANSLAUGHTER CHARGE'. The article explained how New Delhi police charged an elephant with manslaughter and bound her in chains after she trampled a man to death in the Indian capital. The article reported: 'Police said they would not release the

44 year-old elephant named Champa until the judge hearing the bizarre case granted bail. Champa was being detained in a makeshift pen at the police compound where she munched on banana plants and grass, ignoring officers standing guard with rifles.'

Between 3,000 and 10,000 people were killed by release of poisonous gas from the Union Carbide Corporation (UCC) chemical plant in Bhopal, India, 1984. There is a very high level of proof that the company UCC (the forty-seventh largest company in the USA) was criminally negligent. The Chief Executive of UCC flew out to India three days after the disaster and was arrested by police when he got off the plane. Unlike the elephant case above, however, the executive was released within two hours and never charged.

7   A single additional factor may not be sufficient on its own, and sometimes there are other factors like the location in *Holloway* (below) where the deceased was killed in his own kitchen.

8   His conviction was quashed on appeal, on a technical point: the trial judge was held to have misdirected the jury on the meaning of 'recklessness'. See *R v Prentice and others*, [1993].

9   The classic illustrative case (Abercrombie, 1960, p. 31) is known as *The Three Triangles*.

*The Three Triangles*. (Read the statement in each triangle.) (*After* R. Brooks)

Most people read in the statements in the triangles as 'Paris in the Spring, Once in a lifetime, Bird in the hand'. Viewers become blind to the words which are not part of the expected pattern.

10   His or her only previous experience is likely to be secondary experience like training exercises, television police drama, or documentaries rather than first hand experience of a death at work. Of the 18 officers I interviewed, only one had encountered a death at work before. Most officers will have other experience of death acquired in the course of their work, owing to the much higher number of road traffic fatalities, and a number of suicides. There are, annually about 4000 road traffic deaths and 3,500 suicides (*Department of Transport Statistics*, 1993/4; Home Office Statistical Bulletin *Statistics of Deaths Reported to Coroners: England & Wales 1993*, April 1996 and 1997).

11   I am not arguing that phenomena understood from scientific experimentation in vision and perception have direct applicability to the more abstract, hermeneutic realm of social judgement and categorisation; I say merely that perception and comprehension are epistemologically comparable processes.

12   *Safety Management*, December 1991, p. 6.

13   See for example Lord Mackay's opinion in *Pepper (Inspector of Taxes) v Hart* [1992], (using Hansard to assist statutory interpretation); and Lord Keith in *R v R* [1992] (marital rape).

14   The only scenario I have been able to discover in which a *de facto* death at work is likely to be unclassified as such is where the worker is self-employed and died a few months after suffering a serious injury in the course of his or her work. If s/he died at the scene,

then it is more likely that the police will, as standard procedure, contact the HSE. Such notification is much less likely where the injured person is just taken to hospital. Because of interpretative difficulties, hospital records of emergency admissions cannot be relied upon to disclose any useful information (e.g. is someone who was 'cleaning out a barn' employed at that time). On 8 October 1994, at the Metropolitan Police Forensic Science Laboratory (MPFSL) in London, I interviewed a number of doctors connected with the criminal justice system. Of 28 whom I asked to think of ways in which death at work could slip through the system, five mentioned that self-employed people who met with fatal accidents could, as far as they could see, end up outside the officially recorded figures of deaths resulting from work accidents. I am grateful to Dr Frances Lewington of the MPFSL for all her cooperation and for helping me with my inquiries.

The latest statistics show that of the 452 deaths at work 1992–93, 63 were self-employed people.

15  In 1979 Blair Peach was killed in public during a charge of the Special Patrol Group on people walking away from a demonstration against the National Front in Southall, London. The case brought forward several witnesses who said that they saw the deceased being hit over the head by a police officer. Mr Peach died from severe head injuries. After a highly contentious conduct of the inquest (Scratton, 1984; National Council for Civil Liberties, 1980) a conclusion of 'misadventure' was returned by the jury.

16  The Brodrick Committee Report (1971) identified five functions which a modern inquest should carry out. According to the committee it should:

(i)   determine the medical cause of death;
(ii)  allay rumours or suspicion;
(iii) *draw attention to the existence of circumstances which, if unremedied, might lead to further deaths*;
(iv)  advance medical knowledge;
(v)   preserve the legal interests of the deceased person's family, heirs or other interested parties [emphasis added].

17  Coroners did this in six of the 40 cases (15 per cent). Additionally, one inquest was, against the law, held without a jury. This was case 30. In a death at work case, the coroner has no discretion about a jury, he must summon one: Coroners Act 1988 s. 8(3) (c). See also Jervis, 1993, pp. 10–25.

18  The jury would not, by virtue of the Coroners Rules 1984 (r.42), be permitted to appear to determine the criminal liability on the part of a named person. There are, circumstances, though, where it will be obvious that a particular person (not named in the verdict) was responsible for the death (Home Office Circular, No. 187 of 1987, App. C, para. 11).

A conclusion of unlawful killing must be recorded if appropriate (Jervis, 1993, p. 252). Thus, after the Hungerford killings, which occured when a gunman went on the rampage, the Berkshire coroner directed an unlawful killing conclusion although it was obvious this only referred to Michael Ryan (*The Independent*, 30 September 1987).

19  This is a legal requirement. The rules are contained in the Reporting of Injuries, Diseases and Dangerous Occurrences Regulations 1985, and are examined in the notes to chapter 3.

20  In ordinary cases, like those where someone had been stabbed, pushed down stairs or shot, the inquest will be adjourned immediately after it has been opened so that the verdict of the inquest will not prejudice the trial. If the suspect is convicted of the homicide the inquest would be superfluous so one is not held. If the suspect is acquitted then there could be an

inquest but in most cases there is not. See Matthews and Foreman (Jervis), 1993, pp. 261–6; Wells, 1991.

21  Coroners Rules, 1984:

r.22(1)  No witness at an inquest shall be obliged to answer any questions tending to incriminate himself.

(2)      Where it appears to the coroner that a witness has been asked such a question, the coroner shall inform the witness that he may refuse to answer.

22  Court Service/Lord Chancellor's Department 1997.

23  The number of cases dropped before Crown Court trial in one year was 8,046 (*Annual Report*, 1996/97). For the criticism, see for example, articles in *The New Law Journal*, (1994), Vol. 144, No. 6655 (8 July); *The Times*, 2 June 1992.

24  The inquiry into Exports of Defence Equipment and Dual Use Goods to Iraq, chaired by Sir Richard Scott, London, 1994 (*The Guardian*, 12 May 1994, p. 8).

25  House of Commons Debates, volume 483, column 681, 29 January 1951. Cited in the Code for Crown Prosecutors 6.1.

26  An equation proved to the satisfaction of some by the fact that the reader pays to read the paper and, therefore, endorses its editorial slant – even although many purchasers have as their primary interest the paper's coverage of sport, specialist themes, fashion, astrology or bizarre news.

27  *The Guardian*, 25 May 1994. He was later sentenced to 18 months imprisonment (*The Independent*, 9 July 1994).

28  S.3 states: '(1) It shall be the duty of every employer to conduct his undertaking in such a way as to ensure, so far as is reasonably practicable, that persons not in his employment who may be affected thereby are not thereby exposed to risks to their health or safety'.

29  Those who work for Robin Thompson & Partners, and Brian Thompson & Partners (two related national firms) are cases in point. These firms have served the trades union and labour movement for over 70 years. W.H. Thompson started his practice on his own account in 1920 and acted largely for trade unions and members of the labour movement. He qualified as a solicitor before the first world war and was in prison for 18 months as a conscientious objector. He became the country's leading expert on workmen's compensation. Upon his death in 1947, his practice was continued by his sons.

30  There was no representation in cases 2, 4, 5, 11, 12, 15, 21, 24, 25, 27, 28, 29, 32 and 40.

31  A good illustration of this is provided by the throngs of unemployed men who gather in certain places in cities early in the morning in the hope of being picked for a day's work on construction sites (see for example the A5 between Kilburn and Cricklewood, where unemployed labourers gather between 6.00 am and 7.30 am in the expectation of work on a site in the city (*The Independent*, 3 December 1994, p. 13). The arrangements are cash-in-hand pay and no awkward questions from the employer. This way, the agent is able to buy labour at a cheaper rate than he would through standard recruitment procedures; an arrangement eminently satisfactory to the agent because he is given a lump sum with which to hire labour over a specified period or in respect of a particular job, which effectively means the more he saves, the more he personally gains.

32  *The Advice Service Second Report*, Public Concern at Work, 42 Kingsway, London WC2B 6EN.

33  Following the Trade Union Reform and Employment Rights Act 1993, all employees, irrespective of age, length of service or hours of work, now have the right to complain to

an industrial tribunal if they are dismissed or subject to any other 'detriment' for leaving their workplace or taking other appropriate action in the face of what they 'reasonably believed' to be 'serious and imminent danger'. Safety representatives and 'designated' employees enjoy similar protection for carrying out their health and safety duties, and other employees have some limited protection if they raise health and safety grievances with their employers. The provisions of 'Framework' Directive No. 89/391 EEC have largely been incorporated into English law by the Management of Health and Safety at Work (MHSW) Regulations 1992. This includes such measures as placing primary responsibility on employers to inform workers of the risk of 'serious and imminent danger' and to take action and give instructions to enable workers to stop work and leave if there is such a danger. Section 22A of the Employment Protection (Consolidation ) Act 1978 (as amended) states: 'an employee has the right not to be subjected to any detriment by any act, or any deliberate failure to act, by his [her] employer' on certain protected health and safety grounds. Under s.57A a dismissal will be *automatically* unfair if the reason or principle reason for dismissal falls within the protected grounds. Similarly, an employee's selection for redundancy will *automatically* be unfair if the reason, or principle reason for selection was an 'inadmissible reason'.

34  Bulletin, December, 1991.

35  *Risky Business,* BBC1, 12 January 1992.

36  I am not arguing that potential witnesses in 14 cases did not testify through intimidation; simply that, as there is a high percentage of all work deaths which take place in an environment of casual and tenuous employment contracts, the legal safeguards do not protect them. The larger the exposed, unprotected portion of the workforce, the higher the number of actually intimidated potential witnesses.

37  In a footnote (1980, p. 167) the authors state:

> we are not arguing that the media cause behavioral boundaries or that they are a perfect mirror of popular moral sentiment. Rather, in the stories covered and the words used to describe events, symbols are utilized that both depend upon and reinforce shared meanings. Thus, while readers may disagree as to the content of particular reports, that content is nonetheless recognizable as a definition of the situation to which the report pertains. These are the meanings that we have sought to identify in the analysis ....

# 6 The Historical and Economic Context

The regularity of such a high number of occupational deaths each year (often more than the annual number of reported personal homicides)[1] suggests that the propensity of companies to conduct their affairs in ways that result in death or serious injury is not attributable to erratic influences like the occasional enterprise of a few extraordinarily careless or unscrupulous firms.

This chapter will first examine ways in which deaths at work are affected by the economic environment in which they occurred. Next it turns to the challenges from the political economy faced in the regulation of work safety. Finally, the chapter examines how the political economy can generate the axioms which influence the outlooks of those personnel examined in the previous chapter.

Certain aspects of crime have been shown to be affected by the economy (Box, 1987; Field, 1990; Taylor, 1994). This study suggests that deaths at work in general, and, therefore, particularly those of them which could be seen as prosecutable crimes using contemporary law and prosecution codes, are circumstantially promoted and facilitated by economic factors. Not only are economic considerations the triggering factors in particular incidents, but the political economy is also responsible for the scale and contours of the annual toll of work-related deaths. For example, the number of fatal injuries to employees and the overall fatal injury rate in 1992/3 dropped to the lowest levels ever reported. But, as the HSE annual report for that period conceded (1993, p. 84):

> the fall in the rate largely reflects changes in the pattern of employment with a shift away from the higher risk injuries into the generally lower risk service sector.

Employment in the coal industry, for instance, in 1992/3 was one-third of the level in 1986/7 and the numbers of people employed in both manufacturing and construction rose to a peak in the 1980s and have since dropped by over 15 per cent. In contrast, employment in the lower-risk service industries increased steadily in the 1980s, rising by 10 per cent between 1986/87 and 1990/91.[2]

The changing patterns of accidents and occupational ill health revealed by the latest statistical analysis (*HSC Annual Report* 1996/97) indicates that fatal accident rates are at an historically low level. Although this trend has been important in recent years, it is unlikely to continue indefinitely and the prospects are not so good. Accidents at work kill over 300 people every year and the rate of fatalities per 100,000 workers is estimated to rise from 1.0 to 1.2, which represents a return to the level seen in 1993/94. This is mainly because the number of self-employed killed in workplace accidents has gone up again – 83 in 1997 compared with 49 in 1996 and 81 in 1994/95. Looking at individual sectors, the fatal injury rate is expected to rise in manufacturing where provisional figures suggest that deaths rose to 57 from 42 in 1996 (1.5 per 100,000 workers); in construction which is likely to rise to 5.9 per 100,000 workers, also a return to the level seen earlier in the 1990s; and agriculture which is likely to rise to 11.1 per 100,000 – the highest figure in the past five years. Only in the extractive and utility supply industries is the fatal injury rate likely to fall with services likely to remain static (ibid.).

The findings in some studies (Carson, 1979 and 1982), including this one, suggest that the predominant factor in determining law, practice and policy in relation to deaths at work is the economy. Mr Justice Stanwick hit on this point in his judgement in a case in 1968. He noted that economic considerations are an important element in determining the nature and extent of some legal duties (*Stokes v Guest, Keen & Nettlefold (Bolts and Nuts) Ltd.* [1968], p. 1784 B–C; see chapter 5).

In the cases this writer examined, 24 (60 per cent) of the deaths were attributable to the pressures of the profit-system economy.[3] Thus, the work practice being used, the disregard for safety equipment or training, were the result not of ignorance but of an unwillingness or inability to pay the necessary extra in order that the work would be safe. For example, in one London case (case 5) a man and his partner were undertaking work for which they were not properly qualified or experienced. They did not have suitable equipment. The man's son told an inquest that his father was a metal craftsman who, having been made redundant from a regular job several months before the incident, had teamed up with a friend and workmate, to do self-employed repair and construction work, sometimes, as in this instance, for large companies. In a twist compounding the economic setting of this fatality, the deceased's friend, very distressed, gave evidence to the inquest about how the accident had occurred: the deceased was on a roof trying to reclaim some asbestos sheeting which was to be used elsewhere on the site when he had fallen through a skylight and crashed some 15 feet below, smashing his head on a concrete floor. The two men were only doing this work because their real skills were made economically 'redundant'; the large company only engaged their services because they were less expensive than engaging a specialist firm; and, ironically, the work in question was reclaiming old asbestos for use elsewhere because this was cheaper than the purchase of new asbestos.

In some cases there was no persuasive evidence that the deceased had met his death as the result of an economic factor. It was judged that in several of these, if one were to give a wide compass to the consideration of 'cause', an economic factor would soon be met. These would, however, be virtually impossible to prove to any acceptable standard because there are a number of unknown elements that could be given a proper answer only by the deceased. In case 1, for example, a workman was crushed to death by a huge slab of concrete which fell on him when he removed a safety prop prematurely. At first sight this was nothing other than an awful error. The working practice of the employer was not called into question, neither was the equipment. Testimony from his widow, however, sets the event in a possibly more telling perspective. She stated that his 'usual job' was steel erecting. She said:

> when he started the job in Benton, he said he was working with large pre-cast concrete and that he didn't like it [because] they were difficult to position. He said he'd been trying his hardest.

If he was a steel erector – a specialist occupation – then why was he not doing that to earn his living? Not because he preferred working with concrete. His wife said he did not have such a preference. It seems likely that this man was doing this dangerous work because he could not get the sort of employment he was trained for. This could afford an economic explanation for the death but, equally, he could have been distracted by a headache or something else at the critical moment. The only cases included in the category of 'deaths attributable to the economy' were those where the facts present a clear *prima facie* case that there was a failure in safety standards or procedure, directly or indirectly, attributable to a cost-related decision. In making such calculations, it was assumed that a decision not to conduct a business or a single operation in a reasonably safe, reasonably well-known way was related to cost where such cost would be significant. Clearly, where a business, choosing between a reasonably safe method of work and a cheaper, more risk-laden method, resolves to employ the riskier choice, it could be doing so mistakenly believing its choice to be the safer. That, of course, would be very unlikely. In the final analysis, such a genuine, honest mistake would have taken the case outside of the category 'deaths attributable to economic factors', as the unsafe system would have been precipitated simply by misinformation rather than parsimonious management. In studying all the testimony from the 24 cases whose occurrence presented as, *prima facie*, related to economic considerations, none was, in fact, explicable on the grounds of mistake.

However, in each of the 24 cases that could be attributed to the pressures of the profit-making economy, it can be demonstrated, on the facts, the workings of the invisible hand of the market. Five cases (detailed in chapter 5) can illustrate the point in question. In the leisure centre case (case 6), when the assistant manager was killed, evidence showed that the centre had been very badly wired. The system was defective and dangerous and could not have been installed by a properly qualified electrician. The evidence further suggested that those engaged to do the work may have been selected because they were cheaper than rival bids. This error was compounded by the fact that those responsible for running the centre had again tried to save money by not having any of the statutory maintenance checks, so the error, gross and easily detectable as it was, was not spotted before it killed one of its employees.

Similarly, the life of the mine worker (case 8) would almost certainly not have been lost (indeed he may not have even been injured) if three features of the mine had been different on the day in question. These three features were known hazards – known nationally and at the colliery in question – and the only reason why they were left in the dangerous condition was to avoid the expense of changing them. The arch overhanging the conveyor belt on which the deceased was travelling out of the mine was too low according to regulations. It was dangerous. The colliery would have had to incur expense to have it altered. They chose not to do so. There was a safety gate a few feet after the point at which the men travelling out of the mine were supposed to move into an upright position and alight from the belt. If, for any reason, a man did not arise (e.g. he had fallen asleep) when his body knocked open the gate as he passed through on the moving belt, the opening of the gate would electrically stop the belt thus saving him from being carried on to the end of the belt and tipped over the edge.

The electric safety gate on the conveyor belt in question was defective so that the victim's body (fainted, asleep or unconscious) passed through without the belt stopping. It was unclear, however, whether the main fault in the belt was (a) electrical (it appeared on being tested to only work erratically) or (b) that its bottom was too high above the conveyor belt so that the body actually went under it without the gate's opening. There was evidence that the electrical fault had not been corrected because of (cost-related) maintenance failures at the colliery. The reason for such gates sometimes being set too high is also an economic one: if you set the gate low, then coal (which also travels on these belts) can form into little piles and open the gate, stop the belt and consequently slow down production, as it takes several minutes to re-set.

The third case involved a worker in a cash and carry warehouse being killed as the result of being asked to perform a highly dangerous work practice – being 'travelled' in a cage, supported by a forklift truck, 18 feet above a concrete floor (case 14). The company employing him had not trained most of its forklift truck drivers. These training courses are relatively expensive for employers and the resulting certification can precipitate claims for higher wages from the trained workers. The deceased had been checking stock stored on pallets stacked very high. To conform to the regulations and not be moved more than a few inches at a time in the raised cage would have considerably slowed down the process of stocktaking in this busy cash and carry warehouse. The dangerous practice was openly condoned by managers at the warehouse, one of whom greeted the deceased as he was being perilously carried aloft (in fact, as it turned out, to meet his death). The employee driving the truck from which the victim fell said in evidence:

> I am aware there is a risk associated with this practice but using the cage in this manner speeds work up and *we wouldn't be able to complete all the jobs we were expected to do over the shift otherwise because of the deadlines set by the managers* ... It was normal to do the job the way I did, it was a matter of routine to ignore the instruction [emphasis added].

Apart from all of this, the truck and cage were woefully defective. The cage had never been maintained, none of the safety devices on the truck or cage were working and it appeared that one or two had been deliberately defeated so as not to slow down work. It was possible to drive the platform along with an individual raised on it with no restriction on the speed of the truck; the person on the platform had no emergency stop device and no control over the vertical movement of the platform. Control of the platform was completely in the hands of the operative of the forklift truck. Communication between these two people was limited to shouting.

The cash and carry warehouse company is clearly able to pass on some of its assiduous cost savings to the customer. Newspaper advertisements at the time of the inquest and even at the time of writing proudly boast of the firm's

'Low, low prices'. The advertisements say nothing about the level of its safety standards.

In the case of the exploding tank (case 38), a worker was killed when the tank of chemicals whose gauge he had been instructed to fix exploded, devastating his body and throwing it over 100 feet. The tank contained a potentially dangerous chemical, toluene. The evidence here suggested that the information about the chemical supplied to the firm where the deceased worked was both highly inaccurate and incomplete. It did not give sufficient warning to the purchaser about the chemical's flash point or flammability. The testimony at the inquest showed that the supplier was fastidious about the financial and contractual details of its arrangement with the farm fertilizer company, but much less conscientious when it came to the chemical details of its wares.

The fifth example (case 39), involved the death of the quarry worker when the tipper truck he was driving (for his employer) on the ridge of a deep quarry failed to stop after a reversing movement and careered down into the quarry. Tests showed that the firm's truck, although very heavy and frequently used at the top of the quarry, had almost no serviceable brakes. The company had evidently tried to cut back on its maintenance costs. There were over 20 large vehicles (lorries and tipper trucks) owned by the company but it employed an unqualified mechanic who had no training from the vehicle manufacturer on how their vehicles should be serviced. The employer was a small family firm run by one man (the other named directors were his parents). The director, when he gave evidence at the inquest, tried to stress that the deceased was a good personal friend, and that, by implication, he would not have knowingly exposed him to any danger. Oddly, however, in a letter to the coroner, the director's solicitor tried to blame the victim for causing the death. Before the inquest, the firm had been prosecuted in the magistrates' court for 'having failed to ensure the safety of persons not in their employment', contrary to s.3 of the HSWA 1974. It had pleaded guilty. The letter to the coroner said:

> ... we thought that it may assist you by way of background that the basis of the [guilty] plea, and therefore the conviction was: that it took account of the relevant case law which indicated that in deciding guilt it was the result achieved rather than the effort put in respect of maintenance that was relevant ... there was considerable potential action which would have avoided the accident because it was avoidable: possibly (in view of alternative explanations set out in the defence experts report), applying the foot brake, parking brake, emergency brake (e.g. select neutral, turn engine off), or any failsafe operation.

... and definitely, steering across the slope (NB effect of articulation of dump truck), selecting forward low range or four wheel drive (to arrest reverse and/or drive up slope) tipping the load, *or jumping* [emphasis added].

This effectively says that the victim died because he did not have the same presence of mind as a lawyer (sitting in a comfortable office looking at the incident with coffee and hindsight) to realise, in the 3–4 seconds it took him to roll over the precipice, that he should have simply leapt out of the truck cabin. This advice is evidently proffered to deter anyone from surmising that the victim died because his truck did not have any proper brakes because his employer did not want to run to the expense of a proper mechanic or proper servicing arrangements.

## The Regulation of Work Safety in Industry

Historical and contemporary evidence suggests that much (not all) of the law and practice of safety enforcement has been governed or strongly influenced by the interests of capital (Marx, 1954, 1887; Carson, 1979; Reiman, 1979; Box, 1983; Calhoun and Hiller, 1986; Norrie, 1993). For employers, profit maximisation means that attention is constantly directed to savings on cost along with the potential gains which are seen to accrue from economic efficiency (Moore, 1991), while safety is regarded as a debilitating 'on cost' (a negative residual).

Pressures from the working class, or those sympathetic to it; the threats of action from the inspectorates; moral imperatives; and, latterly, the threat of litigation, have all helped to shape developments. The contribution of certain individuals has been influential – in particular, from the USA, Ralph Nader, author of *Unsafe at Any Speed*, and Mike Cosentino, the heroically-regarded and highly-skilled state prosecutor in the Ford prosecution in Elkhart, Indiana; and from the UK, the lawyer Louise Christian, the academic Celia Wells, and the campaigner David Bergman.[4] These people have done much to alter public perception in recent years and have already precipitated slight changes in the official response to deaths at work. The contribution of particular individuals to the historical development of any given period or set of circumstances was recognised by Marx:

> World history would indeed be very easy to make, if the struggle were taken up only on condition of infallible favourable chances. It would, on the other hand,

be of a very mystical nature, if 'accidents' played no part. These accidents themselves fall naturally into the general course of development and are compensated again by other accidents. But acceleration and delay are very dependent upon such 'accidents', which include the 'accident' of the character of those who at first stand at the head of the movement (Marx and Engels, 1959, p. 464).

Apart from what can be classified as the personal forces – charismatic force in the Weberian sense – influencing legal and social changes, or at least a graver official response to deaths at work, there is also the factor of litigation. Litigation can be expensive to defend and very expensive if damages have to be paid; there is also, from a company's point of view, the possible detriment of adverse publicity if poor safety standards are exposed. In the shadow of such menaces, firms are more likely to pay attention to basic safety requirements, or at least (wherever possible) to settle as expeditiously as possible claims against them arising from safety violations (Kagan in Hawkins, 1990, p. 453). Litigation, like literacy, is a two-edged sword. Both were developed by and for members of élites but, once developed, both could be used by ordinary people, by the 'masses' against the élites.

Demotic literacy was largely developed to assist the owners of industry who were in need of regular cohorts of trained workers to deal with the work generated by the growing commerce of the nineteenth century (Williams, 1961).[5] What, however, had been developed for one purpose, was used by workers to promote their own ends: trade unionism and other working class organisations. The first reformers had to get around the representative opinion (cited ibid., p. 135) of a Justice of the Peace in 1807:

> It is doubtless desirable that the poor should be generally instructed in *reading*, if it were only for the best of purposes – that they may read the Scriptures. As to *writing* and *arithmetic*, it may be apprehended that such a degree of knowledge would produce in them a disrelish for the laborious occupations of life.

Once achieved, general working class literacy became something which assisted that economic class in its own organisation, *vis-à-vis* the interests of the ruling class.

Similarly with civil litigation. Certain aspects of the criminal law were evolved to cater to the needs of merchants and those trading with them (Hall, 1952). Comparably, the civil legal process was not historically developed in order that peasants or, latterly, workers should be able to enforce their rights, a point aptly summed up by Mr Justice Darling in his ironic observation that:

'the law courts of England are open to all men, like the doors of the Ritz Hotel' (Drewry, 1975, p. 138).

Like literacy, though, litigation, while evolved to suit the needs of merchants, became an instrument that could be used by workers where the costs were being met by trades unions. This also has put companies on their guard. Of the 40 cases in this study of workplace deaths, firms were legally represented at 80 per cent of inquests. However, there would have been no need for employers to have had representation at the inquest in eight of these cases because the deceased was the managing director of the firm, or a close relative of the director, etc. Of the remaining 32 cases, all the firms (100 per cent) had representation at the inquests to put the firm in the strongest position in relation to any impending litigation (or criminal proceedings).

These findings suggest that the predominant factor in determining law, practice and policy in relation to deaths at work is the economy; the very point noted by Mr Justice Stanwick in his judgement in 1968 (supra) when he recognised that economic considerations are an important element in determining the nature and extent of some legal duties.

Similarly, at the close of the Ford trial, after the jury had heard evidence of the company's cost-benefit analysis which was coldly prepared to countenance the burning of people as a cheaper option than a mass recall and refit exercise, Jim Neal, attorney for the company said (Cullen et al., 1987, p. 291):

> If this country is to survive economically, we've got to stop blaming industry and business for our own sins. No car is now or ever can be said to be safe with reckless drivers on the road.

Balancing safety and cost is a similar operation to balancing the control of crime and cost. The problem of reducing crime levels is largely a question that hinges on resources and a political balance: certain sorts of crime could perhaps be substantially reduced or even eradicated if there was enough of an inroad into civil liberties. Both of these points will now be briefly addressed.

First, on the matter of resources, the issue seems to be more openly articulated in current public debate than it was previously. A study by the management consultants Coopers and Lybrand (*Prevention Strategy for Young People in Trouble*, 1994) calculated that the total cost of crime is £17 billion a year. The proportion attributed to people aged 10 to 20 is £7 billion which includes £444 million of criminal damage, £170 million on motoring offences, £160 million on damage during burglary and £582 million for violence against people. In such a context the state can calculate the cost-effectiveness of particular policies. A classic example of William Petty's 'political arithmetic' (Wiles, 1971, p. 174). The report proposed youth work schemes as a method of diverting people from criminality. As might be expected from business consultants, the report is concerned principally with the *financial* cost of crime, and clinically observes that to be 'cost effective' each scheme would need only to prevent one in 75 offenders from committing one crime a year.

Similarly, the degree of safety which any given employer is legally obliged to afford to the worker is usually calculated on the basis of 'reasonable practicality' (e.g. Health and Safety at Work Etc. Act 1974, ss. 2–6). The burden is on the accused to prove that (s.40):

> it was not practicable or not reasonably practicable to do more than was in fact done to satisfy the duty or requirement, or that there was no better practicable means than was in fact used to satisfy the duty or requirement.

The resolution of these issues, as the cases show,[6] is ultimately a matter of resources. This has been openly conceded by Frank Davies, the chairman of the Health and Safety Commission. Speaking after the publication of HSE research (HSE, 1994) showing that it is generally cheaper for companies to avoid accidents than to pay for the consequences of them, he noted that it would not be 'cost-effective' to 'eliminate all risk of injury at work'.[7]

Regarding the second point here, the political balance, Orwell's *Nineteen Eighty-Four* is probably the clearest modern portrayal of a scenario where ordinary crime has been considerably suppressed by totalitarianism, being a little-glossed version of the experiences of Nazi Germany and the Soviet tyranny from which he drew his fears.[8] The recent spate of adoptions by councils of camera surveillance systems for their streets is a case in point.[9] The pioneering project in England and Wales in Newcastle upon Tyne began in 1992. It achieved an 18 per cent reduction in crime in the city over a 12 month period. This reduction, however, made no impact on the national crime figures covering the same period. During that time crime rose nationally by 6 per cent; violent crime and vehicle crime (i.e. those sorts aimed to be cut by cameras) rose by 7 per cent and 3 per cent, respectively. Offenders were evidently just moving out of camera focus, into the nearest area without them. Perhaps if there was no corner of Britain left unmonitored in such a way then street crime would be virtually eliminated but the social cost, concomitant political tension, and pent up dissent, would be enormous.

The level of safety at work or in rail, sea and air travel operates on a similar way: cost and expediency are balanced against known dangers, their chances of materialising, the number of people who would be hurt in the event of such materialisation and the gravity of injury to them. As Asquith LJ put it in one case:

> As has often been pointed out, if all the trains in this country were restricted to a speed of five miles an hour, there would be fewer accidents, but our national life would be intolerably slowed down. The purpose to be served, if sufficiently important, justifies the assumption of abnormal risk.[10]

The precise nature of this negotiation between commercial interests and best safety practice has been exposed in relation to the safety of 'roll-on, roll-off' (roro) ferries. In the aftermath of the Zeebrugge disaster, in which 192 were killed when the *Herald of Free Enterprise* capsized on 6 March 1987, several reports resulting from marine engineer studies recommended that all of these large ferries should be installed with bulkheads in the lower deck. If this huge open area which houses the lorries and cars is not partitioned at intervals, then any water entering this deck sloshes about along the whole length of the vessel causing rapid instability. This means that the vessel will sink very quickly, in a matter of minutes, so most passengers and crew die inside the ship as they cannot get out. The installation of bulkheads would provide a critical extension of perhaps 30 minutes – retarding the destabilisation – so that people can get into lifeboats. The trouble, for passengers, is that these bulkheads must be part of the design of vessels built after 1990; they are not fitted on most older vessels. Shipping companies could adapt the existing ships but they do not on grounds of expense. For the last few years there has been a pressure on the companies to change their policy but to no avail. The companies all insisted that the alterations that they had made in the light of the Sheen Report in the *Herald* disaster (like closed-circuit television enabling the bridge to check the bow doors are closed before sailing) were sufficient. Then the ferry *Estonia* sank in the Baltic sea on 28 September 1994, killing over 900 people (small children were not registered as passengers so the toll could have been significantly over 900). Most of these people died in the vessel because they did not have sufficient time to get on to the upper deck. Had the ferry been fitted with bulkheads the sinking would have been delayed long enough for everyone to have escaped from the ship.[11]

Following Zeebrugge, the United Nations body, the International Maritime Organisation (IMO) convened a special conference and eventually passed the Safety of Life at Sea Regulations (SOLAS 90). Regulation 8 of SOLAS 90 states that all roll-on, roll-off ferries (so-called because lorries drive in through the bow and out through the stern at the destination) must be able to stand upright long enough for passengers to evacuate. Although this applies automatically to vessels built after April 1990, it does not apply to those built before that date. This is a remarkable compromise with safety, but one which is normal in the commercial world. If a parent found that a brand of toy he or she had just bought a child was unsafe and put the child at serious risk, the parent would be most unlikely to say 'well keep that one but I shan't be getting you another one of those!'. Clearly, the dangerous toy would be taken from the child. The only justification for keeping the old ferries without bulkheads, once the newer safer design had been stipulated for post-1990 vessels, is an economic one. The cost of installing such bulkheads, if it was to be passed on to passengers, would increase fares by between 18 and 19 pence per ticket.[12] In an age of great competition between ferry companies (and air and train travel) this, apparently, according to the operators, makes a significant difference to the fortunes of the operators. The standards agreed as suitable in SOLAS 90 have been repeatedly postponed. They will now not be fully operative until 2005.

The contradiction between this postponement and best safety practice was put to Dr William O'Neill, President of the IMO, during the television interview in June 1992.[13] He answered the questions put to him thus:

Q. It does look like some of the member countries, and in the end enough to carry the day, basically felt that safety standards cost too much.

A. No. I don't think that they felt that safety standards cost too much. I think that they felt the *level* that was prescribed might have been more than they were willing to apply to the existing ships. But the safety standards are still improved. They are still elevated. So the acceptance of increased safety standards is still there.

Q. But commercial interests won out?

A. No. Commercial interests did not win out.

Q. But if safety cost too much then commercial interests won out.

A. No, no. Commercial interests had their part to play in the decision-making process.

Three years later, after 900 people had died in the *Estonia*, Dr O'Neill made several contributions to news stories[14] in which he emphasised that the matter of the compulsory installation of bulkheads would be urgently reviewed. No new research was cited by the president, so he was evidently responding to nothing more than the huge death toll: 900 grieving families and world alarm over ferry safety evidently spoke more eloquently to the president than all the cogent evidence from naval architects and safety groups which he had been repeatedly given in the wake of Zeebrugge, and which he had repeatedly rejected.

Shipping interests seem to have considerable influence on the political process. After the Zeebrugge disaster, the Prime Minister, Margaret Thatcher announced that:

> It is the fundamental design of the ferry that I understand is the problem. That is a factor that will have to be looked at very quickly because public confidence has been severely jolted.[15]

The factor was indeed examined very quickly and immediately rejected. Three days later the Secretary of State for Transport, John Moore, told the House of Commons: 'I have no evidence to support the view that the disaster was due to the design of the ship' (*Hansard* [Commons] Vol. 112, No. 1410, Col. 21, 9 March 1987).

This seemed to ignore the evidence of a conference held in London in 1985 by the Royal Institute of Naval Architects at which a paper was presented detailing the urgent need for design changes in roll-on, roll-off ferries in the wake of the capsize of the vessel *European Gateway* off Harwich in 1982.[16] Six people were killed in that incident. Several senior members of the Institute are recorded in the minutes of the conference as urging quick change to the design of roro vessels before an even larger scale of incident occurred. One address from a senior Institute member blames 'commercial pressures' for stopping ship owners and governments from insisting on the installation of transverse bulk heads, and ends thus: 'The question must still be asked: what happens if a vessel of this type carrying 1000 passengers instead of 34 suffers a similar accident?'[17]

Two years later, 192 people were killed when the *Herald of Free Enterprise* sank off Zeebrugge. The Department of Transport was represented at the 1985 conference and was furnished with a full report of the research demonstrating the perils of open vehicle decks, so it seems inexplicable that just 18 months after his department had been explicitly warned (by the most suitable body in

Britain to do so) of danger to ferry passengers the minister could claim to the House of Commons that he had 'no evidence' that the design of the ferries was unsafe.

There followed repeated public statements of concern that nothing was being done to correct what had been identified as a serious contributory factor (the undivided vehicle deck),[18] and to require all ferries to install bulkheads. Once again however nothing was done. Meanwhile, relatives of the *Herald* victims expressed fury when the chairman of P&O European Ferries, Sir Jeffrey Stirling, was ennobled in Mrs Thatcher's resignation honours; this notwithstanding the observation of Mr Justice Sheen in his official report that P&O was a company in which:

> All concerned in management, from the members of the Board of Directors down to the junior superintendents, were guilty of fault in that all must be regarded as sharing responsibility for the failure of management. From top to bottom the body corporate was infected with the disease of sloppiness.[19]

The news of the new peerage was treated with dismay by some newspapers. One headline ran: 'It's Lord Zeebrugge'.[20]

While relatively unsafe ferries plied their trade into and from British ports, the government and the IMO were allied to commercial interests. In another telling television interview in the documentary mentioned above, Lord Caithness, then minister responsible for shipping, was asked whether he would be prepared to publish a list of all the ferries that had thereto conformed *in full* with the SOLAS 90 standards, i.e. had fitted bulkheads. The minister replied to the camera that he would have no objection. Then, in an extraordinary turn of events, a voice was heard off-camera asking for the film to be stopped. The film, perhaps unknown to the minister, was not stopped, so the viewer saw a man in a suit clasping a batch of paper walk on to the set and talk in grave tones to the minister. The documentary then cut to what was a retake of the original question. This time the minister said that he would *not* publish such a list (despite the fact this would assist British travellers to select the safest ferries) because it would prejudice the business interests of some British operators whose foreign rivals (from northern and western Europe) would gain from such disclosure. This was the second take:

> Q. In an era of open government can we have your assurance that the details of which ships comply to Solas 90 will be published?

> A. I think that every country ought to do that.

Q. And will you do it?

A. I think that every country ought to do that and it can only be done effectively on a complete basis with every country doing it. *It isn't going to be beneficial* by just one country doing it because it puts at a severe commercial disadvantage that country [emphasis added].

Here the minister sees the interests of passengers and commerce as identical, whereas there is a clear conflict. It obviously *would* be 'beneficial' to customers to be able to make properly informed decisions about the safest ferry to travel on, even if the shareholders of British operators were not best pleased that passengers were choosing to travel on ferries operated by foreign firms. In October 1994, only one ferry operating in British waters had bulkheads, and this is operated by a Belgian company, Ostend Lines.

The coach industry also seems to have an extraordinary persuasive power over government. Each year about 30 children are killed and hundreds are seriously injured when the coaches in which they travel crash on motorways and trunk roads.[21] Most would have been saved were they to have worn seatbelts. They do not wear seatbelts because these are not generally fitted on coaches. It is not really something about which much expert technical knowledge is required in order to understand the need for seatbelts to be fitted in coaches. They are compulsory in other vehicles and on aeroplanes. Even so, there is now much expert evidence to support such a request. The coach industry in Britain is reluctant to fit its coaches with such life-saving devices because of the cost, and the government has repeatedly stalled on introducing legislation to compel such fixture. Despite all the evidence suggesting that, in the event of a crash, seat belts save lives, the Bus and Coach Council, which represents bus operators, has steadfastly opposed the mandatory installation of belts, arguing that it is not satisfied with the current cogency of evidence.[22] The roads minister, Robert Key, almost directly exposed the cost-benefit based reasoning of the government when he said (*Guardian*, 1 July 1994, p. 2):

> We don't need legislation to [make seatbelts compulsory]. If we were to do it we'd have the whole problem of enforcement. We're talking about hundreds of thousands of people in the community being transported safety without any incident every day. We're also talking about a tragic but tiny number of things going wrong.

This focuses attention on the rarity of 'things going wrong', but the central point of the debate is what measures should be taken to minimise harm when things *do* go wrong. The logical consequence of the minister's argument is to cast doubt on whether we need have special 'burns units' in hospitals or kidney dialysis machines as these would only ever be used, taking society as a whole, on a tiny number of cases where things go wrong.

The reasoning would appear as more repugnant if it expressly articulated the 'costs' of a certain number of children killed and maimed, as against the 'cost' of enforcement; a similar calculation to the one used by the Ford Motor Company (below). That part of the calculation is left implicit. The argument about enforcement did not prevent the legislation in the 1980s which made seatbelts compulsory in cars; quite why it here becomes critical is not clear.

Perhaps the best challenge to address at this juncture is posed by Kramer (1983, p. 167):

> We need ... to develop an understanding of the political economy of corporate violence; we need to know how and why a corporate capitalist economy systematically generates such violence, and why the state in a capitalist economy is so impotent in its attempts to control these acts. We need also to understand how organizational environments, goals, and structures relate to corporate violence.

It is helpful to begin to address Kramer's query with a brief history of the state's response to death and injury incidental to employment. The first piece of health and safety legislation came in 1802 in response to the appallingly inhuman conditions in which child apprentices were worked in the mills (Carson, 1979; Engels, 1969, 1845, pp. 170–81). The Health and Morals of Apprentices Act prohibited the employment of children for more than 12 hours a day and provided for the eventual cessation of night work by children. Some rudimentary provision was also made for the physical and intellectual well-being of these children with minor requirements concerning clothing, sleeping arrangements and their education. A further Act of 1819 fixed the minimum age for working in a cotton factory at nine years, and prohibited the employment of those under 16 for longer than 12 hours a day (excluding meal times). By 1831 these rules were extended to night working. As Carson notes, these measures were almost wholly ineffectual because enforcement was left to the Justices of the Peace who, if they carried out any inspections, were evidently quite uncritical and perfunctory in their checks. In view of the fact that these people shared the same class status and clubs as those whom they were supposed to police, this reluctance may not be surprising (Field, 1990). Looking at the possibility of making violations of safety legislation punishable as an ordinary crime, a Royal Commission in 1833 rejected the idea with the conclusion that such a change would: 'create a serious objection to the investment of capital in manufacturing industry in this country' (Carson, 1979, p. 42).

Instead, the Act decided that the appropriate sanctions would be a relatively low level of fines with an additional cushion that where the magistrate found that a violation was neither wilful nor grossly negligent the defendant could be discharged or given a minimal penalty. The ensuing legislation did create four inspectors and a number of superintendents to work under them, but they were under instructions to be 'in communication exclusively with employers, with the view of making the law acceptable to them' and it was not long before the inspectors were reporting that the new law *was* being generally adhered to. Carson notes (ibid., p. 43) that the enforcement policy here came close to 'an outright conspiracy'. Before the final phase of the 1833 legislation was to come into effect, bringing 12–13 year-olds within the law, the factory inspectorate were actually persuaded by mill owners to oppose such a change on the grounds that it would make life impossibly difficult for them; a consideration which appears to have held greater sway than the interests of the thousands of children who were being worked to death.

Legislation was drafted to postpone the change but it was not promulgated. One of the problems of enforcement was that the owners of industry tried, in periods of economic adversity, to improve their performance by cutting labour costs and by extending the hours worked. This was not just restricted to the poorer less reputable firm. According to witnesses (ibid., p. 50; Marx, 1954, 1887, p. 232), masters even admitted quite openly that it was easier to pay the occasional mitigated fine than to incur the costs involved in obeying the law or lose the profits accruing from its violation. Sixty-eight per cent of all fines imposed between 1836 and 1842 involved sums of £1 or less (£1 being the minimum stipulated fine, although it could be less in exceptional circumstances). The average fine following from a death in the construction industry in London 1988/90 was £1,282. The state of affairs today is very similar. The level of penalty an employer can expect for serious infringements is relatively low: the average penalty imposed on companies guilty of health and safety offences in 1992/93, while representing a 17 per cent rise on the previous year (Slapper, 1994d) was still only £1,384. The average fine for prosecutions by HSE which resulted in conviction (excluding fines of £100,000 and over) has in fact been decreasing each year since 1993/94 for the extractive and construction industries, although increasing each year since 1993/94 for the agriculture and service industries. For the manufacturing industry the average fine decreased for the first time since 1992/93.

Overall, the average fine for 1996/97, based on figures for the whole of HSE, was £5,421 – if the 10 highest fines are discounted, the average is £3,266 (HSC statistics 1996/97).

There is also today, as in the nineteenth century, very little chance of being inspected, with one inspector to every 690 registered premises – not counting the estimated 40 per cent of sites and premises which do not register[23] (Whitfield, 1992). For companies, a visit from a government safety inspector is likely only once in four or five years (Nelken, 1994; Tye, 1989).

Hutter's study (1994, cited in Clarke, 1990, p. 209) of four Environmental Health Offices highlights the limits to effectiveness built into the EHO's remit. They are employed by local authorities and not central government, which means their status, funding and independence may vary from authority to authority and reflect political control of authorities. They have extremely diversified responsibilities which are often shared with other regulatory agencies such as the Health and Safety Commission. Finally the penalties in the cases which they take to court are statutorily limited to relatively small fines. EHOs, she argues, have a vital job to do in ensuring that the public as customers and employees are not poisoned by substandard food from shops, restaurants and canteens, and ensuring that tenants, especially those in difficult circumstances, do not suffer from damp, structural defects and the failure of landlords to maintain properties. Yet the chances of their achieving anything like rigorous enforcement are remote indeed. Given their very wide-ranging responsibilities many offences are inevitably undetected as the number of premises constituting potential sites for inspection is vastly greater than can be coped with on a regular basis. Legal action, she argues, is deterred by the limited nature of the penalties involved and by the diversion of time from inspection which preparing a case for court entails.

Bergman (1994) also argues that part of the failure of the enforcement agencies to conduct adequate and competent investigations arises out of a starvation of resources supplied to the regulatory bodies but, he argues, part is also attitudinal – an apparent lack of will to criminalise employers' conduct, however culpable they may have been.

It is worthy of note in passing that even if a site has been inspected, it is unlikely to be properly followed through, for economic reasons. A report by the National Audit Office (1994) notes that staff shortages and under-resourcing at the HSE means that it is failing to process reports on dangerous industries. At the time of the audit (1994) it had failed to assess 132 of 331 reports on major hazard sites in Britain. The Merseyside office, for example, was still assessing 25 out of 39 reports on safety which had been submitted in 1989.

Having gained the advantages of legislation which, although creating criminal wrongs, contained only regulatory offences, the employers were then afforded the additional advantage in the policy, developed by inspectors, of only prosecuting when there was evidence that there had been a *mens rea* of intention on the part of the employer, e.g. the offence in question was committed in violation of an earlier warning from the inspectorate.

Carson concluded that the operation of the law developed in this way in order not to constrain the economic development taking place in the nineteenth century (1979, p. 57). In his later study of the high death rate in the North Sea oil fields, he notes that by the middle of the 1970s the rate of 'accidental' death in the oil industry was 11 times higher than that for construction, nine times higher than that for mining and six times higher than that for quarrying. His evidence indicates that the accidents were not simply what is only to be expected when an industry undertakes hazardous operations at the very frontiers of technology, but rather the result of factors like poor communication, failure of equipment, poor working practices and lack of safety precautions. Throughout the 1970s the British government was under considerable pressure to extract North Sea oil as rapidly as possible for economic reasons, including a pressing balance of payments problem. The government was heavily dependent on the expertise and resources of the major transnational oil companies, who would only act quickly if they were left relatively unhampered by any requirement for costly and time-consuming safety precautions. The government eventually acceded to their demands about the legislative framework in which the companies were to operate. Carson concludes that most of the 106 deaths which had occurred up to December 1980 could have been avoided if the 'political economy of speed had not been allowed to prevail over the 'political economy of employee's lives'. He was struck by the parallels between the history of North Sea oil safety and that of the earliest efforts to impose statutory controls upon the operations of the 'dark satanic mills' of the nineteenth century. In both periods there were 'immutable laws of capital' which rendered it imperative that regulation should be minimised (1981, p. 302).

One of the survivors of Piper Alpha, the world's worst offshore disaster, blames the culture of profit and greed in the North Sea for the tragedy which killed 167 husbands, fathers and sons on 6 July 1988 (*The Guardian*, 6 July 1988). Ten years on, the survivors and friends and families of the bereaved are still attempting to understand the events of that fateful night, which began with a gas explosion and has continued as an interminable battle against the corporate might of the oil industry to discover where the true fault lay and who was responsible. The Cullen inquiry, the longest running in British legal history, led inexorably to the conclusion that there was a gross failing in the platform's safety procedures. Yet no prosecutions were ever brought against the company, Occidental Petroleum. The only people found culpable in law were two workers who died on that night, after a judge held them responsible when insurance companies sued to get their compensation back.

Occidental was never even fined and it has been suggested (*The Guardian*, 6 July 1998) that, with tax relief to build the replacement Piper Bravo platform, insurance cover and the rise in oil prices which followed the disaster, the corporation may even have turned a profit on the events of that night. The survivors and bereaved received only meagre compensation. On Piper Bravo the unrelenting production drive continues round the clock, while the survivors and bereaved continue to campaign for a 'corporate killing' law in the hope that, at least in the long term, these gigantic corporations cannot shroud human tragedy behind the bureaucracy and culture of the corporate structure.

The flight of dangerous capital to jurisdictions with the least stringent controls (often because they wish to encourage the investment to assist with a developing economy) is acknowledged by Beck (1992, pp. 20, 41, 44). This does not, however, always bode well for the place where it lands. A catastrophic materialisation of this principle occurred a couple of years after Carson made the point: the leak of toxic gases at Bhopal, India on 3 December 1984, the worst chemical disaster the world has seen. Estimates of those who died in the immediate aftermath vary from 2,500 to 10,000. Apart from these immediate casualties, it has been reported that two people still die each week in Bhopal from the aftereffects of the disaster (Jones, 1988, p. 1), and 20,000 people will probably go blind (Beck, 1992, p. 43). The disaster illustrates the dangers of the flight of capital, because Union Carbide Corporation (UCC), a major US-based chemical multinational company, exported to Bhopal a pesticides manufacturing plant that was defectively designed and dangerously deficient in terms of safety, and there is evidence that this plant had been previously rejected on safety grounds in Canada (Jones, 1988, p. 296, n. 3).

The paramount economic priority of companies is to be profitable concerns. It is their essential purpose. Scruples, moral considerations and legal restraint, in different measure for different people, restrict injurious conduct in the quest for profit. Lord Lauderdale sought to deny chimney girls and boys a right to life by arguing that neither morality nor ethics had anything to do with market efficiency (Strange, 1982; Easton, 1984: Moore, 1991). During a recent drought when water supplies were simply exhausted in some parts of England, at least two groups of young men were discovered trying to *sell* buckets of water to old, housebound people. Their conduct may be regarded as morally repugnant but it was not illegal and it was, in a strict sense, within the province of what has been described as 'enterprise culture'.

The economic environment exerts a strong pressure on companies to take risks. Work practice is governed by a state of affairs characterised by William Morris as 'modern commerce – the counting-house forgetful of the workshop' (1947, 1877, p. 35). This pressure was directly conceded by Dr John Cullen, the former Chairman of the Health and Safety Executive, when he stated:

> The enterprise culture, the opening up of markets, and the need to survive competition place businesses under unprecedented pressure ... the scale and pace of technological change means that increasing numbers of people – the public as well as employees – are potentially at risk (*The Guardian,* 4 March 1989).

The amoral nature of the operation of modern commerce has been a feature of the social system since its inception, as a factory inspector's report from 1841 demonstrates:

> It is certainly much to be regretted that any class of persons should toil 12 hours a day, which, including the time for their meals and for going to and returning from their work, amounts, in fact, to 14 of the 24 hours ... Without entering into the question of health, no one will hesitate, I think, to admit that, *in a moral point of view*, so entire an absorption of the time of the working classes, without intermission, from the early age of 13, and in trades not subject to restriction, much younger, must be extremely prejudicial, and is an evil greatly to be deplored ... [emphasis original] (Leonard Horner, Reports of Insp. of Fact. for 31 Dec., 1841, cited in Marx, 1954, 1877, p. 264).

The immorality of such ravages did not, in itself, call the conduct to a halt. It was only when moral indignation and philanthropic reforming zeal were joined by parallel desires for change from the owning class (who recognised that some regulation was in their best long-term interests) (Marx, 1954, 1887, ch. 10; Engels, 1969, 1845; Carson, 1970a and 1979) that the legislation became feasible.

Marx showed how, at every legislative restriction on the factory owners, many industrialists strove to do the most that they could to undermine or limit its intended effect. The 1833 Factory Act left it optional with the factory owners during the 15 hours, from 5.30 am to 8.30 pm, to make every 'young person' and 'every child' begin, break off, resume, or end his 12 or eight hours at any moment they liked, and also permitted them to assign to different persons, different times for meals. The factory owners, far from using the discretion with any compassion, immediately resorted to a 'system of relays' which completely thwarted the inspectors' attempts to check who, if anyone, was being overworked. They ensured that 'the labour-horses were not changed at fixed stations', but were constantly re-harnessed at changing stations (Marx, 1954, 1887, p. 266). Again, the 'lynx eye of Capital' discovered that the Factory Act of 1844 did not allow five hours work before midday without a pause of at least 30 minutes for refreshment, but prescribed nothing of the kind for work after midday.

> Therefore, it claimed and obtained the enjoyment not only of making children of 8 drudge without intermission from 2 to 8.30 pm, but also of making them hunger during that time (ibid., p. 272).

As many business people often claim, from its launching onwards, the process of running a company is constantly beset with a variety of risks. Companies are relentlessly having to remain 'competitive' by keeping their expenditure as low as possible. Clearly, most companies today will not knowingly jeopardise the lives of their customers or the general public, but there are enough documented instances of such risks apparently being knowingly taken to demonstrate the compelling pressure of commercial competition.

Vehicle manufacture provides another source of illustration. On 13 September 1978, the Ford Motor Company was indicted in Indiana, USA for reckless homicide. A Grand Jury decided after three days of deliberation that Ford was to be tried as a responsible party for the deaths of three teenagers, who were burnt to death when their Ford Pinto burst into flames following a low-speed, rear-end collision. Many people had died in similar incidents all over the USA. Dowie has stated that 'by conservative estimates Pinto crashes have caused more than 500 deaths' (1977, p. 14).

Fighting strong competition from Volkswagen for the lucrative smaller car market, the Ford Motor Company rushed the Pinto into production in much less than the usual time. The normal time span from conception to production of a new car model is about 43 months, whereas the Pinto schedule was set at 25 months (Dowie, 1977, p. 16). The man behind this project was a young executive, Lee Iacocca, who had been 'head-hunted' from General Motors, and then gained a reputation after the enormous success of his first project – the Mustang. Ford engineers discovered, however, in the pre-production crash tests of the Pinto, that rear-end collisions would rupture its fuel system very easily. Because assembly-line production was already tooled (i.e. the factory plant and machinery to be used in making the cars) when engineers found this defect, a decision had to be taken at the highest levels within the company that production should nonetheless proceed.[24]

The actual homicide trial resulted in the company being acquitted[25] but evidence was led in the case which demonstrated that Ford was aware of the danger posed by the Pinto but had used a cost-benefit calculation to decide that the cars should be left, unaltered, with their owners. It would have cost less than $11 per car to remedy the defect, but calculations had shown that subsequent insurance claims resulting from the number of people predicted to be killed and maimed would be $49.5 million[26] whereas it would cost $137 million to recall and alter all the Pintos it had sold (see Appendix 1). This sort of cost-benefit analysis, which relegates human life below the considerations of profit, is not peculiar to Ford Motor Company or to recent developments. It is a feature endemic to the system of commerce.[27]

The way that the economic imperatives of commerce can prompt decisions which imperil life was commented upon by Max Weber. In 1904 he observed that:

> After their work, ... [Chicago] workers often have to travel for hours in order to reach their homes. The tramway company has been bankrupt for years. As usual, a receiver who has no interest in speeding up the liquidation, manages its affairs; therefore, new tramcars are not purchased. The old cars constantly break down, and about four hundred people a year are thus killed or crippled. According to the law, each death costs the company about $5,000 which is paid to the widow or heirs, and each cripple costs $10,000, paid to the casualty himself. These compensations are due so long as the company does not introduce certain precautionary measures. But they have calculated that the four hundred casualties a year cost less than would the necessary precautions. The company therefore does not introduce them (quoted in Swigert and Farrell, 1980, p. 166).

The calculation made in the Pinto case should, however, be put in its socioeconomic context. As Swigert and Farrell note (1980, p. 176) cost-benefit analysis is not unique to the Ford Motor Company. Corporate profits depend upon a rational calculation of income and expenses.[28] It has also been argued (Epstein, 1980, p. 19; Swigert and Farrell, op. cit.) that consumer safety regulations themselves encourage such calculations:

> when, therefore, the prosecution said that Ford had made a conscious choice to 'trade' cost against safety, the answer is that this is precisely what the tort law ... establishes as the limit of its legal obligation....

Cost-benefit analysis says that if the cost is greater than the benefit, the prospective project should not proceed. It can be seen as the quintessential calculation of capitalism. The analysis is also not significantly different from the formula used in the United States to determine whether the defendant has been negligent: the defendant is guilty of negligence if the loss caused by the accident, multiplied by the probability of the accident's occurring, exceeds the burden of the precautions that the defendant might have taken to avert it.[29] Posner (1972, p. 69) notes that this is an economic test. The burden of precautions is the cost of avoiding the accident. The loss multiplied by the probability of the accident is the cost that the precautions would have averted. If a larger cost could have been avoided by incurring a smaller cost, efficiency requires that the smaller cost be incurred. Quite openly then, a company can decide on how safe its workers, passengers or consumers will be using a cost calculation in conjunction with human conscience.

In the United Kingdom, Dunlop faces having to pay more than £1 million to two families involved in a head-on car crash which left a child dead, a woman blinded and seven people injured after defective tyres were blamed for the accident. Lord Justice Judge, sitting with Lord Justice Auld and Lord Justice Nourse at the Court of Appeal, said Dunlop had concealed defects in the SP4 radial to protect their commercial viability (*The Times*, 21 January 1998). In relation to corporate crime it might be thought that the fine was a perfect disposal because, unlike individuals whose criminal conduct is often committed whilst affected by alcohol, drugs or passionate emotions (and are thus not considering the current sentencing tariffs when they commit crimes), corporations generally behave rationally. They conduct business through decision-making processes that *are* susceptible to rationally predictable outcomes like profits and fines. Businesses use cost-benefit analysis as a routine procedure. The trouble is that such calculations are as much based on the likelihood of *being caught* as they are upon the level of fine if caught and convicted.

As noted earlier in this chapter, there were often good economic reasons for factory and mill owners to support some of the reforms restricting the working day if they believed that the legislative requirements would be manageable and would detrimentally affect their smaller rivals. There is even an example of the smaller firms helping to fund agitation by workers in the larger firms to promote legislation for a nine-hour day when the smaller firms saw this as being in their economic interests (Marx, 1954, 1887, p. 257, n. 2). The pattern of larger firms having better safety records is something which has continued into our contemporary setting. Health and Safety Executive research has shown (Thomas, 1991) that in manufacturing firms employing under 50 workers there seems a 20 per cent greater risk of major injury than in medium or larger enterprises, and a 40 per cent greater risk than in the very largest workplaces.

There were other reasons why the owners of industry lent support to legislation relating to control over working conditions, but, critically, these reasons are related to the economic interests of that class rather than moral or humanitarian case for change. For one thing, in the interests of preserving the working class from being over-plundered, the Factory Acts were necessary, in Marx's words (1954, 1887, p. 229), to 'curb the passion of capital for a limitless draining of labour-power'. He reflects that:

> Apart from the working class movement which daily grew more threatening, the limiting of factory labour was dictated by the same necessity which spread guano over the English fields. The same blind eagerness for plunder that in the one case exhausted the soil, had, in the other, torn up by the roots the living force of the nation.

That the working class was in danger of being pummelled so badly that its wealth-creating ability would be significantly reduced is corroborated by medical data concerning epidemic illness and the declining physical condition of military recruits (ibid.). Capitalists were also prevailed upon with two further economic arguments against over-working their servants. First, that this would shorten the life, and therefore duration of labour-power, of a worker; that the rate at which workers need to be replaced would increase; and, therefore, that the cost of the social reproduction of labour-power would increase (ibid., p. 253). Second, that 'all work and no play' would reduce the ingenuity, dexterity and general productivity of workers (ibid., p. 261).

There is evidence to suggest that another factor lending support to the regulation (apart from the pressure of reformers, and the enlightened economic self-interest of certain capitalists) was that it assisted in the discipline and regimentation of the workforce: that with its emphasis on regularity and uniformity, upon records of machinery operation, upon times of entry and departure from the mills, it helped inculcate 'habits of obedience' (Thompson, 1967; Carson, 1979).

There is also evidence (ibid., p. 45) to show that the efforts of the early factory inspectors to impress upon employers that the provisions relating to the education of children in the 1833 Act should be complied with, helped to disseminate awareness of the advantages that might accrue to labour discipline from education of the factory children. The results of one survey of employers showed that those who had installed schools enjoyed an enhanced level of what the inspectorate labelled the 'habits of subordination'.

Sometimes the economic pressures of the market system even prevail where the operation in question is supposed reduce the risk of injury and death. The railway crash at Clapham Junction station on 12 December 1988 was such an example. A crowded commuter train ran into the rear of a stationary train just south of Clapham Junction station. The death toll was 35, with an additional 500 people injured, 60 of them seriously. The immediate cause of the disaster was a loose wire in a relay controlling signal which allowed the display of a yellow light instead of a red one. A senior technician had re-wired this particular signal two weeks earlier as a part of the Waterloo Area Resignalling Scheme (WARS), and had left the old wire hanging loose which was his usual practice. In fact, British Rail standard procedures required the old wire to be cut back and removed or tied back. The Report of Anthony Hidden QC[30] on this disaster clearly reveals the way in which culpability can be traced back from individual error, through lax and indifferent management, to wider economic issues (Field and Jörg, 1991). The technician himself could be the sole target of blame for having violated a departmental instruction, 'S.I. -16' which stipulated that disconnected wires should be insulated and secured. Nonetheless, another departmental instruction demanded that an 'independent wire count' be conducted by the technicians supervisor or the area Testing and Commissioning Engineer after the work had been completed. These procedures did not operate. The technician could not recall any occasion on which his work had been checked in this way. Some of his mistaken techniques had been long-standing ones which had never been corrected or even discovered by BR management.

The violation of S.I. -16 takes on a different meaning when it is discovered that the technician received very little proper training and never even received a copy of the instruction in question; neither was his supervisor aware of the requirement for an independent wire count. The area Testing and Commissioning Engineer did not realise that he had overall responsibility for ensuring that the necessary testing was carried out. All this ignorance was attributable to failures of management to communicate with its employees. The wire count instruction had been issued with no accompanying explanation, training or monitoring. The WARS was worked on a tight schedule, dependent upon high levels of overtime. These levels were never monitored. In the 13 weeks before the accident, 28 per cent of the workforce had worked seven days a week and another 43 per cent had worked 13 days out of 14. One witness told the inquiry that staff were 'shell shocked by the pressure of work'.

A situation which Moore (1991, p. 23) notes can only be described as 'paradoxically bizarre, in as much as workers were forced to work to the point where they were almost comatose from nervous exhaustion while installing a system designed to improve safety'. The technician in question, who was under great personal financial pressure, had taken only one day off work in the preceding three months. Such levels of overtime had been going on for years at BR. Writing over 120 years earlier (in 1866), Marx addressed a similar incident (1947, 1877, p. 242):

> A tremendous railway accident has hurried hundreds of passengers into another world. The negligence of the employees is the cause of the misfortune. They declare with one voice before the jury that ten or twelve years before, their labour only lasted eight hours a-day. During the last five or six years it had been screwed up to 14, 18 and 20 hours, and under a specially severe pressure of holiday-makers, at times of excursion trains, it often lasted for 40 or 50 hours without a break. They were ordinary men, not Cyclops. At a certain point their labour-power failed. Torpor seized them. Their brains ceased to think, their eyes to see. The thoroughly 'respectable' British jurymen answered by a verdict that sent them to the next assizes on a charge of manslaughter, and, in a gentle 'rider' to their verdict, expressed the pious hope that the capitalistic magnates of the railway would, in future, be more extravagant in the purchase of a sufficient quantity of labour-power, and more 'abstemious', more 'self-denying', more 'thrifty', in the draining of paid labour-power.

In the Clapham incident the technician made a mistake (possibly a worse one than he was routinely making) through exhaustion and ignorance. He was tired because he had been overworking because that was the only way he could afford to meet his financial obligations, so his error tracks back to the economy. He was ignorant because of lax management, and this is attributable (Field and Jörg, 1991) to the low priority that safety was accorded within BR for commercial reasons -again the fault, this time indifference, is traceable to the economy.

## The Social Axioms

A society in which the social production of goods and services is dominated by commercial considerations will be likely to generate a certain human sacrifice. These are portrayed as people who die for the greater good of the majority. What originates as a necessary consequence of the economic structure is translated into a social axiom.

The problematic force, then, is social – it originates systemically – and the decisions, made by individuals, which endanger life are results of the hypostatic grammar of economic reasoning which underlies capitalism. We are cautioned against seeing the origin of economically motivated recklessness in individuals by Marx, who noted (1954, 1887, p. 257) that all the life lost in industry does not depend on the good or ill will of the individual capitalist but rather on external coercive economic laws.

He goes on to examine cases where individual capitalists with a conscience pricked by the suffering of children in their factories could not behave any more compassionately to their 'hands' because to do so would jeopardise their position *vis-à-vis* their competitors. In a footnote (ibid.), for example, he notes that in the beginning of 1863, 26 firms owning extensive potteries in Staffordshire, including Josiah Wedgwood & Sons, petitioned for better legislation to govern the employment of children because: 'Much as we deplore the evils before mentioned, it would not be possible to prevent them by any scheme of agreement between the manufacturers ...' (Children's Employment Comm., Rep. 1, 1863, p. 322).

At the time of the Robens committee's examination of health and safety law (1972), Nicholas (1984) observed that the considerations of profit maximisation and cost cutting, along with the organisational authority of maintaining managerial authority, would inevitably be put before safety by employers. This is not just because employers enjoy membership of a modern equivalent of Dickens' 'Association for the Mangling of Operatives', nor is it simply a result of the employers' callous disregard for the welfare of workers and the public interest. Rather such consequences are a logical outcome (Moore, 1991) of the profit system. This inevitability is recognised by the Organisation for Economic Co-operation and Development (OECD) (1989). There is widespread agreement in OECD member countries on the need for government regulation to play a major role in this area. It acknowledges that (1989, p. 6):

> protection against work accidents has historically tended to be the first area of government intervention into the workplace. Such intervention has been based on the belief that the predominance of the private market would lead to socially unacceptable levels of occupational injury, disease and death.

The legal framework of protection and compensation has historically upheld the primacy of free markets and managerial authority (Moore, 1991; Posner, 1972) which originates within nineteenth-century master and servant legislation. Thus, working class moves for forms of joint control over safety have been fiercely opposed by the state and employers. Such forms remained very rare[31] until the 1974 legislation, and even then the legislation did not permit the scarcely unreasonable trade union request to be able to stop work in situations of extreme risk. This has now (in 1993 legislation) been achieved, 160 years after the first factory legislation in 1833. Employees now have the right not to be dismissed or subjected to detrimental treatment on the grounds that they left or proposed to leave their place of work, or any dangerous part of the workplace, 'in circumstances of danger which he or she reasonably believed to be serious and imminent' and which the employee could not reasonably have been expected to avert.[32] The idea that the servant was fair game for any risk to which the master wished to expose him and that he consented to danger by virtue of his contract, has been eroded. The 'employee' now has a similar nominal and civil status as his or her 'employer', but this change has itself been used as the basis to decriminalise certain lethal risk-taking with the lives and limbs of workers. Now, following from the new, 'civilised', cordial employment relations in some workplaces where managers and workers all wear the same smart company clothes and eat together in the same staff canteens, the inherently lawful, virtuous nature of the relationship is accentuated whenever anything goes drastically wrong. However grave are the faults exposed in an investigation, the company will be able to stress the respect which it is accorded in the community and the esteem in which it is held by its personnel.

So clearly and widely is it now recognised that the engines of industry and commerce are primarily controlled by financial factors that these have been reverted to by health and safety campaigners as the key to promoting safety at work. Appeals to companies for humane working practices, threats of criminal proceedings, educational campaigns, equipping workers with the right knowledge, and all sorts of negotiated compliance strategies have still left a high toll of death and injury. In a publication (HSE, 1994), the Health and Safety Executive estimates that £16 billion is lost to the British economy each year through accidents and ill health at work. The loss to industry is calculated at £360 a year for every worker. More than 2.2 million people suffered from ill-health which was wholly or partly caused by work and 750,000 of them took time off as a result, leading to the loss of 11.5 million working days. Work-related illnesses forced 70,500 people to stop work permanently.

The message to owners of industry is, essentially: take better safety precautions for your workers (in training, equipment and procedure) because it will cost you more if they are killed and injured than the sum you will have to spend to avoid such exigencies. This replicates the Hand formula (above) used in the USA to determine whether a defendant has been negligent. Frank Davies, chairman of the Health and Safety Commission, was quite explicit in his admonition to employers: 'Accidents hurt your profit and loss account'.[33]

The headline of a newspaper story[34] examining the provisional findings of the Health and Safety Commission research (before the report was published) captured the import very succinctly: 'Profits "at risk from accidents at work"'. Company losses through accidents were between eight and 36 times greater than insured costs.

The report followed a detailed study of accidents and illnesses at a construction site, a creamery, a transport haulage company, a North Sea oil production platform and a NHS hospital, each of which had a previously established above average record of safety. It shows that the construction firm lost £700,000 a year through accidents and ill-health, the creamery almost £1 million, the transport company £196,000, the hospital £400,00 and the oil production platform £3.7 million. The relevant costs include the payment of compensation to injured workers or relatives, replacing staff involved in an accident and repairing damaged equipment. It estimates the direct cost to employers of accidents and work-related ill-health at between £4 and £9 billion, equivalent to 5–10 per cent of all British-based company profits.

The reasoning may be correct and persuasive. Once it is conceded, however, that the considerations of profit are the ultimately determinative factor, not just in business strategy, but also in respect of human safety, then it is to that factor we must pay very special attention. It may be true that the profit principle can be harnessed to improve safety, in the way the HSE envisages, by persuading companies that avoiding a funeral is cheaper than paying for one. But, suppose certain assumptions inherent in the current reasoning began to change. Suppose that the proposals to deregulate business safety law (Lashmar, 1994) which were eventually dropped in the face of much opposition (June 1994) were to be resurrected, and were duly promulgated. The regulations and practice governing the *quantum* of damages payable in respect of fatal injuries could also change.[35] In such changed circumstances it may suddenly become possible, using the already adopted principle that we should follow the dictates of the market, to argue that it is cheaper to allow people to die through lack of safety than to foot the bill for avoiding such risks. Once it is accepted that the economic pressures of the market system are, ultimately, more powerful influences upon work safety practice than moral imperatives, then the very limited potential for legally engineering the problem of commercial carnage out of industrial society becomes apparent. In support of this one contemporary development can be noted.

Consider the proposition that the legal system, its criminal laws, criminal sanctions and consequential gravamen can, ultimately, substantially overcome or manage corporate recklessness.

The evidence suggests that many corporate actors are so socially powerful that not only do they enjoy relative immunity from the criminal law but that the current 'economy of illegalities' (Foucault, 1977) is such that they are *de facto* beyond the criminal law (Box, 1983; Ermann and Lundman, 1992; Croall, 1993; Jamieson, 1994; Pearce and Tombs, 1994). It is notable that 500 transnational corporations control 70 per cent of world trade and take 30 per cent of its income. The forms of industrial organisation have been transformed over the last century. The rise in the level of industrial concentration has been especially pronounced. As Leslie Hannah observes (1979, p. 1), the structure of British industry has, over the last century, been transformed 'from a disaggregated structure of predominantly small, competing firms to a concentrated structure dominated by large, often monopolistic corporations'.

Throughout much of the nineteenth century, British capitalism was highly competitive, with such a high number of small firms in each industry that none of them was large enough to exercise a perceptible influence over their own markets, let alone over the economy as a whole. Hannah considers it likely that the largest 100 firms in 1880 accounted for less than 10 per cent of total manufacturing output. Over the last century however, *aggregate* concentration has steadily risen: the largest 100 firms accounted for about 16 per cent of net manufacturing output by 1909, 24 per cent by 1935, 32 per cent by 1958, 37 per cent by 1963, 42 per cent by 1968, and nearly 50 per cent (perhaps even more) by the mid 1970s. Between 1949 and 1970 the largest 100 firms share of output increased two and a half fold (ibid., pp. 15, 215–25). Moreover, as Campbell indicates (1981, pp. 60–80), taking net manufacturing assets rather than output as the measure, current aggregate concentration is found to be even higher, and also to have been increasing at a faster rate. The proportion of the UK's manufacturing assets held by the largest 80 companies increased from 38 per cent in 1957 to 70 per cent in 1978, an annual growth rate of 7 per cent. Even within the top 100 companies themselves concentration, as Campbell shows, has been rising: in 1968, of the 42 per cent of total output emanating from the largest 100 firms, over 75 per cent was accounted for by the largest 50. The degree of concentration increased again in the 1980s with an unprecedented large wave of mergers (Pearce and Tombs, 1994). Accompanying the increasing domination of a smaller number of very large firms, not surprisingly, is the decline of the smaller firm (those employing 200 people or fewer). Between 1935 and 1963, their share in manufacturing output declined from 35 per cent to 16 per cent. Aaronovitch (1979) has observed that 'without any exception, giant firms dominate the key industrial and financial sectors of all advanced capitalist economies'. Ireland (1992) has noted that reflecting the massive increase in aggregate concentration is a corresponding growth in '*market* concentration, that is growth in the domination of particular industries by a small number of large firms'.

Using a 'concentration ratio' measure based on the proportion of an industry's sales accounted for by the largest five firms in it, Aaronovitch and Sawyer (1975, pp. 92–102) calculate that in 1968, 30 per cent of manufactured goods come from industries where five firms or fewer account for at least 90 per cent of that industry's sales, while nearly 50 per cent come from industries where five firms account for at least 70 per cent of that industry's sales. Thus, nearly half of all sales of manufactured goods are in markets where five firms or fewer control at least 70 per cent of the market between them. The average five-firm concentration ratio was 52 per cent in 1935, by 1968 it had risen to 69 per cent and in 1974 it was estimated to be around 76 per cent. Increasingly high levels of industrial concentration are not confined to British industry but are, according to Hannah (1976, p. 116) 'one of the better attested facts of the recent economic history of most economically advanced Western countries'. The growing might of corporate power has major implications for the jurisprudence and operational policy of regulatory and criminal justice agencies (*The Guardian*, 'Analysis', 15 February 1998).

If there is any way that the criminal law could, arguably, be used to chasten a dangerously reckless company it would surely be for that company to be indicted in a major national criminal trial accused of manslaughter. This was, of course, exactly what happened to the Ford Motor Company when it stood trial for manslaughter of three girls in Indiana in 1978. Ford was acquitted but a number of evidential revelations must have been highly detrimental to its image. There was, for instance, the callous cost-benefit analysis it used to sacrifice '180 burn deaths' as a cheaper option than refitting the defective Pintos (see Appendix 1). According to his statements, Henry Ford himself was very concerned about the case. He is quoted as saying at one point:

> the lawyers would shoot me for saying this, but I think there is some cause for concern about the car. I don't even listen to the cost figures – we've got to fix it ... The Pinto ... recall campaign is a matter ... of great concern to Ford Motor

Company and to me personally (*Washington Post*, 26 August 1978, cited in Swiggert and Farrell, 1980, p. 175).

All this apparently grave concern, however, and the full sobering effect of being tried as a homicidal company which took terrible risks with the lives of those who travelled in its cars, did not have the result it might have done. Although Ford Motor Company was acquitted of the three homicides in question in Elkhart, Indiana, it stood morally convicted of a very dubious policy in relation to safety. This conviction evidently did little to chasten the company. Fifteen years later in May 1993, under headlines like 'Ford cars fare badly in crash safety study',[36] British newspapers reported that a Department of Transport study had discovered that nearly all of their models had safety records below the national average. Ford's fortunes have, nevertheless, continued to grow (Cullen et al., 1987, p. 297).

A similar point can be made in respect of ferry safety in the UK after the prosecution for manslaughter of P&O European Ferries (Dover) Ltd. Evidence was heard at the inquest which showed the senior management to have been highly cavalier towards the safety of passengers and even facetious to captains who suggested the need for safety improvements.[37] The Sheen Inquiry found, *inter alia*, that 'from top to bottom the body corporate was infected with the disease of sloppiness'. Like the Ford Motor Company, P&O was acquitted of the formal charge but publicly exposed as being more concerned with making profits than with some aspects of passenger safety. After the tragic loss of nearly 200 lives and the public chastisement entailed in the criminal trial at the Old Bailey, there would be good reason to imagine that the company (and others which might, watching the trial, have whispered 'there but for the grace of God go I') was shaken into scrupulous safety consciousness. Such a belief would be mistaken. In the following years, bow door safety became an issue constantly returned to by campaigning bodies and the news media. Yet the *Estonia* capsized in the Baltic sea killing over 900 people in 1994. Water entered the vessel through defective bow doors. Six weeks after this sinking, a report from the Department of Transport's Marine Safety Agency discovered that of the 107 roro ferries it had inspected, bow door faults were found in one in three vessels.[38]

The chrematistic pressures of commerce evidently prevail over the most obvious and urgent, if time-consuming and interruptive, dictates of safety.

The paramount aim of companies and employers in the commercial system is to make a profit. Some are concerned with collateral issues, like doing business ethically and others who, for example, produce or distribute arms or torture equipment are not racked by such considerations. In any event, whatever the moral code of the business directors (or the deep psychological factors motivating them to engage in business), the *sine qua non* of their operation is profitability. Consequently, although companies can afford occasionally to run into debt, condone certain losses and discount certain items, these must be only intermittent and temporary. The quest for profit is a continuous and vital part of business operation: a business needs profit like a swimmer needs air.

The preservation of human life and welfare is not the abiding, supreme governing principle of capitalism. Human welfare is a desideratum that prevailing ideology suggests must be sought as far as commercial considerations make this a realistic, achievable goal. Each year about 300 people are killed and over 36,000 seriously injured at work. Most of these fatalities are avoidable. Most occur through economically-related causes concerning training, supervision, equipment and working environment. The degree of moral culpability (measured by the criminal law's criteria of gross negligence and recklessness as these apply to the crimes of manslaughter and serious assault) from which the commercial carnage results is strikingly similar to that of conventional crime. There is, though, a pressure for what is engendered by commercialism as a regular toll of mayhem not to be regarded as endemic crime. If that became too sharp and commonly accepted a social perception the cost would be twofold: it would be grist to the legitimation crisis mill (Habermas, 1976, pp. 33–94) and it would undermine a core part of the ideology of the market system, namely that a system which is posited on the promotion of social good by the pursuit of individual gain in a competitive economy (Smith, 1976, 1776, p. 456, para. 9) best promotes the public interest. Smith argued that:

> As every individual, therefore, endeavours as much as he can both to employ his capital in support of domestick industry, and so to direct that industry that its produce may be of the greatest value; every individual necessarily labours to render the annual revenue of the society as great he can. He generally, indeed, neither intends to promote the publick interest, nor knows how much he is promoting it. By preferring the support of domestick to that of foreign industry, he intends only his own security; and by directing that industry in such a manner as its produce may be of the greatest value, he intends only his own gain, and he is in this, as in many other cases, led by an invisible hand to promote an end which was no part of his intention. Nor is it always the worse for society that it was no part of it. By pursuing his own interest he frequently promotes that of the society more effectually than when he really intends to promote it. I have

never known much good done by those who affected to trade for the publick good. It is an affectation, indeed, not very common among merchants, and very few words need to be employed in dissuading them from it.

In the context of promoting safety, it is clear from the general history of factory legislation (Marx, 1954, 1887; Carson, 1971, 1979 and 1981) that the public interest is not best promoted by Smith's nascent laissez-faire policy. On the contrary, the evidence suggests that, in the same way as there is a constant downward pressure on wages from capital, there is a constant downward pressure on the expense of safety. Smith's dichotomy between, on the one hand, the shameless pursuit of individual interests, and, on the other hand, the altruism of 'those who trade for the public good' is no longer the most appropriate set of historical alternatives. The real historical alternative to aggregated individualism is a non-market economy. Crump has emphasised the essential similarities between the hitherto established forms of capitalistic society, forms in which capital is controlled privately and by the state. He notes (1987, p. 45) that the society envisaged by non-market socialists would remove all these divisions at one stroke, by realising the communal ownership of the means of production. Since capitalism is an integrated economic system whose market encompasses the whole world, he argues, 'it can be removed only by an equally world-enveloping system which displaces the market'.

Attempts to deal effectively with cavalier attitudes to safety within one nation can only have limited effect because, as was seen with the dangerous plant refused a licence in Toronto only to end up in Bhopal, the problem is then exported by capital to another jurisdiction. Like water running down a hill, capital follows the path of least resistance.

The standard middle class definition of crime, a London magistrate once remarked, is 'the sort of thing I don't do'. Much the same thing is postulated by corporate concerns and their political and legal public relations agents. Karl Mannheim observed (1936, p. 36) that:

> There is implicit in the word 'ideology' the insight that in certain situations the collective unconscious of certain groups obscures the real condition of society both to itself and to others and thereby stabilizes it.

The more powerful the group, the less likely will its misdeeds be perceived and classified as crimes. As an old Polish proverb has it: if you are caught stealing a chicken you are branded a common chicken thief, if you steal a Kingdom you will be hailed as a King.

This exculpation of corporate entities is further facilitated by the criminal law which, as has been shown (chapter 2), evolved and was adapted and sustained to deal with individual offending. After four centuries of development, corporate liability in criminal law only begins in substance in the 1940s. Since then there have been several jumps forward culminating in the latest proposals from the Law Commission to legislate for the crime of corporate manslaughter. The next chapter will examine the impact of contemporary empirical research upon existing theory on corporate crime and upon the changes favoured by certain writers and the Law Commission.

## Notes

1    The number of annual deaths at work in 1992–93 was 432. The annual number of reckless homicides for the same period was generally fewer than 200. According to 1996/97 figures, there has been no significant change (see Health and Safety Commission Statistics 1996/97 and Criminal Statistics England and Wales 1997, Cm 4162, Home Office).

2    I am grateful to the Health and Safety Executive Statistical Unit in Bootle for this information.

3    Cases 3, 5, 6, 8, 10, 11, 13, 14, 15, 16, 20, 22, 23, 24, 27, 29, 30, 32, 33, 34, 36, 38, 39, 40.

4    In some ways Nader's book has been as influential upon public consciousness as Edwin Sutherland's essays *White Collar Criminality* (1940), as it gave the iniquities of commercial misconduct a wide readership. It is a book that had been read by very many of the HSE inspectors and managerial personnel and lawyers whom I interviewed or with whom I discussed my research.

Mike Cosentino's work on the Ford prosecution was a remarkable display of skill, dedication and public-spirited devotion to dealing firmly with antisocial commercial conduct. The Ford case was a landmark in helping to change public perception. It has had prosecutorial repercussions all over the world (Field and Jörg, 1991; Jones, 1988; Swiggert and Farrell, 1980; Stessens, 1994), and Mr Cosentino's role here was critical (Cullen et al., 1987). A personally less dedicated state prosecutor would have allowed history to develop less dramatically.

Louise Christian, a partner in the firm Christian Fisher & Co., has represented clients in many cases of alleged corporate crime, both 'ordinary' cases like construction deaths, and high profile public cases like the private prosecution for manslaughter arising from the sinking of the *Marchioness*. She acts for unions like the Union of Construction and Allied Trades and Technicians (UCATT), and General, Municipal, Boilermakers and Allied Trades Union (GMB), and has been engaged in political action to legislate a Corporate Liability Act.

Both Celia Wells and David Bergman have written widely on this theme. The measure of their impact on public perception and public policy can be gauged from the recognition they are given in the Law Commission's consultation paper on Involuntary Manslaughter (Law Commmission, 1994a, pp. 90, 127).

5    Although, like the process of litigation – for whose historical development I would suggest several causal factors including the personal, the organisational and the structural – there were various reasons which account for its expansion. Williams (1961) includes among

these: the genuine response to the growth in democracy, the new version of 'moral rescue', and the economic argument.

6   This is essentially a cost-benefit exercise (on which, see later in this chapter). The generally accepted formula today is one taken from a case which was actually deciding the meaning of the words 'reasonably practicable' in relation to s.102 of the Coal Mines Act 1911. Asquith LJ said:

> 'Reasonably practicable' is a narrower term than 'physically possible' and implies that a computation must be made in which the *quantum* of risk is placed in one scale and the sacrifice involved in the measures necessary for averting the risk (whether money, time or trouble) is placed in the other, and that, if it be shown that there is a gross disproportion between them – the risk being insignificant in relation to the sacrifice – the defendants discharge the onus upon them (*Edwards v National Coal Board* [1949]).

The 'money, time or trouble' in the formula are all reducible to the same thing: wasted time is an 'opportunity cost' and trouble is a 'resource cost'. The standard test in the USA to determine whether there has been negligence is one which considers whether the loss caused by the accident, multiplied by the probability of the accident occurring, exceeds the cost of avoiding the accident. If so, there has probably been negligence (Posner, 1972, p. 69).

7   *The Guardian,* 10 February 1994, p. 6. There are many other examples of the tension and inversitive relations between safety and commercial pressures. The following reports are good examples: 'Fire risk on Tube "does not justify cost of changes"', *The Independent,* 9 September 1992, p. 7; 'BR axes £600m safety measures', *The Independent on Sunday,* 7 November 1993, p. 6; 'Firms balk at unhealthy cost of safety management', *The Sunday Times,* 24 July 1994, p. 7.

8   See George Orwell, 1970.

9   See 'Long Lens of the Law', Stewart Hennessey, *The Independent,* 6 July 1994.

10   *Daborn v Bath Tranways Motor Co., Ltd & Trevor Smithey* [1946] 2 All ER 333 at 336.

11   *The Independent,* 29 and 30 September and 1 and 4 October; *The Observer,* 2 October; *The Guardian,* 29 and 30 September and 1, 3, 4 and 26 October 1994.

12   This is based upon an outlay of £866,000 for a large ferry, like the *Pride of Calais,* where (as is normal practice) the cost is spread over several years. This calculation was made by an independent marine expert, David Byrne, managing director of Transmarine. He made his calculation for the BBC *Panorama* programme *Fatal Flaw,* 28 November 1994, Marshall Meek, former president of the Royal Institute of Naval Architects, states that even on the most lavish estimate of required expenditure, the added cost per ticket would not be above 50 pence (personal communication) 27 January 1995.

13   The documentary was made for *Check Out 1992,* and broadcast on Channel 4 on 24 June 1992. The interviewer was Mike Embley.

14   For example *The Independent,* 8 November, 1994, p. 3.

15   *The Times,* 8 March 1987; BBC Radio 4, 8 March 1987.

16   'The Technical Investigation of the Sinking of the Ro-Ro ferry *European Gateway*' delivered by John Spouge, 17 April 1985, at Royal Institute of Naval Architects, 10 Upper Belgrave Street, London, SW15 8BQ. The paper incorporated suggested 'improvements to ship safety … which might help prevent the loss of life which is possible if such an accident occurs again' (RINA Transactions, 1986, p. 49).

17   Royal Institute of Naval Architects, 1986, p. 63. This was put by Marshall Meek (a Fellow

of RINA. who personally confirmed to me (26 January 1995) that the Ministry of Transport had been made aware of the design dangers of open car-decks before and after the 1985 conference, but such warnings had been consistently ignored.

18  *The New Law Journal*, David Bergman, 26 October 1990. See also the publications of *Disaster Action*, e.g. 'Disasters: A New Agenda for Dealing with Corporate Violence', 1993.

19  Mr Justice Sheen's inquiry was held under the Merchant Shipping Act, 1950. Report of the Court, No. 8074. Dept. of Transport, 1987, para. 14., *M. V. Herald of Free Enterprise*.

20  *Daily Mirror*, 21 December 1990. It is worthy of note that P&O has for a long time been in the list of the top 10 corporate donors to the Conservative party, the party in government at the time of the sustained reluctance to prosecute (see chapter 2) and the ennoblement of Jeffrey Stirling. In 1993 it was the second largest donor. Reproduced from Labour Research Department, Fact Service, Vol. 55, Issue 19, 13 May 1993.

21  *The Independent*, 16 May 1994 and 1 July 1994; *The Guardian*, 1 July 1994.

22  *The Independent*, 19 November 1993, p. 3.

23  This is a national average, In the West Midlands there are 35 factory inspectors to inspect 25,000 registered workplaces, one for each 714 places. Research by the West Midlands Health and Safety Advice Centre found that 79 per cent of all major accidents and injuries were not investigated by the HSE (Bergman, 1994).

24  Heightening the anti-safety pressure on Pinto engineers was an important goal set by Iacocca known as 'the limits of 2000'. The Pinto was not to weigh an ounce over 2,000 pounds and not to cost a cent over $2,000. An engineer gave evidence that Iacocca enforced these limits 'with an iron hand', so even when a crash-test showed that a one-pound, one-dollar piece of metal stopped the fuel tank from being punctured as it was pushed against the differential housing, it was rejected as extra cost and extra weight (Dowie, 1977, p. 17). The engineer remarked that: 'This company is run by salesmen, not engineers: so the priority is styling, not safety'. The company was prepared to go to any lengths to retain and expand its share of the car market. One piece of evidence led by the prosecution in the Ford case concerned the company's prior convictions. The court heard (Cullen et al., 1987, p. 282) that in February 1973 Ford had been convicted of 350 (sic) criminal counts of filing false reports to the Environmental Protection Agency and was fined a total of $7 million. The crimes occurred in 1972 when the company performed unauthorised maintenance on test vehicles and submitted falsified data certifying that the emission levels of its 1973 models (including the Pinto) met the standard prescribed by the 1968 Clean Air Act. This was a straightforward case of lying in order to make financial gain. The cost to the environment and the people who would, to varying extents, be poisoned was completely dismissed.

25  The defendant was probably acquitted because it managed to raise a doubt about the causation of the three deaths in question. It contended that the vehicle in which the three victims were travelling was hit at a speed in excess of 50 mph, a collision in which many types of vehicle suffer a ruptured fuel tank and would burst into flames. Vehicles were not legally obliged to be structurally able to withstand a collision in which they were hit at 50 mph. For this account to be true, however, the victim's vehicle would have had to have been stationary at the moment it was hit in the rear, whereas several eye-witnesses testified that the victim's vehicle was moving when it was hit. Ford adduced 'scientific' evidence to support its contention that the Pinto in question was hit by something travelling at more than 50 mph, but the tests which showed this had been conducted in their own grounds by an expert whom they paid $22,000 (Cullen et al., 1987, pp. 265–307).

26  The calculation was made on the basis that a life was worth $200,000. Rather than produce the figure itself, Ford had, in conjunction with other motor companies, procured the Highway Traffic Safety Administration to make the necessary calculations and in 1972 it did so estimating the price at $200,725 (Dowie, 1977, p. 20).

27  Some disturbingly callous considerations feature in this type of calculation. Discussing *The Value of Life* in cost-benefit analysis, Mishan (1971, p. 220) mentions an example of 'premature burial', i.e. that when the actuarial scientists calculate funeral expenses, these must be set higher where the deceased is young because an untimely death will usually mean higher funeral expenses. He notes that 'if the unfortunate person dies at a very early age, some useful savings may be effected from the lower cost of a smaller coffin'. It is difficult to know whether this is written facetiously but, because it *could* be serious, that *per se* is indictment enough of the sort of calculations which men are called upon to make.

28  The authors note that it is a matter of speculation why the Ford company in this instance became subject to the charge of homicide whereas others had escaped on similar evidence against them before. They suggest the reasons might include the facts that Ford made a point of (unsympathetically) fighting every civil case against it arising from Pinto deaths and injuries; and it failed to cooperate with the Grand Jury's request for certain very senior personnel to appear as witnesses. It fought liability, in other words, tooth and nail. Similar cases also appear after the Ford prosecution but there have been no major prosecutions. General Motors, for example, produced a model which, evidence suggests, had a faulty rear wheel brake with a tendency to prematurely lock. This has resulted in 1,700 complaints, 71 known injuries and 15 deaths. GM fought the case bitterly (Hills, 1987, p. 7) but has not been indicted for homicide, possibly in the light of the expensive failure to convict Ford.

29  *United States v Carroll Towing Co.* [1947].

30  Investigation into the Clapham Junction Railway Accident, 1989, Anthony Hidden QC, Cm. 820. London, HMSO.

31  There were exceptions. The 1872 Coal Mines Regulation Acts did provide for a right to bilateral process of safety regulation.

32  Ss.22A (1)(d) and 57A (1)(d) of the Employment Protection (Consolidation) Act, 1978 as amended by the Trade Union Reform and Employment Rights Act 1993.

33  *The Guardian*, 10 February 1994, p. 6.

34  *The Independent*, 24 November 1994, p. 6.

35  The government was, in 1994, sufficiently enthusiastic about reducing compensation payable to victims of crime that its alteration of the regulations without proper parliamentary consultation was ruled unlawful by the Court of Appeal: *R v Secretary of State for the Home Department*. Law Report, *The Independent*, 10 November 1994.

36  *The Independent*, 15 May 1993, p. 6.

37  *R v H.M Coroner for East Kent ex parte Spooner and others* [1989] at p. 13.

38  *The Guardian, The Independent* and *The Times*, 8 November, 1994.

# 7 Legal, Criminological and Social Science Perspectives

In a grotesque footnote to a story on the report, one newspaper noted that 30 corpses have still not been recovered from the wreckage of the Piper Alpha under the North Sea because the oil company thinks it would be too expensive to retrieve them (Foley, 1990, p. 25).

The mosquito knows full well, small as he is
he's a beast of prey
But after all
he takes only his bellyful
he doesn't put my blood in the bank (D.H. Lawrence).

The academic discussion arising from work deaths (and serious injuries) (Wells, 1989, 1992, 1993a, 1993b and 1997b; Field and Jörg, 1990; McColgan, 1994; Gobert, 1994a and b; Pearce and Tombs, 1990 and 1991; Tombs, 1995, 1996 and 1999) has for the most part been generated from theoretical debates alone, as opposed to empirical evidence garnered by the writers. The legal and evidential difficulties which beset any attempt to use the law of manslaughter against a company (Bergman, 1991 and 1994: Wells, 1991 and 1993a; Field and Jörg, 1992; Slapper, 1992a, 1992d and 1993b; Gobert, 1994a) were thrown into sharp relief by the factual profiles of the cases in this study. The empirical evidence I collected from the 40 cases, and from interviews with personnel from every branch of the official response to deaths at work, indicates that myriad factors are influential upon what legal responses are made to such fatalities. Immediately, the work of coroners, coroners' officers, police officers, HSE inspectors, crown prosecutors, and lawyers is determined by the legal framework which governs their respective occupations. The latent discretionary power inherent in virtually all of the rules enables those personnel to legislate effectively as they give practical implementation to the rules. In understanding this latter process, it is necessary to appreciate the precepts and perceptions which are part of the occupational subcultures of the various people involved. Identification and evaluation of those occupational

202

perceptions begs questions about their origin; inquiries which necessitate examination of the political economy. This study found the preponderance of deaths at work attributable to the operating principles, and consequential culture, of the profit-system.

People in our age, as in previous ages, are circumstantially encouraged to perceive their surroundings not as part of a dynamic, developing phenomenon, but rather as a 'reality' whose fundamental features are immutable; history, for many, is something which stopped on the last page of their final school history book. Beholding a huge meat processing plant in Chicago at the beginning of the century (one of the largest concentrations of labour and capital in the world at that time) the lead character in Upton Sinclair's *The Jungle* is arrested by wonderment (Sinclair, 1906, p. 51):

> ... it was a thing as tremendous as the universe – the laws and ways of its working no more than the universe to be questioned or understood. All that a mere man could do, it seemed to Jurgis, was to take a thing like this as he found it, and do as he was told; to be given a place in it and share in its wonderful activities was a blessing to be grateful for, as one was grateful for the sunshine and the rain.

Most aspects of human life involve some adventure into conduct after calculation of risk. Often this process is routine and almost subconscious: crossing the road, overtaking another vehicle on a road, travelling on a ship or an aeroplane, etc. It is probably safe to say that this is an endemic feature of human life (Beck, 1992) irrespective of how we are socially organised. Under certain conditions of social organisation, however, the degree to which we are exposed to avoidable risk to life is, arguably, enhanced by factors which do not arise simply from the balance between maximum safety (e.g. not travelling, eating only organic food, etc.[1]) and expedition. In a competitive, commercial environment actors are frequently pressed to engage in a decision-making process which incorporates the well-being not only of society and of particular individuals, but also (and, often, determinatively) of bank balances and corporate welfare. The ultimate justification for this is that, as wealth is produced and distributed by companies, and, further, as wealth must cascade down from the rich at the top of the economic pyramid to the poor at the base, what is best for the company is, ultimately, best for society. The nature of this cost-benefit calculation is exemplified in all its exquisite horror in the arithmetical sacrifice of life the Ford Motor Company was prepared to make in declining to recall its defective cars and refit them as it was cheaper to pay compensation for death and maiming that would certainly follow from a decision not to recall the vehicles (chapter 5).

This calculation can also be found daily in more modest, mundane circumstances. Deaths from severe head injuries following falls from scaffolding are quite common. In case 32, Mr Morris died in such circumstances because, ultimately, there was a reluctance to incur the additional expense that would have been entailed in acquiring extra scaffolding to raise the painting platform being used to a suitable height for work. This scenario is mordantly reflected in the remark of a plumbing contractor quoted by Haines from her study of deaths at work in Australia (1992, p. 8):

> if you tender for a contract and it's a contract where you are a recommended sub-tenderer, in other words you are going to get the job whether you are £10,000 dearer or not, then you can put in all the safety parts you like into it. But if you tender for a job, especially at the moment, you might be one of 150 people who are tendering so therefore you've got to keep the job as low as you can … there are always short cuts that you do … or you will see bricklayers who are working where they are and the bricks need to go another four feet but the elevator is not high enough, so they throw the bricks up and catch them at the other end. *Nobody is going to go to the job and then go out and hire another scaffold for $700 or $1000 and get it erected by steel erectors, nobody is going to do it, so they throw them up in the last 10ft or 7ft or whatever* [emphasis added].

Offending against best safety practice or the law is not, of course, a universal or persistent phenomenon. The question then arises: why do some companies under pressure offend while others do not (a question with a direct counterpart in the criminology of ordinary crime)?

The answer suggested by the work of Box (1987 and 1983) and Clinard and Yeager (1980) concerns the degree of economic pressure (real and perceived) acting upon employers and corporations. Following the prolific growth in the number and influence of companies this century (see chapter 6), the (consequential) steep rise in corporate crime is clearly, in some part, a recording phenomenon, i.e. not necessarily a 'real' rise but one which becomes apparent through the establishment of improved inspectorates and the bureaucratic apparatus for recording the statistics. It may also be the case that companies offend against the law at the point at which economic pressure necessitates that some safety corners are cut as a survival mechanism – a corporate parallel to the individual phenomenon observed by Engels, who noted that offending occurs when 'the influences demoralising to the working-man act more powerfully, more concentratedly than usual' (1969, 1845, p.

159). The scale of industrial killing is way beyond that of ordinary personal homicide (see chapter 2), and the scale of fraud and theft in the context of business belittles the annual total of goods stolen in conventional crime[2] (Box, 1983; Nelken, 1994).

Further evidence to support this analysis is offered by Jamieson (1994). Using officially recorded information, she examines structural and environmental factors that influence corporate executives to engage in anti-competitive means to achieve corporate goals. Her focus is narrow but sharp: she looks at just one sort of offence (antitrust offences, whereby businesses limit block competition and deny consumers access to goods or services at normally competitive prices) amongst large manufacturers. She uses a comprehensive quantitative analysis and qualitative approach, drawing on interviews with leading federal officers responsible for antitrust enforcement. Companies are structured to bring about profit most efficiently; in the process of creating an internal structure designed to secure profit, they often create both incentive and opportunity for employees to violate the law. The competitive characteristics of corporate operating environments may contribute to corporate deviance. A 'turbulent' economic environment is likely to increase offending and 'maladaptive behaviours are expected to be most prevalent where the incongruity between rational internal structures and uncertain operating environments is greatest' (ibid., p. 25).

Again, in a wide-ranging exploration of organisational crime in the nursing home industry, insider trading, industrial water pollution, the cartage industry in New York and the savings and loan industry, the authors Tonry and Reiss (1993) show a plethora of ways in which the pressures of the economy trigger illegality in organisations.[3] One of the main purposes of the papers is to obtain a better understanding of the 'structural influences that shape organisational crime'. The authors chart a number of limitations of the existing white collar crime literature, like its propensity to deal with large companies and senior managers, and show how the papers in the text extend those boundaries. Peter Reuter's description of collusion in the cartage industry, for example, demonstrates how organisational offending is grounded in the behaviour of many small-scale entrepreneurs in one of the most demeaned occupations – garbage collection.

In her paper on insider trading, Nancy Reichman suggests (ibid., p. 91) that we need to recognise 'organisational capabilities to adapt to regulatory environments and to shape the regulatory apparatus that governs their behaviour'. There is much evidence (Box, 1983; Carson, 1979 and 1981; Jones, 1988; Field, 1990) that in the realm of corporate affairs the nature of legal right is still appreciably influenced by mercantile minority might.

The authors in Ermann and Lundman (1992) address what the editors call the 'origins of corporate and governmental deviance' (ibid., p. 7) with a rich range of illustrative material. Their analysis, however, is restricted to a close-up look at the factors *within* organisations, like the influence of organisation élites, which engender deviance. There is no attempt to examine the wider environment of political economy, in particular the abiding pressures of capitalism, with a view to developing a general theory of corporate deviance. In each of the 11 studies (and additional ones cited by the editors) people have aided and abetted in the causing of harm, generally against their own better judgement,[4] as a result of commercial pressures. This even applies to the soldiers in Vietnam (Kelman and Hamilton, 1989) who were sent there in furtherance of American economic interests rather than as, for example, part of a moral crusade. The importance of setting these case studies in their historical and economic contexts is that, without taking such a view, writers can too easily fall into prescribing changes in legislation or public attitude as a means of solving the problems. A wider, historical-economic analysis might show such proposals to be idealistic. Social actors (including campaigning legal reformers) ignorant of history may be doomed to repeat it.

Wells (1993a) has gone much further than most in seeking to examine the criminality of corporations in a broad context of the political economy. Using the analytic instruments of many disciplines, including jurisprudence, philosophy, penology and economics, she has made much path-breaking progress to the move to a better comprehension of corporate crime.

For the most part of its existence, the criminal law has not had to deal on any significant scale with juristic corporations. The criminal law originated and developed to deal with individuals. Today, however, companies are enormously influential actors in every aspect of social life. Each year hundreds of people are killed and thousands are injured in circumstances where companies can be seen as blameworthy. Debate about what response the state should make to corporate offending of this sort raises many important questions. The issues are wide-ranging and have generated some forceful and animated argument (e.g. exchanges on the 'formal policing' versus 'negotiated compliance' approaches to controlling industrial safety between Pearce and Tombs, 1990 and Hawkins, 1991).

Wells advances a powerful polemic for corporate criminal liability. She presents David Garland's observations about 'penality's role in the creation of culture' (1990, p. 249) – punishment as both a product of and influence upon culture – as analogous to her contention that notions of criminal responsibility cannot be separated from the social context in which they develop. It is necessary, she argues, in the context of corporate crime, for the law to develop a clearer understanding of 'recklessness' in the sense of 'practical indifference', an attitudinal state manifested in conduct, and less elusive than a mental state. Following Duff (1990), she commends the principle as applicable to corporations: 'The crucial question is to determine what attitude the defendant's action displayed rather than to look for a hidden mental state or feeling' (Wells, 1993a, p. 83).

All this provides the foundation for an analysis of core questions about corporate liability. Wells argues that whatever their metaphysical nature, corporations can be regarded as morally responsible 'persons'. We should, she contends, develop a form of liability which supplements the corporation's vicarious liability for all its employees in strict liability offences and unimaginative 'identification doctrine' used for ordinary crimes. Liability could be based on the corporation itself with an aggregation of employees' knowledge.

The conspicuous challenge Wells leaves us with is that of determining the extent to which there are any significant amendments to the criminal law which can be made to control corporate violence within the current political economy. Wells carefully examines many options in respect of the criterion of blame (e.g. different ways to determine recklessness); the identification of the corporation as wrongdoer (by widening the identification doctrine, allowing for aggregated fault, etc.) and a range of alternative sanctions including community service, equity fines, adverse publicity.

The suggestions on forms of corporate punishment call for some critical reply. There is no clearly established body of law (or theory) on how companies and company directors convicted of criminal offences in relation to their enterprise should be dealt with by the courts.

## Fining Companies

Since its emergence and development during the later stages of Anglo-Saxon law, the fine has always been a problematic sanction. In recent history there is evidence (Jones, 1988; Ermann and Lundman, 1992; Tonry and Reiss, 1993; Jamieson, 1994) that many offenders see the penalty as a risked 'add-on' cost to their criminal enterprise and, if the prospective gain from crime is sufficiently high, are undeterred; if caught, paying the fine will be seen by the offender simply as a form of taxation on crime. Econometric criminologist Gary Becker, (who trained as an economist), suggested in some detail (1968) just how such calculations may be made by individual offenders.

In relation to corporate crime it might be thought that the fine was a perfect disposal because, unlike individuals whose criminal conduct is often committed whilst affected by alcohol, drugs or passionate emotions (and are thus not considering current sentencing tariffs when they commit crimes), corporations arguably generally behave rationally (Bergman, 1994). They conduct business through decision-making processes that *are* susceptible to rationally predictable outcomes like profits and fines. Businesses use cost-benefit analysis as a routine procedure. The trouble is that such calculations are as much based on the likelihood of *being caught* as they are upon the level of fine if caught and convicted. As there is a very low chance of being inspected (in London, for example, there are about 20 inspectors for 200,000 sites), many companies decide to take the risk of unsafe systems. There are numerous documented case studies of such corporate malpractice. Often the money to be made from evading regulations is of a different order from anything the company is likely to be fined if caught. Another problem with the corporation-as-rational-actor model is that quite often many corporations do not act as unified rational entities (Tombs, 1995). They are beset with tensions and conflicts within and between various levels of management; contradictions which may result (Reed, 1991) from incompatible organisational goals.

The record for the largest fine ever imposed on a construction company for a heath and safety offence in Britain was broken in April 1993 when a London firm was fined a total of £160,000 and ordered to pay £28,000 costs at Knightsbridge Crown Court, following the electrocution of a worker on the London Water Ring Main Project. The record was broken again in November 1993 at Maidstone Crown Court when a fine of £200,000 was imposed on the Channel Tunnel consortium TML after it pleaded guilty to failing to ensure the safety of a worker crushed to death between two trains (Slapper, 1994d). The five UK construction companies in the Transmanche-Link consortium were each ordered to pay £40,000. Then, in 1997, the record was again broken when four companies were fined £1.7 million following the collapse of a walkway on the Kent coast. Two Swedish companies who designed, built and installed the walkway at the Port of Ramsgate were fined a total of £1 million, the port £200,000 and Lloyd's Register of Shipping, which gave the device a safety certificate, £500,000. This was the first criminal conviction for the Register in its 237-year history (*New Civil Engineer*, 6 March 1997).

Relatively large fines have also been imposed on smaller companies and their directors. In December 1993 the owner of an outdoor activity centre, and his company, were fined £15,000 each after admitting to breaches of the Health and Safety at Work Etc. Act 1974 which led to the death of an 11 year-old girl on a school holiday. The company had employed an unqualified instructor who was supervising a group of 30 children on a night hike. The girl received fatal head injuries after falling down a steep bank when the instructor decided that the group should take a short-cut down a 55 degree slope, a move which was criticised by the court as 'stupid'. The girl was only attended to by a doctor 75 minutes after the accident owing to company safety procedures which were 'nothing short of lamentable'.

This raises the question as to whether heavy fines are an appropriate way to deal with corporate wrong. It can be argued, for example, that the burden of such fines is inappropriately borne by shareholders or, if the fine affects the company very badly, by employees who are eventually made redundant, or by consumers. A dramatic illustration of this effect arose in 1994. Manchester City Council was fined £25,000 for a 'disastrous programme' of ineptitude in wrongly fitting gas heaters into council properties, resulting in one resident's death and the imperilment of over 800 others. Who will ultimately bear the burden of that £25,000 fine (remembering one cannot insure against criminal liability)? The answer is: the people who pay a community tax to Manchester City Council, including the relatives of the killed man and the 800 people mortally endangered by the council (Slapper, 1994d). Even local government funds from central government are taken from tax revenue. The fine was necessary to register the gravity of the offence but it is arguable that the £25,000 could have been better used to fund improved safety training or equipment.

The trouble is, however, that the general deterrent effect of this sort of corporate punishment on large firms is questionable (general deterrence being the effect upon corporations who observe one of their kind being punished). There is some evidence that punishing one corporation with an appropriately serious sanction for an offence has a chastening effect upon others. There is, however, equally, evidence that companies are not deterred by watching other companies get pulled through the criminal justice system.

In October 1997, Chrysler, the third largest car manufacturer in America, was ordered to pay a record $262.5 million (£162 million) damages to the parents of a six year-old boy who was killed as the result of one of its mini-vans. A South Carolina jury awarded the parents of the boy, Sergio Jiminez, $12.5 million in actual damages and $250 million in punitive damages. A faulty latch allowed the boy to be thrown from the vehicle after it was involved in a collision. The jury said that Chrysler was negligent in the design and testing of the mini-van, that it had known about these faults but had tried to cover them up. One particularly damaging document revealed in court was an internal memo from the vice-chairman to the president and chairman of the company which said: 'If we want to use political pressure to try to squash a recall letter [i.e. a compulsory recall of all similar Chrysler vehicles on the road] we need to go now' (*The Guardian*, 10 October 1997). However, an almost exactly similar case to this Chrysler scandal, involving the Ford Motor Company (see chapter 6) 10 years previously – a case with major international high-profile coverage – failed subsequently both to ensure a good safety design policy at Chrysler, and then, when the fault became known, to chasten the company into ordering a prompt recall.

In the case of the Pinto, the Ford Motor Company (the largest car manufacturer in America) allowed an unsafe car to go on the roads and failed to recall it, with the result that many lives were lost in dreadful circumstances. A prosecution for corporate manslaughter failed but, in the light of very negative evidence about the company's attitude to safety which was elicited during the trial, many civil claims against the company were settled.

The temptation for some directors to try anything to avoid a huge corporate cost (like large-scale vehicle recall) seems irresistible in the light of the gains to be made if such atrocious behaviour succeeds in its aim.

Noting that a small fine on a corporation may have no impact and a large one might simply be passed on to the shareholders or consumers, causing injustice, Punch (1996) records the alternatives used in the American system – probation, adverse publicity, equity fines, community service, making a company lend an executive to a charity for a year, direct compensatory orders and punitive injunctions.

Punch also notes (1996, p. 261) an unprecedented judgement from a judge in Virginia in which a company was 'jailed' for involvement in price-fixing (*The Economist*, 10 September 1988):

> Judge Doumar made it clear that he did not actually expect to have the company incarcerated, but said that he could have all [the company's] facilities padlocked for the full three years of the sentence. He said that it was unfair for a company to make large illegal profits and then get away with a simple fine.

In the event, Mr Doumar relented a little. He suspended the sentence (and $50,000 of the £1 million fine), placed the company on probation and ordered four of its senior executives to work full-time for the community for up to two years.

## Corporate Enquiry Reports

A cogent case for an improved system of fining companies, has been put by David Bergman (1992 and 1994). He has noted that presently, when sentencing convicted companies, magistrates and judges do not have the same detailed information of the offender as they do for individuals awaiting sentence; in the case of the latter, educational details, income, expenditure, and antecedents are known and often a social inquiry report will also be furnished with an assessment of the offender's likely response to probation. Whereas (1992, p. 1312):

> No such care is taken in relation to corporate offenders. No police officer or similar person gives evidence and there is no document available to the court similar to the social inquiry report. The court generally remains unaware of the most basic information on the company – its turnover, annual profits, history of relationship with the regulatory agency or its general health and safety record.

In arguing for higher fines, Bergman advocates the use of the 'corporate enquiry' report detailing essential financial and safety information. He cites as a model the system in the United States under which a federal probation officer is required to undertake a pre-sentencing investigation into each convicted company to help the court decide an appropriate level of fine. Since this argument was published, the average penalty imposed on companies guilty of health and safety offences has risen by 17 per cent: from £783 (1989/90) to £1384 (1992/93) to £3061 (1993/94).[5] Largely this seems to reflect the introduction in March 1992 in the lower courts of an exemplary maximum fine of £20,000 for the more serious offences (breach of sections 2–6 of the HSWA 1974, and failure to comply with a notice or court order) and from October 1992, the increase from £2,000 to £5,000 of the maximum fine for other health and safety offences.[6] The average fine for convicted offences against health and safety legislation prosecuted by HSE in 1995/96 was £2,572. This was the first *fall* in average fines since 1992/93.[7]

Bergman (1992 and 1994) has also argued for a disposal known as 'corporate probation' which has been available in the USA since 1987. Under such sanctions the judge can compel the senior management of a company to change how the company devises and implements safety procedures. As with personal probation, conditions can be imposed by the court; for example, insistence on certain safety procedures and the employment of certain safety staff. It seems likely, however, that two of the main advantages of such a system do not transfer well from paper to practice. First, it has been argued that such orders can impose punitive burdens on management which are more difficult to transfer than economic impact of fines. Ultimately, however, additional, court-imposed corporate responsibilities can, just like fines, be paid for by companies. Second, it is sometimes argued that by requiring conditions that lower the reputation of the company in a public manner, probation can impose greater punishment and deterrence than mere economic sanctions. There is no evidence, however, that companies which have been technically disgraced by a conviction and a huge fine for a very serious wrong *are* lowered in the estimation of the public. In 1978, for example, BP was fined £750,000 after an incident in which three workers were killed. This was a major news item at the time yet there is no evidence of any consumer boycott of BP products as a result.

## The Appropriate Level of Fine

What is the appropriate level of fine for a company? In Bergman's view, it is essential for the courts to get the level right because if the fine rises past 'a certain level' (1992, p. 1312), then managers and directors simply pass the burden to consumers, shareholders or workers. The real problem is that fines in general are meant to reflect the seriousness of the culprit's error, not necessarily the outcome of that error (Thomas, 1979). Misunderstanding that point often leads to legally unwarranted journalistic outrage. Consider, for example, a case from France. A man who killed a British skier when he hurtled into her on the French Alps was fined £300 by a French court. He had been convicted of manslaughter and also given a three-month suspended sentence.[8] The sum of money here is clearly not calculated to reflect the value of the deceased's life but to represent the culpability of the mistake of the defendant who was himself badly hurt. Similarly, commenting on the £160,000 fine imposed on the company guilty of offences leading to the electrocution of a worker on the London Water Ring Main (above), Jeff Hinksman, Deputy Chief Inspector with the HSE said:

> This was a bad accident. The *level of fine against the company reflects a widespread corporate failure* and should serve as a warning to all firms in the construction industry to take their management responsibilities for health and safety seriously [emphasis added].[9]

Thus, as fines in this context are legally calculated to betoken a level of criminally culpable error, it seems most improbable that putting artificial ceilings on them to ensure they do not 'rise above a certain level' could operate effectively and fairly equalising the burden in different companies committing the same offence.


## A New Corporate Criminology

The principles of the criminal law were evolved in the common law tradition to cater for individual responsibility. Now, however, corporate actors are a ubiquitous and extremely powerful element in social life, yet the criminal law has not been properly adapted to meet this social development. In much of her pioneering work in this area, Wells has argued for 'the development of liability which is better tailored to the organisational facts of corporate existence' (1993b, p. 565). No sooner do we begin to unravel the appropriate ways for the criminal law to deal with corporations, particularly in respect of issues of *mens rea* and the doctrine of identification (Wells urges a move away from corporate liability derivative from specific individuals), than we are faced with very challenging penological questions. If fining companies or putting them on probation are ineffective sanctions, what about custodial sentences for individual directors? There are many problems here too. Individuals, for example, could thus be easy scapegoats for what really is an organisational fault (Slapper, 1994d).

The Law Commission's report on *Involuntary Manslaughter* (1996, following the consultative paper in 1994) responded to the widespread criticism about the inability of the criminal law to punish companies for homicide by proposing changes that would significantly facilitate the prosecution of companies for manslaughter.

The legal philosophy traditionally applied to mainstream English criminal law and favoured by the Law Commission is known as 'subjectivist theory'. This approach 'rests on the principle that moral guilt, and hence criminal liability, should be imposed only on people who can be said to have *chosen* to behave in a certain way or cause or risk causing certain consequences. The roots of subjectivism lie in a liberal philosophy that regards individuals as autonomous beings, capable of choice, and each deserving of individual respect (4.4).

Three principles have been identified as inherent in this basis of liability: a *mens rea* principle which limits liability to those results intended or knowingly risked; the 'belief principle' which judges people according to what he or she believed he was doing or risking; and the 'correspondence principle' which insists that the fault and harm elements correspond (4.5). Thus, subjectivist theory aims to minimise the role of chance or luck.

In its commitment to subjective fault principles, the Law Commission proposes three offences to replace the current single offence of manslaughter. For the individual offences 'reckless killing' and 'killing by gross carelessness' replace unlawful act and gross negligence manslaughter. A company could be liable for these also but only via the existing identification route.

The Commission's third proposal is for a separate offence of 'corporate killing'. This offence will be exclusive to companies and is testimony, in the wake of much-publicised disasters, to contemporary social concern about the importance of corporate accountability. Corporate killing, which broadly corresponds to its proposal for a general offence of killing by gross carelessness, is based on 'management failure'. What constitutes a management failure is defined in clause 4(2) as follows:

> ... there is management failure by the company if the way in which its activities are managed or organised fails to ensure the health and safety of persons employed or affected by those activities; and such a failure may be regarded as a cause of a person's death notwithstanding that the immediate cause is the act or omission of an individual.

The proposed concept of 'management failure' is an attempt to define what, for the purposes of a corporate counterpart to the individual offence of killing by gross carelessness, can fairly be regarded as unacceptably dangerous conduct *by a corporation*. But it must of course be proved, as in the individual offence, that the defendant's conduct (which in the present context, means the management failure) in *causing* the death falls far below what could reasonably be expected; and that (unlike the individual offence) the corporate offence should *not* require that the risk be obvious or that the defendant be capable of appreciating the risk (8.35). The company's fault lies in its failure to anticipate the foreseeable negligence of its employee, and any consequence of such negligence should therefore be treated as a consequence of the company's fault (8.37).

While corporations may commit any of the three proposed offences, the Commission intends that no individual should be liable for prosecution for the corporate offence, even as a secondary party (Clause 4(4)). This is because the corporate offence is intended as a practical device to ensure that corporations cannot escape liability for killing by gross carelessness merely because their decision-making structures are large and complex. The report envisages that existence of the corporate offence would normally make it unnecessary for the prosecution to charge a corporation with reckless killing or killing by gross carelessness and thus undertake the burden of showing that a 'controlling mind' of the corporation was guilty of the offence charged; even if no such person could be identified, the corporation could still be convicted of a homicide offence if the death was caused by management failure of the requisite gravity (8.77).

The relationship between the liability of a corporation itself and of individuals is a matter receiving increasing attention in the literature (Wells, 1996, p. 549; Sullivan, 1996). As noted earlier (chapter 2), neither the agency nor identification routes as they have evolved to deal with corporate defendants are satisfactory. It is difficult not to concede, therefore, that addressing corporate culpability in terms of 'management failure' may be an acceptable solution to the problem even although it is possible to criticise in some detail any set of law reform proposals. For example, what constitutes 'management failure' seems relatively straightforward. Such a failure will occur in the relevant sense when a death would not have happened had the company been managed or organised differently in terms of health and safety provision. The problem lies in the element of responsibility, and how it will be determined that the failure constituted conduct falling far what could have been reasonably expected of the company in the circumstances (Sullivan, 1996, p. 540).

Wells (1997b, p. 1467) has conjectured that much of the concern to enable companies to be prosecuted for manslaughter might be at variance with the popular 'cultural expectation' that *individual directors* should be made liable for fatal commercial disasters. She argues that a major weakness in the Commission's formulation is that 'management' is not defined. Asking why the prosecution failed in the P&O case, Wells states that, amongst other factors, there might have been a 'confusion in the target of blame'. She says:

> Perhaps it is the directors, those who take the money for making decisions which have far-reaching implications for thousands of employees and even more consumers, to whom the blame is being attached.

This might well be so. Certainly, following the Southall train crash (19 September 1997) there were many renewed calls from lawyers, academics and some campaign groups for tougher action against reckless directors (see *Guardian* letters, 4 October 1997). Similarly, David Bergman (1997, p. 1652) states:

Perhaps the greatest general criticism of the Government's new approach is that it fails to consider the issue of the criminal culpability of individual directors or senior company officers.

In the same vein, Charles Woolfson has written:

Whatever the legal complexities of a new law of corporate killing, and they cannot be exaggerated, there is a fundamental human axiom the efficacy of which is to be commended, particularly with respect to the jailing of individual directors – when one goes down, all sit up (*Guardian* letters, 4 October 1997).

Nevertheless, if there is to be a refocusing of attention on reckless directors, the weakness of such a policy should be fully explored. During the last three years, accompanied by some high profile news coverage, five company directors have been jailed for manslaughter and serious safety offences, yet the rate of deaths at work has undergone no significant change (see chapter 2).[10]

It is clear that there are serious deficiencies in the current law in this area and, as commentators have shown (Wells, 1996 and 1997b: Bergman, 1997: Sullivan, 1996), in the Law Commission's proposals. It is also clear there are difficulties in arguing that heavy fining or personalising criminal liability offer significantly better ways forward.

In the field of crime committed by individuals, the evidence suggests that despite a long history of punishments designed to effect individual and general deterrence, only a tiny fraction of offenders are convicted, and rates of recidivism are high (Pearson, 1992). Home Office evidence suggests that only two crimes from every 100 committed results in a conviction[11] and approximately two-thirds of all young offenders and almost half of all adults are re-convicted at least once within two years of being released from a custodial sentence.[12] Sentencing policies which seek to reduce crime – reductive sentencing – have therefore suffered from a fading credibility and 'just deserts' models have enjoyed wider acceptance. According to the essence of this thinking, punishment is given simply because offenders deserve it.

The emerging criminology of corporate crime, and related questions of sentencing, may be faced with the same chronic problem as the long-established criminology of ordinary individual crime: that policies of legal framework, policing, prosecution and sentencing all appear to have significantly less influence on crime levels than do social and economic factors. Historically, corporations took their legal shape, rights and duties from commercial practices they were engaged in. The legal glove was largely made to fit the hand of commercial practice (Hadden, 1977; Ireland et al., 1987; Gower, 1992). In any event, trade practice evolves to suit its own interests whereas law is made reactively. Whether the criminal law and sentencing can now be successfully adapted to control endemic commercial delinquency is an important question to be addressed.

One cannot help wonder in what way society would operate if Wells' best legal framework was instituted. She states that her text (*Corporations and Criminal Responsibility*) is written on 'certain assumptions' (1993a, p. 148) which amount to the framework of modern capitalism. How far can criminal law be used to control gigantic corporate interests? The criminal justice system is already notably challenged by wealthy, powerful individuals. In three recent prosecutions involving prosperous businessmen, the proceedings against one were discontinued (unprecedentedly) when he became ill (he has since recovered his health); another was convicted for a serious crime but given a short spell in an open prison before being released on health grounds (although he has since made a rapid recovery from a form of senile dementia not normally medically regarded as a passing condition) and the third, while on a £3 million bail, chartered a plane for £50,000 and flew out of the jurisdiction before his trial, breaking the bail (which he has since said he will repay to his surety).[13]

Wells accepts (ibid., p. 37), the 'underlying problem of economic dominance by some large corporations' and the 'realistic approach' of Braithwaite and Pettit (1990, p. 191) that:

> there is almost a sociological inevitability that ruling class constituencies will mobilize their political and economic power so that the enforcement directed against them will be more muted than that which the police deliver against the working class (Wells, 1993a, p. 29).

Given this, it is difficult to agree with her that even though prosecuting companies will be 'of token effect overall' there is 'still something to be said for small gains' (ibid., p. 38).

This outlook is reminiscent of Carson's at the end of *The Other Price of Britain's Oil* – his accomplished and telling study of the way in which the pressures of the profit system resulted in so many fatalities on oil rigs in the 1970s. The study presented a powerful indictment of the political economy and could have been concluded with the contention that the injurious nature of the system was effectively unalterable through legislative reform. Carson acknowledged that the problems he had examined all had their genesis in the structure of capitalism whose forces (1981, p. 297) are surely:

of such massive dimensions and of such inexorable character that there is little point in making piecemeal suggestions or in counselling changes which stop short of basic alterations to the entire social and economic system in which we live.

Ultimately, however, he resolved, as does Wells, to support a number of reforms whilst acknowledging that the system he was proposing to amend would in future, on the whole, be causing the majority of people more harm than good. He said it would be, 'both morally and intellectually irresponsible' (ibid., p. 298) not to have a policy for running capitalism. Insofar as everyone who desires radical change takes this approach then, 'the meantime' will last indefinitely. There is a good case for arguing that radical criminology should be less compromising in its approach to problematic roots.

If law is regarded as a phenomenon separate from its social object and detachable from its historical development, then an optimistic view may be taken as to how instrumental the criminal law can be in dealing with corporate manslaughter. Conversely, if law is seen as a *product* of social relations, not something *extrinsic* to them, then it is less likely that any significant change to the extent of corporate manslaughter can be wrought by the criminal law whilst the social relations and pressures from which the crime arises remain in place. Warrington (1977, p. 29) has observed that:

> Law merely attempts to make what is legitimate (i.e. socially accepted relationships) operate smoothly. Its legitimacy cannot depend upon itself (the law) but on what makes law what it is (society).

The state's prosecutorial policy in respect of corporate manslaughter can thus be regarded as originating in the economic structure and operating precepts of the commercial system. However, the matter is not presented as such but assumes the image of either an independently arrived at legal stance or an accidental cluster of mechanisms and rules. As Engels wrote in 1886 (1973, p. 5):

> But once the state has become an independent power *vis-à-vis* society, it produces forthwith a further ideology. It is indeed among professional politicians, theorists of public law and jurists of private law that the connection with economic fact gets lost for fair. Since in each particular case the economic facts must assume the form of juristic motives in order to receive legal sanctioning and since in so doing, consideration of course has to be given to the whole legal system already in operation, the juristic form is, in consequence, made everything, and the economic fact nothing.

In seeking to explain the development of legal phenomena like prosecutorial policy in *prima facie* cases of corporate manslaughter, materialist analysis, in contradistinction to idealistic or autopoietic theory, is relatively compelling. A view of society as 'a recursively *closed system* which can neither derive its operations from its environment nor pass them on to that environment' (Luhmann, 1988, p. 18) is one which leaves odd but clearly patterned legal phenomena (like the corporate manslaughter problem) unexplained.

A doctor making a study of cholera might reasonably conclude that the problem of the disease is really a social one rather than a medical one; there are appropriate medical responses but, ultimately, the disease is best dealt with by better social sanitation and water systems. Civil engineers, resources and suitable social priorities will solve the problem that doctors alone cannot. In a comparable way, my conclusion here is that whatever clinical legal responses are invoked following death at work (and some responses are more fitting than others), the problem is ultimately one of political economy. Many more people are killed at work than are killed in conventional crime but they are mostly the victims of the perceived imperatives of the commercial system, the accepted face of capitalism.

## Notes

1   The dichotomy between maximum safety and expedition is in many ways false, or, at least, disturbed by awkward choices. Choosing, for example, to forgo all modern scientific benefits which are associated with 'unnatural' risk would presumably entail declining immunisations; a decision which perhaps just changes the type of risk incurred rather than eliminating risk.
2   *The Independent*, 24 December 1994, p. 11.
3   The editors opt for the term 'organisational crime' in contradistinction to 'white collar crime', as the latter phrase now includes many forms of offending (like income tax evasion) committed by *individuals* (who enjoy middle class status) for their own personal benefit. These issues are also discussed in Nelken, 1994.
4   This is relevant to my declared aim (Introduction and Methodology) of moving towards an answer to Box's question (1987, p. 197): 'how do actors bring about the results of which they may be dimly aware, and in their more enlightened moments would not even support?'
5   Health and Safety Commission Annual Report (1992–93).
6   The Offshore Safety Act 1992 s.4, allows for maximum fines of £20,000 to be given by Magistrate's Courts for some specified offences. Subject to maxima legislatively set by particular Acts, or for particular offences, fine is without limit in the Crown Court.
7   HSC Annual Report (1996/97).
8   *The Independent*, 9 December 1993.
9   Health and Safety Bulletin, April, 1993.

10  Peter Kite was jailed in 1994 following the death of four teenagers in the Lyme Bay canoe incident (*New Law Journal*, 1994, p. 1714); Roy Edwin Hill was jailed at Bristol Crown Court in 1995 for violating health and safety legislation (Slapper, 1996, p. 280); two company directors of Calder Felts Ltd of Sowery Bridge were jailed in April 1996 following an incident on a textile garneting machine in which a 19 year-old employee lost his arm (*Yorkshire Post*, 24 April 1996); and Alan Jackson, director of Jackson Transport (Ossett) Ltd was imprisoned in November 1996 on a charge of manslaughter (see chapter 1).

11  Home Office, 1995, p. 25.

12  Home Office, 1990, chapter 9.

13  The prosecution against Roger Seelig, the merchant banker accused of taking part in an illegal scheme to support the Guinness share price, collapsed in February 1992 after Mr Seelig 'became too unwell to continue'. It could be argued that the depression he was diagnosed as having was a natural result of the gravity of charges for which he was standing trial (*The Independent*, 15 February 1992). In August 1990, Ernest Saunders was given a five year sentence after being found guilty of two charges of stealing £8 million. His sentence was then reduced to 30 months and he was released after 10 months. This case is now under appeal again (*The Guardian*, 23 December 1994, pp. 1, 10). Asil Nadir was the businessman who in May 1993 evaded trial by chartering a jet to take him to Northern Cyprus. He skipped his £3.5 million bail, saying that he would not be given a fair trial in England for the offences of theft and false accounting with which he was charged. He also went on record as saying that his sureties would not suffer as he would repay those who had put up bail for him.

# Bibliography

Aaronovitch, S. (1979), *Ruling Class: Study of British Finance Capital*, Macmillan, London.

Aaronovitch, S. and Sawyer, M. (1975), *Big Business: Theoretical and Empirical Aspects of Concentration and Merger in the United Kingdom*, Macmillan Press, London.

Abercrombie, M.L.J. (1969), *The Anatomy of Judgement*, Penguin, London.

Althusser, L. (1984), *Essays on Ideology*, Verso, London.

Andrews, J. (1973), 'Reform in the Law of Corporate Liability', *Criminal Law Review*, pp. 91–7.

Arthurs, H.W. (1985), *Without the Law: Administrative Justice and Legal Pluralism in 19th Century England*, University of Toronto Press, Toronto.

Ashworth, A. (1991), *Principles of Criminal Law*, Clarendon Press, Oxford.

Aubert, V. (1952), 'White Collar Crime and Social Structure', *American Journal of Sociology*, 58, pp. 263–71.

Baker, J.H. (1971), *An Introduction to English Legal History*, Butterworths, London.

Bandura, A. (1977), *Social Learning Theory*, Prentice Hall Inc., New Jersey.

Bardach, E. and Kagan, R. (1982), *Going by the Book: The Problem of Regulatory Unreasonableness*, Temple University Press, Philadelphia.

Bartlett, F.C. (1932), *Remembering*, Cambridge University Press, Cambridge.

Beck, U. (1992), *Risk Society: Towards a New Modernity*, trans. M. Ritter, Sage, London.

Becker, G. (1968), 'Crime and Punishment an Economic Approach', *Journal of Political Economy*, 76 (2), pp. 169–217.

Becker, H.S. (1964), *Outsiders*, Free Press, New York.

Becker, H.S. (1971), *Sociological Work: Method and substance*, Allen Lane, The Penguin Press, London.

Bentham, J. (1975), *Theory of Legislation*, Oceana, New York.

Bergman, D. (1990a), 'Manslaughter in the Tunnel', *New Law Journal*, 3 August, p. 1108.

Bergman, D. (1990b), 'Recklessness in the Boardroom', *New Law Journal*, 26 October, pp. 1496–7..

Bergman, D. (1991), *Deaths at Work: Accidents or Corporate Crime*, Workers' Educational Association, London.

Bergman, D. (1992), 'Corporate sanctions and corporate probation', *New Law Journal*, Vol. 144, p. 1312.

Bergman, D. (1993), *Disasters: Where the Law Fails*, Herald Families Association, London.

Bergman, D. (1994), *The Perfect Crime*, West Midlands HASAC, Sheffield.

Bergman, D. (1997), 'Weak on Crime, Weak on the Causes of Crime', *New Law Journal*, p. 1652.

Blackstone (1996), *Blackstone's Criminal Practice*, Blackstone Press, London.

Blackstone, W. (1979, 1769), *Commentaries on the Laws of England*, Facsimile of First Edition, University of Chicago Press, Chicago.

Boisjoly, R., Curtis, E. and Mellican, E. (1989), 'Ethical Dimensions of the Challenger Disaster' in M. Ermann and R. Lundman (eds), *Corporate and Governmental Deviance: Problems of Organizational Behaviour in Contemporary Society*, Oxford University Press, Oxford.

Bottomley, A.K. (1973), *Decisions in the Penal Process*, Martin Robertson, London.

Bottomley, K. and Pease, K. (1986), *Crime and Punishment: Interpreting the Data*, Open University Press, Milton Keynes.

Box, S. (1983), *Power, Crime and Mystification*, Routledge, London.

Box, S. (1987), *Recession, Crime and Punishment*, Macmillan, London.

Braithwaite, J. (1979), *Inequality, Crime and Public Policy*, Routledge, London.

Braithwaite, J. (1983), *Corporate Crime in the Pharmaceutical Industry*, Routledge and Kegan Paul, London.

Braithwaite, J. and Pettit, P. (1990), *Not Just Deserts: A republican theory of justice*, Clarendon Press, Oxford.

Brazier, M. (1988), *Street on Torts*, Butterworths, London.

British Petroleum plc (1987), *Annual Report*, BP, London.

Brodrick Report (1971), *Report of the Committee on Death Certification and Coroners*, Cmnd. 4810 (Chairman Mr, later Judge, Norman Brodrick QC).

Buchanan, D.R. and Mason, J.K. (1995), 'The Coroner's Office Revisited', *Medical Law Review*, 3, Summer, pp. 142–60.

Burke, K. (1967), *Language as Symbolic Action*, University of California Press, London.

Burles, D. (1991), 'The Criminal Liability of Corporations', *New Law Journal*, 3 May, pp. 609–11.

Burton, J.D.K., Chambers, D.R. and Gill, P.S. (1985), *Coroners' Inquiries*, Barry Rose, London.

Cain, M. (1973), *Society and the Policeman's Role*, Routledge & Kegan Paul, London.

Cain, M. and Hunt, A. (1979), *Marx and Engels on Law*, Academic Press, London.

Calhoun, C. and Hiller, H. (1986), 'Insidious Injuries: Johns-Manville and Asbestos Exposure' in M. Ermann and R. Lundman (eds), *Corporate and Governmental Deviance: Problems of Organizational Behaviour in Contemporary Society*, Oxford University Press, Oxford.

Campbell, M. (1981), *Capitalism in the UK*, Croom Helm, London.

Carlen, P. and Collison, M. (eds) (1980), *Radical Issues in Criminology*, Martin Robertson, Oxford.

Carr, E.H. (1961), *What is History?*, Macmillan, London.

Carson, E.H. (1970a), 'White Collar Crime and the Enforcement of Factory Legislation', *British Journal of Criminology*, 10, pp. 383–98.

Carson, E.H. (1970b), 'Some Sociological Aspects of Strict Liability and the Enforcement of Factory Legislation', *Modern Law Review*, 33 (4), pp. 396–412.

Carson, E.H. (1979), 'The Conventionalization of Early Factory Crime', *International Journal for the Sociology of Law*, 1979, Vol. 7 pp. 37–60.

Carson, E.H. (1981), *The Other Price of Britain's Oil*, Martin Robertson, Edinburgh.

Chambliss, W. and Seidman, B. (1971), *Law, Order and Power*, Addison-Wesley, London.

Cicourel, A.V. (1968), *The Social Organisation of Juvenile Justice*, Wiley, New York.

Clarke, M. (1990), *Business Crime: Its Nature and Control*, Polity Press, Cambridge.

Clarkson, C.M.V. and Keating, H.M. (1994), *Criminal Law: Text and Materials*, Sweet & Maxwell, London.

Clinard, M. and Yeager, P. (1980), *Corporate Crime*, Free Press, New York.

Cohen, S. (ed.) (1971), *Images of Deviance*, Penguin, Harmondsworth.

Cohen, S. (1985), *Visions of Social Control: Crime, Punishment and Classification*, Polity Press, Oxford.

Cohen, S. (1988), *Against Criminology*, Transaction Books, Oxford.

Coleman, J.S. (1982), 'Power and the Structure of Society' in M. Ermann and R. Lundman (eds), *Corporate and Governmental Deviance: Problems of Organizational Behaviour in Contemporary Society*, Oxford University Press, Oxford.

Coleman, J.S. (1990), *Foundations of Social Theory*, Harvard University Press, Cambridge, Massachusetts.

Coleman, J.W. (1987), 'Toward an Integrated Theory of White-Collar Crime', *American Journal of Sociology*, 93, pp. 406–93.

Cooper, D. (1972), *The Death of the Family*, Penguin, Harmondsworth.

Cornish, D.B. and Clarke, R.V. (eds) (1986), *The Reasoning Criminal: Rational Choice Perspectives on Offending*, Springer-Verlag, New York.

Cosin, B.R. (ed.) (1972), *Education: Structure and Society*, Penguin, Harmondsworth.

Criminal Statistics England and Wales (1997), Cm 4162, RDS, Home Office, London.

Croall, H. (1989), 'Who is the White Collar Criminal?', *British Journal of Criminology*, Vol. 29, No. 2, Spring, pp. 157–75.

Croall, H. (1992), *White Collar Crime*, Open University Press, Buckingham.

Cross, R. and Harris, J.W. (1991), *Precedent in English Law*, Clarendon Press, Oxford.

Crown Prosecution Service (1996–97), *Annual Report*, The Stationery Office Ltd, London.

Crown Prosecution Service (1994), *Code for Crown Prosecutors*, The Stationery Office Ltd, London.

Crump, J. (1987), 'The Thin Red Line: Non-Market Socialism in the Twentieth Century' in M. Rubel and J. Crump (eds), *Non-Market Socialism in the Nineteenth and Twentieth Centuries*, Macmillan Press, London.

Cullen, F.T., Maakestad,W. and Cavender, G. (1987), *Corporate Crime Under Attack*, Anderson Publishing, New York.

Dember, W. (1969), *The Psychology of Perception*, Holt, Rinehart & Winston, London.

Devlin, P. (1965), *The Enforcement of Morals*, Oxford University Press, Oxford.

Diamond, S. (1971), 'The Rule of Law Versus the Order of Custom' in C.E. Reasons (ed.), *Sociology of Law: a conflict perspective*, Butterworths, London.

Dowie, M. (1977), 'Pinto Madness' in S.J. Hills (ed.) (1987) *Corporate Violence: Injury and Death for Profit*, Rowman and Littlefield, New Jersey.

Drewry, G. (1975), *Law, Justice and Politics*, Longman, London.

Du Cann, R. (1980), *The Art of the Advocate*, Penguin, Harmondsworth.

Duff, A. (1990), *Intention, Agency and Criminal Liability*, Basil Blackwell, Oxford.

Durkheim, E. (1984, 1893), *The Division of Labour in Society*, Macmillan, London.

Dworkin, R. (1977), *Taking Rights Seriously*, Duckworth, London.

Easton, J. (1989), 'The Climbing Boys', *New Society*, 20.12, pp. 450–2.

Ecclestone, B. (1998), 'Work related deaths', *NLJ Practitioner*, 19 June, p. 910.

Eiser, J.R. and Stroebe, W. (1972), *Categorization and Social Judgement*, Academic Press, London.

Ekblom, P. (1986), *The Prevention of Shop Theft: An Approach Through Crime Analysis*, Home Office Crime Prevention Paper No. 5, Home Office, London.

Ekblom, P. (1987), *Preventing Robbery at Sub-Post Offices*, Home Office Crime Prevention Paper No. 9, Home Office, London.

Engels, F. (1969, 1845), *The Condition of the Working Class in England*, Panther, London.

Engels, F. (1973, 1886), *Ludwig Feuerbach and the End of Classical German Philosophy*, Progress Publishers, Moscow.

Epstein, R.A. (1980), 'Is Pinto a Criminal?', 4 Regulation 15.

Ermann, M.R. and Lundman, R. (eds) (1992), *Corporate and Governmental Deviance: Problems of Organizational Behaviour in Contemporary Society*, Oxford University Press, Oxford.

Field, S. (1990a), 'Without the law? Professor Arthurs and the Early Factory Inspectorate', *Journal of Law and Society*, 17, p. 445.

Field, S. (1990b), *Trends in Crime and Their Interpretation*, Home Office Research Study No. 119.

Field, S. and Jörg, N. (1991), 'Corporate Liability and Manslaughter: should we be going Dutch?', *Criminal Law Review*, pp. 156–71.

Fine, B. et al. (eds) (1979), *Capitalism and the Rule of Law: from deviancy theory to Marxism*, Hutchinson, London.

Fisse, B. (1971), 'The Use of Publicity as a Criminal Sanction Against Business Corporations', *Melbourne University Law Review*, Vol. 8, pp. 107–50.

Fisse, B. (1990), 'Recent Developments in Corporate Criminal Law and Corporate Liability to Monetary Penalties', *University of New South Wales Law Journal*, 13, 1, pp. 15–16.

Fisse, B. and Braithwaite, J. (1988), 'Accountability and the Control of Corporate Crime' in M. Findlay and R. Hogg (eds), *Understanding Crime and Criminal Justice*, Law Book Co. of Australia, Sydney.

Fleming, J.G. (1983), *The Law of Torts*, Law Book Co. of Australia, Sydney.

Foerschler, A. (1990), 'Corporate Criminal Intent: Towards a Better Understanding of Corporate Misconduct', *California Law Review*, Vol. 78, pp. 1286–311.

Foley, C. (1990), *Slaughter on Britain's Building Sites*, Connolly Publications, London.

Foucault, M. (1977), *Discipline and Punish*, Allen Lane, London.

Frank, N. (1987), 'Murder in the Workplace' in S.J. Hills (ed.) (1987), *Corporate Violence: Injury and Death for Profit*, Rowman and Littlefield, New Jersey.

Fry, M. (ed.) (1992), *Adam Smith's Legacy*, Routledge, London.

Garland, D. (1990), *Punishment and Modern Society*, Clarendon Press, Oxford.

Geiss, G. (1967), 'The Heavy Electrical Equipment Antitrust Cases of 1961' in M. Ermann and R. Lundman (eds) *Corporate and Governmental Deviance: Problems of Organizational Behaviour in Contemporary Society*, Oxford University Press, Oxford.

Glasgow University Media Group (1976), *Bad News*, Routledge and Kegan Paul, London.

Glasgow University Media Group (1982), *Really Bad News*, Writers and Readers, London.

GMB (General and Municipal Boilermakers and Allied Trades Union) (1987), *Hazards of Work*, GMB Health and Safety Publication, London.

Gobert, J. (1994a), 'Corporate Criminality: four models of fault', *Legal Studies*, 14, pp. 393–410.

Gobert, J. (1994b), 'Corporate Criminality: New Crimes for the Times', *Criminal Law Review*, pp. 722–34.

Gower, L.C.B. (1992), *Principles of Modern Company Law*, Sweet and Maxwell, London.

Graef, R. (1989), *Talking Blues*, Fontana, London.

Griffith, J.A.G. (1997), *The Politics of the Judiciary*, Fontana Press, London.

Habermas, J. (1976), *Legitimation Crisis*, Heinemann, London.

Hadden, T. (1977), *Company Law and Capitalism*, Weidenfeld & Nicolson, London.

Haines, F. (1992), *Deaths in the Workplace and the Dynamics of Response*, unpublished.

Haines, F. (1993), 'The Show Must Go On: The Response to Fatalities in Multiple Employer Workplaces', *Social Problems*, Vol. 40, No. 4 November, pp. 547–63.

Haines, F. and Polk, K. (1989), *Work Death in Victoria: An Exploratory Analysis*, paper presented at the annual Australian Law and Society Conference, La Trobe University, December.

Haines, F. and Sutton, A. (1992), *Workplace Deaths, Contracts and Ambiguity: Corporate Rationalizations on Economic Reality*, paper presented at the 8th Annual Australian and New Zealand Society of Criminology Conference, St Hilda's College, University of Melbourne, 30 September.

Hall, J. (1952), *Theft, Law and Society*, Bobbs Merrill, New York.

Hannah, L. (1976), *The Rise of the Corporate Economy*, London University Paperbacks, Methuen, London.

Harding, A. (1966), *A Social History of England*, Penguin, Harmondsworth.

Hart, H.L.A. (1961), *The Concept of Law*, Clarendon Press, Oxford.

*Harvard Law Review* (1987), 'Getting Away with Murder: Federal Occupational Safety and Health Administration Pre-emption of State Criminal Prosecutions for Industrial Accidents' (editorial), 101, pp. 535–54.

Hawkins, K. (1984), *Environment and Enforcement: Regulation and the Social Definition of Pollution*, Clarendon, Oxford.

Hawkins, K. (1990), 'Compliance Strategy, Prosecution Policy, and Aunt Sally', *British Journal of Criminology*, Vol. 30, No. 4, Autumn, pp. 444–66.

Hawkins, K. (1991), 'Enforcing Regulation: More of the Same from Pearce and Tombs', *British Journal of Criminology*, Vol. 31, No. 4, Autumn, pp. 427–30.

Hay, D. (1977), 'Property, Authority and the Criminal Law' in D. Hay et al. (eds), *Albion's Fatal Tree*, Peregrine, Harmondsworth.

Health and Safety Executive (1985), *Deadly Maintenance*, HMSO, London

Health and Safety Executive (1986), *Agricultural Blackspot*, HMSO, London.

Health and Safety Executive (1987), *Safety in Roofwork*, HMSO, London.

Health and Safety Executive (1988a), 1987/88, *Annual Report*, HMSO, London.

Health and Safety Executive (1988b), *Blackspot Construction*, HMSO, London.

Health and Safety Executive (1989), 1988/89, *Annual Report*, HMSO, London.

Health and Safety Executive (1990), 1989/90, *Annual Report*, HMSO, London.

Health and Safety Executive (1991), 1990/91, *Annual Report*, HMSO, London.

Health and Safety Executive (1992), 1991/92, *Annual Report*, HMSO, London.

Health and Safety Executive (1993), 1992/93, *Annual Report*, HMSO, London.

Health and Safety Executive (1994a), 1993/94, *Annual Report*, HMSO, London.

Health and Safety Executive (1994b), *The Costs to the British Economy of Work Accidents and Work-related Ill-health*, HSE Books, Sudbury.

Health and Safety Executive (1996/97), *Annual Report,* HMSO, London.

Health and Safety Executive (1996/97), *Statistics,* HMSO, London.

Hills, S. (1987), *Corporate Violence: Injury and Death for Profit*, Rowman & Littlefield, Totowa, NJ.

Hobsbawm, E. (1968), *Industry and Empire*, Weidenfeld and Nicolson, London.

Hoggart, R. (1957), *The Uses of Literacy: Aspects of Working Class Life With Special Reference to Publications and Entertainments*, Chatto and Windus, London.

Holdsworth, W. (1936), *A History of English Law*, Vol. II, Methuen & Co., London.

Holgate, G. (1993), 'Corporate Liability', *Solicitors Journal*, 20 August, p. 826.

Holroyd, J. (1993), 'Convicting Criminal Directors', *Solicitors Journal*, 1218, 3 December.

Home Office (1995), *Digest 3: Information on the Criminal Justice System*, England and Wales, HMSO, London.

Hood Phillips, O. and Jackson, P. (1987), *Constitutional and Administrative Law*, Sweet and Maxwell, London.

Hutter, B. (1986), 'An Inspector Calls', *British Journal of Criminology*, Vol. 26, No. 2, April, pp. 114–29.

Hutter, B. (1988), *'The Reasonable Arm of the Law?'*, Clarendon Press, Oxford.

International Transport Workers Federation (1987), *Relationship between Road Transport Working Conditions, Fatigue Health and Traffic Safety*, ITF, 133–5 Great Suffolk Street, London SE1.

Ireland, P. (1992), *Capitalist Development and Industrial Organisation*, unpublished paper.

Ireland, P., Grigg-Spall, I. and Kelly, D. (1987), 'The Conceptual Foundations of Modern Company Law', *Journal of Law and Society*, Vol. 14, No. 1, p. 149.

James, P. (1992), 'Reforming British Health and Safety Law: a framework for discussion', *Industrial Law Journal*, Vol. 21, No. 2, June, pp. 83–105.

Jamieson, K. (1994), *The Organization of Corporate Crime: dynamics of antitrust violation*, Sage, London.

Jervis, J. (1993, 1829), *On the Office and Duties of Coroners*, see under P. Matthews and J. Foreman, authors of the 11th edition.

Jones, T. (1988), *Corporate Killing – Bhopals Will Happen*, Free Association Books, London.

Joyce, D. (1989), 'Why Do Police Officers Laugh at Death', *The Psychologist*, Vol. 12, No. 9, September.

Kagan, P. and Scholz, J. (1984), 'The Criminology of the Corporation and Regulatory Enforcement' in K. Hawkins and J. Thomas (eds), *Enforcing Regulation*, Kluwer-Nijhoff, Boston.

Keane, A. (1994), *The Modern Law of Evidence*, Butterworths, London.

Kelman, H.C. and Hamilton, V.L. (1989), 'Crimes of Obedience' in M.D. Ermann and R.J. Lundman (eds) *Corporate and Governmental Deviance: Problems of Organisational Behaviour*, Oxford University Press, Oxford.

Kilalfry, A. (1958), *Outlines of English Legal History*, Sweet & Maxwell, London.

Kinney, J.A., Weiss, K., Sufalko, K., Gleason, A. and Maakestad, W. (1990), *Criminal Job Safety Prosecutions*, National Safe Workplace Institute, Kansas City.

Kinsey, R., Lea, J. and Young, J. (1986), *Losing the Battle against Crime*, Blackwell, Oxford.

Kitsuse, J.I. and Cicourel, A.V. (1963), 'A Note on the Official Uses of Statistics', *Social Problems*, 12, pp. 131–9.

Kogan, M. (1978), *The Politics of Educational Change*, Fontana, London.

Kramer, R.C. (1983), 'A Prolegomenon to the Study of Corporate Violence', *Humanity and Society*, 7, May, p. 166.

Kuczynski, J. (1973), *Labour Conditions Under Industrial Capitalism, Vol. 2. The United States of America 1789–1946*, Muller, London.

Labour Research (1990), 'Workplace Death – Who to blame?' *Labour Research*, Vol. 79, No. 9, p. 13.

Lacey, N. (1988), *State Punishment, Political Principles and Community Values*, Routledge, London.

Lacey, N. and Wells, C. (1998), *Reconstructing Criminal Law*, Butterworths, London.

Lacey, N., Wells, C. and Meure, D. (1990), *Reconstructing Criminal Law*, Weidenfeld and Nicolson, London.

Lashmar, P. (1994), 'Death by Deregulation', *New Statesman*, 6 May, pp. 16–19.

Law Commission (1989), *Criminal Law: A Criminal Code for England and Wales*, Vol. I, Report and Draft Criminal Code Bill, Law Com. No. 177, HMSO, London.

Law Commission (1994a), *Involuntary Manslaughter*, Consultation Paper No. 135, HMSO, London.

Law Commission (1994b), *The Year and a Day Rule in Homicide*, Consultation Paper No. 136. HMSO, London.

Law Commission (1996), *Involuntary Manslaughter,* Law Com. No. 237, HMSO, London.

Layard, R. (ed.) (1974), *Cost-Benefit Analysis*, Penguin, Harmondsworth.

Lee, J.A. (1981), 'Some Structural Aspects of Police Deviance in Relations with Minority Groups' in C. Shearing (ed.), *Organisational Police Deviance*, Butterworths, Toronto.

Leigh, L.H. (1969), *The Criminal Liability of Corporations in English Law*, Weidenfeld and Nicolson, London.

Leigh, L.H. (1977), 'The Criminal Liability of Corporations and Other Groups', *Ottawa Law Review*, 9, p. 247.

Leigh, L.H. (1985), *Police Powers in England and Wales*, Butterworths, London.

Lemert, E. (1967), *Human Deviance, Social Problems, and Social Control*, Prentice-Hall, New Jersey.

Lewes, G.H. (1879), *Problems of Life and Mind*, Trübner, London.

Lloyd, D. (1991), *The Idea of Law*, Penguin, Harmondsworth.

London Hazards Centre (1991), *Corporate Manslaughter, Inquests and Deaths at Work*, London Hazards Centre, London.

Luhmann, N. (1988), 'The Unity of the Legal System' in G. Teubner (ed.), *Autopoietic Law: A New Approach to Law and Society*, De Gruyter, Berlin.

Mannheim, K. (1936), *Ideology and Utopia*, Routledge & Kegan Paul, London.

Marx, K. (1955, 1847), *The Poverty of Philosophy*, Lawrence & Wishart, London.

Marx, K. (1970, 1859), *Contribution to a Critique of Political Economy*, International Publishers, New York.

Marx, K. (1954, 1887), *Capital: A Critique of Political Economy*, Vol. I, Lawrence & Wishart, London.

Marx, K. and Engels, F. (1959), *Selected Works*, Vol. 2, Lawrence and Wishart, London.

Marx, K. and Engels, F. (1976), *Collected Works*, Vol. 5, Lawrence and Wishart, London.

Maryon, S. (1993), 'Company Cars', *The Safety and Health Practitioner*, May, p. 4.

Matthews, P. and Foreman, J. (1993), *Jervis on the Office and Duties of Coroners*, Sweet & Maxwell, London.

Maxwell Atkinson, J. (1971), 'Societal Reactions to Suicide: The Role of Coroners' Definitions' in S. Cohen (ed.), *Images of Deviance*, Penguin, Harmondsworth.

McCabe, S. and Sutcliffe, F. (1978), *Defining Crime*, Blackwell, Oxford.

McColgan, A. (1994), 'The Law Commission Consultation Document on Involuntary Manslaughter – Heralding Corporate Liability?', *Criminal Law Review*, pp. 547–57.

Mills, B. (1994), 'The Code for Crown Prosecutors', *New Law Journal*, Vol. 144, No. 6654, p. 899.

Mills, C.W. (1956), *The Power Elite*, Oxford University Press, Oxford.

Milsom, S.F.C. (1981), *Historical Foundations of the Common Law*, Butterworths, London.

Mintz, M. (1985), *At Any Cost: Corporate greed, women and the Dalkon Shield*, Pantheon Books, New York.

Mishan, E.J. (1971), 'The Value of Life' in R. Layard (ed.), *Cost-Benefit Analysis*, Penguin, Harmondsworth.

Moore, R. (1991), *The Price of Safety: The market, workers' rights and the law*, The Institute of Employment Rights, London.

Morgan, L.J. (1992), 'Corporate Criminal Capacity: Nostalgia for Representation', *Social and Legal Studies*, Vol. 1, pp. 371–91.

Morris, W. (1947, 1877), *On Art and Socialism: Essays and Lectures*, John Lehmann, London.

Morrison, A. and McIntyre, D. (1971), *Schools and Socialization*, Penguin, Harmondsworth.

Murphy, P. (editor-in-chief) (1997), *Blackstone's Criminal Practice*, Blackstone Press Ltd, London.

Nader, R. (1965), *Unsafe At Any Speed*, Grossman, New York.

Napier, M. (1990), 'Zeebrugge: the Way Forward', *The Law Society's Gazette*, No. 40, 7 November, p. 2.

National Audit Office (1994), *Enforcing Health and Safety Regulations in the Workplace*, February, HMSO, London.

National Council for Civil Liberties (1980), *The Death of Blair Peach – Report of the Unofficial Committee of Inquiry*, National Council for Civil Liberties, London.

Nelken, D. (1982), 'Is there a Crisis in Law and Legal Ideology?', *Journal of Law and Society*, Vol. 9, No. 2, Winter, pp. 177–89.

Nelken, D. (1983), *The Limits of the Legal Process*, Academic Press, London.

Nelken, D. (1987a), 'Book Review – Without the Law: Administrative Justice and Legal Pluralism in Nineteenth Century England', *Public Law*, pp. 293–5.

Nelken, D. (1987b), 'Critical Criminal Law', *Journal of Law and Society*, Vol. 14, No. 1, Spring, p. 105.

Nelken, D. (1990), 'Why Punish?', *The Modern Law Review*, 53, pp. 829–34.

Nelken, D. (1994), 'White Collar Crime' in M. Maguire, R. Morgan, and R. Reiner (eds), *The Oxford Handbook of Criminology*, Clarendon Press, Oxford.

Nicholas, T. (1984), *The British Worker Question: A New Look at Workers and Productivity in Manufacturing*, Routledge and Kegan Paul, London.

Norrie, A. (1993), *Crime, Reason and History*, Weidenfeld and Nicolson, London.

Office of Population Census and Surveys (1987), *Occupational Mortality*, Decennial Supplement parts 1 and 2, 1979–80, 1982–3, HMSO, London.

Organisation for Economic Co-operation and Development (1989), *Occupational Accidents in OECD Countries*, July, Employment Outlook, Paris.

Orwell, G. (1970), *Collected Essays*, Vol. 4, S. Orwell and I. Angus (eds), Penguin, Harmondsworth.

Owen, T. (1991), *Coroners' Courts*, LNTV (lawyers' training video) transcript.

Parsons, T. and Bales R.F. (1956), *Family: Socialization and Interaction Process*, Routledge and Kegan Paul, London.

Pashukanis, E.B. (1983, 1924), *Law and Marxism – A General Theory*, Pluto Press, London.

Pearce, F. and Tombs, S. (1990), 'Ideology, Hegemony, and Empiricism: Compliance Theories of Regulation', *British Journal of Criminology*, Vol. 30, No. 4, Autumn, pp. 423–43.

Pearce, F. and Tombs, S. (1991), 'Policing Corporate 'Skid Rows': A Reply to Keith Hawkins', *British Journal of Criminology*, Vol. 31, No. 4, Autumn, pp. 415–26.

Pearce, F. and Tombs, S. (1994), 'Class, Law, and Hazards', paper submitted to *The Permanent Peoples' Tribunal* (Industrial Hazards and Human Rights), 28 November–2 December, London.

Pearson, G. (1994), 'Youth, Crime, and Society' in *The Oxford Handbook of Criminology*, Clarendon Press, Oxford.

Plucknett, T.F.T. (1956), *A Concise History of the Common Law*, Butterworths, London.

Posner, R.A. (1972), *Economic Analysis of Law*, Little, Brown & Company, Boston.

Powis, D. (1977), *The Signs of Crime: A Field Manual For Police*, McGraw Hill, London.

Punch, M. (1996), *Dirty Business: Explaining corporate misconduct*, Sage, London.

Quinney, R. (1970), *The Social Reality of Crime*, Little, Brown & Company, Boston.

Radzinowicz, L. (1948), *A History of English Criminal Law*, Vol. 1, Stevens, London.

Reed, M. (1991), *The Sociology of Organisations*, Harvester Wheatsheaf, Hemel Hempstead.

Reichman, N. (1993), 'Insider Trading' in M. Tonry and A. Reiss (eds) *Beyond the Law: Crime in Complex Organisations*, University of Chicago Press, Chicago.

Reiman, J. (1979), *The Rich get Richer and the Poor get Prison*, Wiley, New York.

Reiner, R. (1978), *The Blue-Coated Worker*, Cambridge University Press, Cambridge.

Reiner, R. (1985), *The Politics of the Police*, Wheatsheaf, Brighton.

Reiner, R. (1988), 'British Criminology and the State', *British Journal of Criminology*, Vol. 28, No. 2, pp. 138–59.

Reiner, R. (1991), *Chief Constables*, Oxford University Press, Oxford.

Reiner, R. (1994), 'Policing and the Police' in M. Maguire, R. Morgan and R. Reiner (eds), *The Oxford Handbook of Criminology*, Clarendon Press, Oxford.

Reuter, P. (1993), 'The Cartage Industry in New York' in M. Tonry and A. Reiss (eds), *Beyond the Law: Crime in Complex Organisations*, University of Chicago Press, Chicago.

Reville, N. (1989), 'Corporate Manslaughter', *Law Society's Gazette*, 19 October, pp. 17–19.

Richardson, G.M., Ogus, A.I. and Burrows, P. (1982), *Policing Pollution: A study of regulation and enforcement*, Oxford University Press, Oxford.

Ridgeway, J. (1980), *Who Owns the Earth*, Collier Macmillan, London.

Robens (Lord) (1972), *Safety and Health at Work*, Report of the Committee (1970-72) Cmnd. 5034, HMSO. London.

Roshier, B. and Teff, H. (1980), *Law and Society in England*, Tavistock Publications, London.

Roth, I. and Frisby, J. (1989), *Perception and Representation: A Cognitive Approach*, Open University Press, Milton Keynes.

Rutherford, A. (1993), *Criminal Justice and the Pursuit of Decency*, Oxford University Press, Oxford.

Sanders, A. (1994), 'Judicial Statistics', *New Law Journal*, Vol. 144, No. 6655, p. 946.

Scratton, P. (1984), 'The Coroner's Tale' in P. Scratton, and P. Gordon (eds), *Causes for Concern*, Penguin, Harmondsworth.

Seigart, P. (1980), *Breaking the Rules*, Justice, London.

Senden, M. (1932), quoted by Abercrombie (1960), q.v.

Sheehy, P. (1993), *Inquiry into Police Responsibilities and Rewards*, Vols. 1 and 2, Cm 2280.1, HMSO, London.

Sinclair, U. (1906), *The Jungle*, Random House, New York.

Sinden, P. (1980), 'Perception of Crime in Capitalist America: The question of consciousness manipulation', *Sociological Focus*, 13, pp. 75–85.

Slapper, G. (1992a), 'Corporate Manslaughter: the difficulties posed by current law', *The Criminal Lawyer*, No. 26, p. 5.

Slapper, G. (1992b), 'Glogg v. South Coast Shipping Co. Ltd. and others (February, 1992) CASENOTE', *Solicitors Journal*, Vol. 136, No. 7, p. 156.

Slapper, G. (1992c), 'The Marchioness Case: Judicial Review', *Solicitors Journal*, 136, No. 25, p. 161.

Slapper, G. (1992d), 'A Safe Place to Work', *The Law Society Gazette*, No. 38, pp. 23–5.

Slapper, G. (1992e), 'Where the Buck Stops', *New Law Journal*, Vol. 144, pp. 1037–8.

Slapper, G. (1993a), 'Manslaughter and Civil Negligence', *Professional Negligence*, Vol. 4, No. 9, p. 52.

Slapper, G. (1993b), 'Corporate Manslaughter: An Examination of the Determinants of Prosecutorial Policy', *Social and Legal Studies*, Vol. 2, pp. 423–43.

Slapper, G. (1994a) 'Manslaughter, Mens Rea and Medicine', *New Law Journal*, Vol. 144, No. 6655, p. 941.

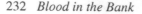

Slapper, G. (1994b), 'Corporate Punishment', *New Law Journal*, Vol. 144, p. 29.

Slapper, G. (1994c) 'Companies, Crime and Punishment', *Business Law Review*, 126, May.

Slapper, G. (1994d), 'Fault lines in Kingston', *New Law Journal*, Vol. 144, No. 1232, p. 16.

Slapper, G. (1994e), 'A Year and a Day', *New Law Journal*, Vol. 144, 748.

Slapper, G. (1994f), 'A Corporate Killing', *New Law Journal*, Vol. 144, No. 6676, p. 1714.

Slapper, G. (1996), 'Manslaughter, Medicine, Medics, and Management', *British Journal of Healthcare Management*, 1996, Vol. 2, No. 5, p. 280.

Slapper, G. (1997), 'Litigation and Corporate Crime', *Journal of Personal Injury Litigation*, December, pp. 220–33.

Slapper, G. (1998), 'Corporate Crime and Punishment', *The Criminal Lawyer*, March/ April, pp. 6–7.

Smith, A. (1976, 1776), *An Inquiry into the Nature and Causes of the Wealth of Nations*, Vol. 1, eds R.H. Campbell and A.S. Skinner, The Glasgow Edition, Liberty Press, Indianapolis.

Smith, D. and Gray, J. (1985), *Police and People in London*, Gower, Aldershot.

Smith, J.C. and Hogan, B. (1996), *Criminal Law*, Butterworths, London.

Smith, N.C. (1990), *Morality and the Market*, Routledge, London.

Smith, R. (1994), 'Judicial Statistics', *New Law Journal*, Vol. 144, No. 6659, p. 1088.

Snider, L. (1991), 'The Regulatory Dance: Understanding Reform Processes in Corporate Crime', *International Journal of the Sociology of Law*, 19, pp. 209–36.

Start, R.D., Delargy-Aziz, Y., Dorries, C.P., Silcocks, P.B., and Cotton, D.W.K. (1993), 'Clinicians and the Coronial System: Ability of Clinicians to Recognise Reportable Deaths', *British Journal of Medicine*, Vol. 306, p. 1038.

Start, R.D., Usherwood, T.P., Carter, N., Dorries, C.P. and Cotton, D.W.K. (1995), 'General Practitioner's Knowledge of When to Refer Deaths to a Coroner', *British Journal of General Practice*, 45, pp. 191–3.

Stephen, J.F. (1883), *A History of the Criminal Law of England*, Macmillan, London.

Stessens, G. (1994), 'Corporate Criminal Liability: A Comparative Perspective', *International and Comparative Law Quarterly*, Vol. 43, pp. 493–520.

Stinchcombe, A. (1963), 'Institutions of Privacy in the Determination of Police Administrative practice', *American Journal of Sociology*, 69/2, pp. 150–60.

Stockdale, E. and Casale, S. (1992), *Criminal Justice Under Stress*, Blackstone, London.

Strange, K.H. (1982), *The Climbing Boys 1773–1875*, Alison Busby, London.

Sullivan, G.R. (1996), 'The Attribution of Culpability to Limited Companies', *Cambridge Law Journal*, 55 (3), November, pp. 515–46.

Sullivan, R.F. (1973), 'The Economics of Crime: An Introduction to the Literature', *Crime and Delinquency*, 19 (2), pp. 138–49.

Sutherland, E.H. (1949), *White Collar Crime*, Holt Rinehart and Winston, New York.

Sutherland, E.H. (1983), *White Collar Crime: The Uncut Version*, Yale University Press, New Haven.

Swigert, V. and Farrell, R. (1980–81), 'Corporate Homicide: Definitional Processes in the Creation of Deviance', *Law and Society Review*, Vol. 15, No. 1, p. 161.

Tappan, P. (1947), 'Who is the Criminal?', *American Sociological Review*, 12, pp. 96–102.

Taylor, I. (1981), *Law and Order: Arguments for Socialism*, Macmillan, London.

Taylor, I. (1994), 'The Political Economy of Crime' in M. Maguire, R. Morgan, and R. Reiner (eds) (1994), *The Oxford Handbook of Criminology*, Clarendon Press, Oxford.

Taylor, I., Walton, P. and Young, J. (eds) (1973), *Critical Criminology*, Routledge & Kegan Paul, London.

Taylor, P. (Lord Taylor of Gosforth) (1993), 'What do we want from our judges?', text delivered as *17th Leggett Lecture*, 26 November, University of Surrey.

Thomas, D.A. (1979), *Principles of Sentencing*, Heinemann, London.

Thomas, M.W. (1948), *The Early Factory Legislation*, Thames Bank, London.

Thomas, P. (1991), 'Safety in Smaller Manufacturing Establishments', *Department of Employment Gazette*, January.

Thompson, A. (1981), 'Law and the Social Sciences: the Demise of Legal Autonomy', paper delivered at University of Kent, March.

Thompson, E.P. (1967), 'Time, Work Discipline and Industrial Capitalism', *Past and Present*, No. 38, pp. 56–97.

Thompson, E.P. (1975), *Whigs and Hunters: the origin of the Black Act*, Peregrine, Harmondsworth.

Thurston, G. (1976), *Coronership*, Barry Rose Publishers, Chichester.

Tigar, M.E. (1990), 'It does the Crime But Not the Time: Corporate Criminal Liability in Federal Law', *American Journal of Criminal Law*, 17, 211, pp. 211–34.

Todd, E. (1985), *The Explanation of Ideology: Family Structures and Social Systems*, Basil Blackwell, Oxford.

Tombs, S. (1990), 'Industrial Injuries in British Manufacturing Industry', *Sociological Review*, pp. 324–43.

Tombs, S. (1992), 'Stemming the Flow of Blood: the illusion of self-regulation', *Journal of Human Justice*, III, 2, pp. 75–92.

Tombs, S. (1995), 'Corporate Crime and the "Management" of Major Hazards' in A. Irwin, D. Lloyd, and D. Smith (eds), *The Strategic Management of Major Hazards*, Routledge, London.

Tombs, S. (1996), 'Injury, Death and the Deregulation Fetish: The politics of safety regulation in UK manufacturing', *International Journal of Health Services*, 26, (2), pp. 327–47.

Tombs, S. (1999), 'Official Statistics and Hidden Crimes: Researching health and safety crimes' in V. Jupp and P. Francis (eds), *Criminology in the Field: The practice of criminological research*, Macmillan, London.

Tonry, M. and Reiss, A.J. (1993), *Beyond The Law: Crime in Complex Organizations*, University of Chicago Press, London.

Transport and General Workers Union (1994), *Fatigue: the hidden killer on our roads*, TGWU, (SW1P 3JB), London.

Treitel, G.H. (1991), *The Law of Contract*, Sweet and Maxwell, London.

Tugendhat, C. (1973), *The Multinationals*, Penguin, Harmondsworth.

Turner, J.W.C. (1966), *Kenny's Outlines of Criminal Law*, Cambridge University Press, Cambridge.

Twining, W. and Meirs, D. (1976), *How To Do Things With Rules*, Weidenfeld and Nicolson, London.

Tye, J. (1989), 'Safety sacrificed at the altar of profit', *The Independent*, 7 October.

Vernon, M.D. (1952), *A Further Study of Perception*, Cambridge University Press, Cambridge.

Vernon, M.D. (1955), 'The Functions of Schemata in Perceiving', *Psychological Review*, 62, p. 180.

Vold, G. and Bernard, T. (1986), *Theoretical Criminology*, Oxford University Press, Oxford.

Ward, J.T. (1962), *The Factory Movement 1830–1855*, Macmillan, London.

Warrington, R. (1977), 'Law – Its Image or its Reality?', *City of London Law Review*, p. 29.

Warrington, R. (1983), 'Pashukanis and the Commodity Form Theory' in D. Sugarman (ed.), *Legality, Ideology and the State*, Academic Press, London.

Wells, C. (1988), 'The Decline and Rise of English Murder: Corporate Crime and Individual Responsibility', *Criminal Law Review*, p. 788.

Wells, C. (1989), 'Manslaughter and Corporate Crime', *New Law Journal*, 7 July, p. 931.

Wells, C. (1991), 'Inquests, Inquiries and Indictments: The Official Reception of Death by Disaster', *Legal Studies*, 11, p. 71.

Wells, C. (1993a), *Corporations and Criminal Responsibility*, Clarendon, Oxford.

Wells, C. (1993b), 'Corporations: Culture, Risk and Criminal Liability', *Criminal Law Review*, pp. 551–66.

Wells, C. (1996), 'Corporate Liability for Crime – *Tesco v. Nattrass* on the danger list?', *Archbold News*, Issue 1, 7 February, pp. 5–8.

Wells, C. (1997a), 'Health and Safety Laws take Corporate Liability for a Ride', *Archbold, News*, Issue 5, 5 June, pp. 5–8.

Wells, C. (1997b), 'Corporate Killing', *New Law Journal*, 10 October, pp. 1467–8.

Welsh, R.S. (1946), 'The Criminal Liability of Corporations', *Law Quarterly Review*, 62, p. 345.

Whitaker, B. (1964), *The Police*, Penguin, Harmondsworth.

Whitfield, M. (1992), 'Cost pressures keep safety on the sidelines', *The Independent*, 9 December.

Wickins, R.J. and Ong, C.A. (1997), 'Confusion Worse Confounded: The End of the Directing Mind Theory?', *The Journal of Business Law*, November Issue, pp. 524–56.

Wiles, P. (1971), 'Criminal Statistics and Sociological Explanations of Crime' in P. Carson, and P. Wiles, *Sociology of Crime and Delinquency in Britain*, Vol. 1, Martin Robertson, London.

Williams, G. (1983), *Textbook of Criminal Law*, Stephens, London.

Williams, G. (1985), 'Letting off the Guilty and Prosecuting the Innocent', *Criminal Law Review*, pp. 115–22.

Williams, K.S. (1994), *Textbook on Criminology*, Blackstone Press Ltd, London.

Williams, R. (1961), *The Long Revolution*, Chatto & Windus, London.

Winfield and Jolowicz on *Tort*, (1994), W.V.H. Rogers, Sweet and Maxwell, London.

Young, J. (1971), 'The Role of the Police as Amplifiers of Deviancy' in S. Cohen (ed.), *Images of Deviance*, Penguin, Harmondsworth.

Young, J. (1994), 'Incessant Chatter: Recent Paradigms in Criminology' in M. Maguire, R. Morgan, and R. Reiner (eds), *The Oxford Handbook of Criminology*, Clarendon Press, Oxford.

Young, M. (1991), *An Inside Job: Policing and Police Culture*, Clarendon, Oxford.

Young, M. (1994), 'Black Humour: Making Light of Death', *Policing and Society*.

Young, R.T. (1981), 'Corporate Crime: A Critique of the Clinard Report', *Contemporary Crises*, 5, pp. 323–36.

# APPENDICES

# Appendix 1

**Benefits and Costs Relating to Fuel Leakage Associated with the Static Rollover Test Portions of FMVSS 208**

### Benefits

*Savings:* 180 burn deaths, 180 serious burn injuries, 2,100 burned vehicles.
*Unit cost:* $200,000 per death, $67,000 per injury, $700 per vehicle.
*Total benefit:* 180 x ($200,000) + 180 x ($67,000) + 2,100 x ($700) = $49.5 million

### Costs

*Sales:* 11 million cars, 1.5 million light trucks.
*Unit Cost:* $11 per car, $11 per truck.
*Total cost:* 11,000,000 x ($11) + 1,500,000 x ($11) = $137 million.

The above table appears in a seven page internal memorandum of the Ford Motor Company: *Fatalities Associated with Crash-Induced Fuel Leakage and Fires*. Using a cost-benefit analysis it argues that Ford should not make an $11 improvement to its vehicles even although these would save 180 lives per year. It would be less costly for Ford to wait until people in their defective vehicles are killed or injured and then meet the compensation claims.

Source: S. Hills (ed.) (1987), *Corporate Violence: Injury and Death for Profit*, Rowman & Littlefield, New Jersey.

# Appendix 2

**The Courts**

I attended inquests at 18 locations: towns and cities throughout the country. Geographically the courts were selected from all major regions, north, south, east and west (with the exception of the outlying west). The jurisdictions of these courts represent a typical demographic mixture of Britain and present a variety of occupation and employment patterns. If local custom, the typical local nature of occupationally-related deaths, assumptions or evolved bureaucratic *modus operandi* had any appreciable effect upon the way cases were processed, or their outcomes, I wanted to be able to identify and control for this. Hence the choice to travel to and witness the proceedings in person and to interview those personnel (coroners, coroners' officers, Health and Safety Executive personnel, lawyers, pathologists and police officers) involved in the process which is the official response to death at work.

Throughout the text the names of the courts, locations, officers and people involved in the proceedings have been altered.

*Eastshire* – a large county with some heavy and much light industry. The county also contains a fair spread of arable farming. Medium population density. The court sits principally in two large towns.

*Star Fields* – a jurisdiction covering a large sector of a major city. The area is heavily populated with much light industry with a high concentration of transportation systems and service industries.

*Castlebridge* – a large old industrial town with a high but declining concentration of heavy industry. This town has suffered badly in the economic recession.

*Stonetown* – a medium-sized industrial town, on the outskirts of the conurbation of a major city. Another area hit badly by the recession.

*Blueport* – the jurisdiction here is a small, commercial district of a city.

*Downton* – a once-thriving industrial town, now presents only a very attenuated residuum of light industry and service sector operations.

*Rossford* – a relatively modern medium-sized town, near a city, the coast and a busy port.

*Valeton* – a new town, in a predominantly rural environment. The surrounding area is rural with some light industry.

*Colneford* – an historic county town. Mining, farming and light industry and trading are the main areas of employment in the county.

*High Hills* – a small town in a rural county where farming and agricultural work account for much employment.

*Marfield* – mining and manufacturing industry are the main areas of employment in the jurisdiction of this court which sits in an old, small industrial city.

*Buthorpe* – a large, industrial town in the conurbation of a major city. This town has undergone notable economic redevelopment during the last 25 years.

*Paveton* – a small industrial city, with a concentration of factories, suffering from economic degeneration.

*Brickmere* – the jurisdiction of this court is that of a large sector of a major city.

*Flintford* – an old city; the court's jurisdiction is that of a county with mining, industry, farming and trading as major areas of employment.

*Lynton* – an ancient city near the coast. Much of the work in this jurisdiction is in farming and fishing.

*Fortbury* – an old industrial city with much manufacturing industry.

*Salsworth* – a large city and major port which economic recession has made industrially desolate in many areas.

## Case 1

EASTSHIRE CORONER'S COURT
Before Dr Colborn

*Inquest into the death of Mr David Green (23) who was killed when a four ton slab of concrete fell on him at a construction site where he was working.*

Cause of death: extensive multiple crush injuries. Toxicologist's report: negative.

The deceased was employed as a concrete erector on a site in Benton. At 2.00 pm on 25 April he was on the first floor of a building under construction when he apparently removed a metal prop which was supporting a four ton

slab of concrete forming part of a lift shaft. The concrete fell down and crushed him. He was certified dead at the scene.

Death was due to extensive multiple injuries to head, chest, back, abdomen and all the limbs. There was 'severe disruption of the body with extensive lacerations and bruises. Extrusion of the lungs, liver, intestines and kidneys. Massive crush injuries with caving in of the chest is present' [from pathologists report].

*Verdict*: open verdict.

HSE prosecution: none.

## Case 2

EASTSHIRE CORONER'S COURT
Before Dr Colborn

*Inquest into the death of Mr Stephen Flemming (31) who was killed when a roof he was demolishing caved in and fell on top of him.*

Cause of death: diffuse cerebral damage, due to severe head injury. Toxicologist's report: negative.

On 17 April, the deceased was working at a house in Benton, demolishing a roof connected to some outbuildings (approximately 10 feet high), when it caved in on top of him. There was no evidence of any other person being involved and it appears that following some drilling, the deceased was hit on the head by a piece of concrete and received fatal injuries.

*Verdict*: accidental death.

HSE prosecution: none.

## Case 3

STAR FIELDS CORONER'S COURT
Before Dr Austin

*Inquest into the death of Mr White (56) who was crushed to death by a fall of heavy pipes on a British Gas site in Westbridge.*

Cause of death: bronchial pneumonia following major crush injury. Toxicologist's report: negative.

The deceased had, alone, been moving large pipes (over 40 feet x 1 feet) on to a pile and chocking them. He had been using a crane to hoist each pipe into position. While he was out of the crane cabin, to adjust something on the pile, a pipe hanging over him broke free from the chain connecting it to the crane arm and crushed Mr White.

*Verdict*: injuries and death due to the breakdown of safety procedures and lack of supervision.

HSE prosecution: yes (s.2 HSWA); court: Magistrates; disposal: £2,000 fine.

**Case 4**

STAR FIELDS CORONER'S COURT
Before Dr Austin

*Inquest into the death of Mr Peter Johnson (61) who died when he fell from a roof in a timber yard.*

Cause of death: severe head injuries. Toxicologist's report: negative.

The death occurred at a large timber yard which was run, along with an adjacent builders suppliers, by the deceased and his adult son and daughter.

The father came into the yard on the morning in question collected a long piece of timber from a stack and walked off with it on his shoulder. The son asked a question about what his father was going to do but received no clear reply and formed the impression that his father was going to do some repair work. About half an hour later the son was summoned by phone from the building supplies yard to the timber yard next door as there had been a terrible accident. He ran there to find his father at the bottom of a ladder with severe head injuries. The ladder was placed up against an area of timber roofing. The deceased, working alone, had evidently fallen either from the top of the ladder or from the roof itself. He said nothing coherent between being injured and dying some time later in hospital.

*Verdict*: accidental death.

HSE prosecution: none.


## Case 5

STAR FIELDS CORONER'S COURT
Before Dr Austin

*Inquest into the death of Mark Lawrence (46) who died after falling through an asbestos roof in Redwood.*

Cause of death: severe head injury. Toxicologist's report: negative.

Mr Lawrence and his working partner did repair and construction work.

The deceased was on a roof trying to reclaim some asbestos sheeting which was to be used elsewhere on the site. He had fallen through a skylight and crashed some 15 feet below, smashing his head on a concrete floor. It was 11.00 am. They had only been there for one morning.

*Verdict*: accidental death.

HSE prosecution: Yes (s. 3(1)); court: Crown; disposal: £10,000 fine.


## Case 6

CASTLEBRIDGE CORONER'S COURT
Before Mr Watts

*Inquest into the death of Mr Brian Styles (29) who was electrocuted in the roof of the leisure centre where he was an assistant manager.*

Cause of death: electrocution; cardiac arrest. Toxicologist's report: negative.

Brian Styles went up into the roof of the leisure centre – the part of the roof that was above the indoor swimming pool – to investigate a leak in the roof which was letting rain down on to the spectators' gallery. Some of the rain had made the electrical circuitry in the roof dangerous and Brian, when he came into contact with a piece of metal, was electrocuted.

*Verdict*: accidental death.

HSE prosecution: yes, breach of prohibition notice; court: Crown; disposal: £50,000 fine.

## Case 7

BUTHORPE CORONER'S COURT
Before Mr Christie

*Inquest into the death of Mr Eric Staple (24) who fell from a mezzanine deck (15 feet) while building part of a new terminal at a city airport.*

Cause of death: severe head injury and severe pulmonary oedema. Toxicologist's report: negative.

Mr Staple was a suspended ceiling fitter. At the end of one shift on this site he was seen to fall from about 15 feet from a mezzanine deck on to a concrete floor. The safety guard rail near to where he had been standing had been detached at one end.

*Verdict*: misadventure.

HSE prosecution: none.

## Case 8

COLNEFORD CORONERS' COURT
Before Mr Wentworth

*Inquest into the death of Michael Roberts who died after suffering a severe head injury whilst travelling on a conveyor belt out of a mine at the end of a shift.*

Cause of death: cerebral contusions, due to fractured skull from severe head injury. Toxicologist's report: negative.

The deceased was a contract tunneller, working for a firm that was subcontracted by a large concern. Leaving the mine one morning at 7.00 am after a night shift, Mr Roberts failed to meet with a workmate at a given point. The workmate went back and eventually found Mr Roberts unconscious and badly injured. Mr Roberts had continued on a conveyor belt (which also carried coal) beyond the point where travellers are supposed to alight, through safety gates and had toppled over a precipitous edge, dropping about nine feet on to another, hard-surfaced conveyor belt below.

*Verdict*: accidental death.

HSE prosecution: none.

## Case 9

ROSSFORD CORONER'S COURT
Before Mr Elton

*Inquest into the death of Mr Derek Wiles (38) when the digging machine he was operating overturned and crushed him.*

Cause of death: asphyxia due to crush injuries. Toxicologist's report: negative.

Mr Wiles was the driver operator of a Maniton maniscopic shovel at a company which produced bricks and concretes. On the day in question he had, as usual, been scooping up limestone dust with a mechanical shovel and depositing it into a large hopper where it is mixed with cement. The machine overturned on to its side, crushing Mr Wiles, who had half fallen out of the cabin. The safety cage trapped him across the chest and abdominal area. It is believed he died at the scene.

*Verdict*: accidental death (7–2 majority).

HSE prosecution: none.

## Case 10

BUTHORPE CORONER'S COURT
Before Mr Christie

*Inquest into the death of Mr Vincent Tressell (51) who fell through a hole in the first floor while moving tanks from an old factory.*

Cause of death: right-sided cerebral contusions, due to fractured skull. Toxicologist's report: negative.

Mr Tressell was part of a team contracted to remove motors, tanks and other machinery from premises to go to other firms. On the day in question he had encountered problems with the crane that the team was using to hoist the tanks out of position. They had put chains around one tank. Mr Tressell had walked around the tank to check the connections and then fallen through a hole in the floor and crashed to the concrete floor of the open area on the lower level. There were more than six of these unprotected holes in the floor; they had resulted from the earlier removal of other equipment by another firm.

*Verdict*: misadventure.

HSE prosecution: none.

## Case 11

PAVETON CORONER'S COURT
Before Mr Christie

*Inquest into the death of Mr Nigel Millard (27) who was crushed under a large precast concrete Bison beam when it snapped through an unchaffed sling.*

Cause of death: adult respiratory disease syndrome, due to multiple injuries. Toxicologist's report: negative.

Mr Millard was working as part of a small team unloading large (30 feet), very heavy precast concrete slabs from a lorry. They were being removed from the open back of the lorry by a crane and it was Mr Millard's job to help 'sling' each beam, i.e. take the slings at the end of the crane's arm's chains, and attach them to the beams (at a distance of 100 cms from each end). They had unloaded a few of these by about 7.30 one morning. Mr Millard was getting off the lorry, having just loaded a beam, when one of the slings failed. The concrete block which was being lifted up by the crane crashed down on top of Mr Millard. He suffered severe multiple injuries from which he died.

*Verdict*: misadventure.

HSE prosecution: HSWA (s.2); court: Magistrates; disposal: £3000 fine, £50 costs.

## Case 12

BRICKMERE CORONERS' COURT
Before Mr Johnstone

*Inquest into the death of Denis Porter (31) who died when a large boat (114 feet long) he was repairing on the bank of a river running through a city slipped from its props and crushed him against the wall of a concrete berth.*

Cause of death: traumatic rupture of the heart and severe chest compression. Toxicologist's report: trace alcohol, well below limit for driving, therefore insignificant.

Mr Porter was working for his father's firm of boat repairers. He, his father and two men were working on a boat that need repairs requiring it to be lifted out of water. Just before the incident, the boat was on several sets of stilts and jacks. One of the jacks sheered through the concrete floor (in a berth on the quayside) and the boat began to slip down. Denis Porter tried to dodge from under the boat and leap over the berth way to avoid the lurching vessel but he was not quick enough and the boat pinned him against the wall and crushed him.

*Verdict*: accidental death.

HSE prosecution: none.

## Case 13

BRICKMERE CORONERS' COURT
Before Mr Johnstone

*Inquest into the death of James Farmer (34) who died when he was buried alive in a hopper of gravel.*

Cause of death: traumatic asphyxia, due to compression of the chest. Toxicologist's report: negative.

The firm in question made various bitumen, tarmac and concrete materials. To do this it had to mix different 'recipes' of gravel and granular substances. At the plant were a row of 13 very large skip-shaped containers with tons of different gravels and sands in each container. Each container had a hole about 2–3 feet in diameter in the middle of the bottom. Underneath that hole there was a short conveyor belt which would take the discharged contents of each 'hopper' on to a long single conveyor belt which would deposit the mixture or 'aggregate' in a large container. By speeding up or slowing down the rate of each hopper's feeder belt, the proportion of the final mixture's constituent parts could be altered.

Mr Farmer, along with a workmate, had been told to clean out a hopper as someone was coming later that day to fit a new pump to a feeder system on the hopper (an industrial size, i.e. a large container similar to the rubbish skips parked in streets but larger and with a funnel opening in the middle of the bottom). Mr Farmer was cleaning out the hopper with a shovel when he slipped and was drawn into the centre bottom of it and covered in an avalanche of the grit aggregate. He was buried and crushed as he was drawn into the funnel leading out of the hopper at its bottom.

*Verdict*: accidental death.

HSE prosecution: HSWA s.2; court: Magistrates; disposal: £10,000 fine.

**Case 14**

PAVETON CORONER'S COURT
Before Mr Christie

*Inquest into the death of Mr Paul Stanford (26) who died from a major head injury when he fell from a forklift truck whilst working on a platform at a cash and carry warehouse.*

Cause of death: cerebral contusions from fractured skull. Toxicologist's report: negative.

Paul Stanford was an employee in a large cash and carry warehouse. Just before the end of his night shift (at about 7.00 am) he was helping another employee to take stock. The stock was set in long wide aisles, stacked on pallets that were placed on metal shelves up to about 25 feet high. Paul was being moved whilst he was in a metal cage supported on a forklift truck. The forks were fully raised, placing Paul at least 18 feet off the ground. The cage hit some pipes running across the ceiling and dislodged the cage. It fell with Paul in it. Both crashed to the ground, falling separately and Paul smashed his head on the concrete floor, breaking his skull.

*Verdict*: misadventure.

EHD prosecution: HSWA s2; Provision and Use of Work Equipment Regs. 5(3), 6(1), 9(1)(a), 9(1)(b); court: Magistrates; disposal: £22,000 (total), £5,724 costs.

**Case 15**

PAVETON CORONER'S COURT
Before Mr Christie

*Inquest into the death of Mr Arnold Campbell (42) who fell from a ladder while painting the wall of a warehouse.*

Cause of death: severe head injury. Toxicologist's report: negative.

Mr Campbell was a decorator who had his own firm Arnold Campbell & Co. He was engaged on a job painting large industrial premises – the job had to be carried out not during the normal week but from Thursday nights to Monday mornings. He was working on one wall with his brother-in-law. He was up a ladder with his feet about 14 feet off the ground when the ladder slipped and Mr Campbell fell, suffering a severe head injury from which he later died.

*Verdict*: misadventure.

HSE prosecution: none.

## Case 16

FLINTFORD CORONERS' COURT
Before Mr Bray

*Inquest into the death of Nicholas Settle (42) who died after a flash fire where he was doing some work at a large power station.*

Cause of death: adult respiratory distress syndrome, from severe burns. Toxicologist's report: negative.

The work in question was being carried out in the oil pump house. The pump and pipework were to be upgraded. One of the three pumps in the room had been removed. Cutting equipment was being used; an oxyacetylene cutting torch run from a mixture of gas and oxygen; and electric-arc welding and cutting equipment. For obvious reasons, all the surfaces in the room had been thoroughly cleaned before this equipment was used. Oil was still being pumped through the pipes connected to the two working pumps. Areas of the flow could be isolated by turning off valves and this had been done on the removed pump.

A new pump arrived one Friday and it was decided to fit it over the weekend. The team from the firm Mr Settle was employed by would not be able to commission the pipe to use but they were to fit it. Beside the boiler was an instrument panel, a large panel on two steel legs each of which had a further stabilising leg protruding from it at 45 degrees at their lower levels. The feet of each of the four legs were welded to the floor. A cluster of thin copper pipes (like household pipes in central heating systems) came out of the back of the panel, from behind the gauges, and led into the pump systems. The gauges indicated the oil pressures.

Very hot oil ran through the pipes to the two pumps that were still in operation.

The new pump to replace the one which had been taken out was a slightly different shape. Fitting it was not possible with the panel in its current position. Seconds after the final leg of the panel had been cut a trouser leg of one of Mr Settle's workmates caught fire. He ran out, then there was a massive explosion and conflagration. Mr Settle caught fire, received severe 70 per cent burns and died 12 days later.

*Verdict*: accidental death.

HSE prosecution: HSWA s3 against both the power company and the main subcontractor; court: Crown; disposal: power company – £10,000 fine plus £28,000 costs; subcontractor – £35,000 plus £14,000 costs.

## Case 17

STAR FIELDS CORONERS' COURT
Before Dr Austin

*Inquest into the death of Gerald Hastings (27) who died while working down a drainage tunnel when a lifting frame became detached from a tower crane and fell on him.*

Cause of death: traumatic head injury. Toxicologist's report: negative.

The deceased was working at the bottom of a concrete tunnel 80 feet deep. He was unloading cement from pallets which were being sent down in a large, very heavy metal cage attached to the chains hanging from a large crane (100 feet high). After unloading one consignment, the cage was hoisted up the height of the tunnel. It then became detached from the chain hook and plummeted down on to Mr Hastings, killing him.

*Verdict*: accidental death.

HSE prosecution: none.

## Case 18

STAR FIELDS CORONERS' COURT
Before Dr Austin

*Inquest into the death of Thomas Pennett (56) who died when he fell down a lift shaft while working on the construction of a new wing for Hall Street Hospital.*

Cause of death: severe head injury (depressed skull fracture). Toxicologist's report: negative.

Mr Pennett was a foreman carpenter. He returned from lunch one day to continue with his work, which was cladding a lift in the new building so that it could be used by workmen as their materials lift. His workmate could not open the lift door, so Mr Pennett took him to another lift, opening the door with a master key. He peered in but the lift was not there and he fell down into the shaft.

*Verdict*: accidental death.

HSE prosecution: none.

## Case 19

LYNTON CORONER'S COURT
Before Mr Clarkson

*Inquest into the death of Lee Sullivan (27) who died when he was crushed by an excavator bucket while reloading an anchor on to a barge.*

Cause of death: bilateral compression of the chest, from traumatic crush injury. Toxicologist's report: negative.

A barge had been washed up near Fenworth on the Telshire coast. It had on it building materials of Engineering Co. Ltd, Mr Sullivan's employer. There was a plan to refloat the barge, which was being carried out when the incident occurred. Before it could be re-floated, the barge had to have its anchor put back. This was done by connecting the anchor to one end of a strop, connecting the other end to the bucket of a mechanical digger, raising the digger arm to hoist the anchor on to the deck and then lowering the arm until the strop was slack, when it could be released. After the anchor had been replaced on the deck, Mr Sullivan moved forward into a danger zone. At the same moment the shovel of the digger jolted sidewards, first penetrating his head and then crushing Mr Sullivan against a deck generator.

*Verdict*: accidental death.

HSE prosecution: none.


**Case 20**

LYNTON CORONER'S COURT
Before Mr Clarkson

*Inquest into the death of Stella Norton (30) who died when she was crushed between a fence bar on a farm and the equipment at her rear on a tractor she was driving while working on a farm.*

Cause of death: traumatic asphyxia. Toxicologist's report: negative.

Stella Norton was working as a farmhand. She came back from work one early evening saying to Martin Neville, her common law husband, that she had to go back to the farm briefly later to clear muck from a field. She duly left. When she had not returned much later Mr Neville went in search of her. He eventually found her in a dark field sitting on a small tractor, trapped between the back of her seat behind her and a large wooden horizontal bar at the perimeter of the field. The tractor was still on but she was lifeless.

*Verdict*: accidental death.

HSE prosecution: HSWA, s.2; court: Magistrates; disposal: £500 fine, £555.82 costs.

**Case 21**

HIGH HILLS CORONER'S COURT
Before Mr Vickers

*Inquest into the death of Mr Duncan Morhall (66) who died at the farm where he was working when he was run over by a mechanical shovel driven by a fellow worker.*

Cause of death: multiple injuries, from a crushed chest. Toxicologist's report: negative.

Mr Morhall was a farm worker. A six-and-a-half ton lift truck was being used to load barley from a barn on to a lorry. There came a point in this operation when the deceased, one of two men sweeping the residues left in the barn by the mechanical bucket, left the sweeping to collect a shovel. He went behind the vehicle and it knocked him down and then, reversing again, ran over him completely crushing his chest.

*Verdict*: accidental death.

HSE prosecution: none.

**Case 22**

SALSWORTH CORONER'S COURT
Before Mr Fenshaw

*Inquest into the death of Mr Clive Byrne (51) who died at Salsworth docks when he was crushed by a container which was lowered on to him on a ship while he was helping with the loading.*

Cause of death: multiple injuries including a transected spine. Toxicologist's report: negative.

Mr Byrne worked at the docks. He was a 'plan man', i.e. he was responsible for ensuring that the large containers (the size held on articulated lorries) were loaded into the correct bays and the correct cells of a freight ship. The cells are metal frameworks in bays which run laterally across the deck of the ship. Containers are lowered three of four high into these cells. There are five or six cells running from starboard to port across the ship.

Clive was on the quayside, then he decided to go on to the ship to check the loading. It was a six or seven minute walk on the quay up the length of the ship (1,000 feet long overall), on to the ship and then back down to the point in question at bay 18. The container was being lowered on to the deck by a gantry crane. The cells are filled sequentially. At the time he was crushed, Clive Byrne was standing in a cell that was not due to be loaded. The crane driver made an error, moving the container over and passed the assigned cell and dropped it into the one where Mr Byrne was standing.

*Verdict*: accidental death.

HSE prosecution: none.

## Case 23

FORTBURY CORONER'S COURT
Before Mr Treacy

*Inquest into the death of Mr Graham Finch (40) who was crushed to death by a fall of concrete when part of the building he was helping to demolish collapsed on him.*

Cause of death: multiple injuries. Toxicologist's report: negative.

Mr Finch was a demolition worker. He was working in a city demolishing an old building. On the day in question his team of three had pulled down three of the bays on a second floor along with the roofs. As they got to the fourth bay they removed the section near to the gable end.

At about 2.55 pm Mr Finch was on the roof cutting away concrete. He then shouted and was seen to lose balance as the floor beneath him gave way. A large slab of concrete hung by a small connection as Mr Finch fell about 15 feet to the concrete floor below and then, after he landed, collapsed on top of him. When they went to the place where he had fallen, his workmates could only see a small part of Mr Finch's back exposed. It was impossible for them, however, to remove the heavy concrete from him.

*Verdict*: accidental death.

HSE prosecution: Construction (Working Places Regs., 1964, R. 33(1)(a); court: Magistrates; disposal: £1,000 fine.


## Case 24

FORTBURY CORONER'S COURT
Before Mr Dalloway

*Inquest into the death of Mr Simon Thornton (44) who was killed by a fall through the roof he was trying to repair at his tyre garage.*

Cause of death: brain damage, due to fractured skull, due to severe head injury. Toxicologist's report: negative.

Mr Thornton was the owner of a tyre garage on the outskirts of a city. He would, from time to time, go up on the roof of his garage to repair it. It often leaked and had been the point of entry for burglars on more than one occasion. He was doing such a repair one morning when he crashed through the perspex roofing surface and fell 30 feet to a concrete floor. His son, who was amongst several of the employees who witnessed the incident, tried to administer care but Mr Thornton's head injuries were severe.

*Verdict*: accidental death.

HSE prosecution: none.


## Case 25

MARFIELD CORONER'S COURT
Before Mr Frenton

*Inquest into the death of Mr Albert Frank (68) who received fatal injuries when a bolt from the hydraulically operated valve (on a farm tractor) that he was helping to clean, sprung out and penetrated his head.*

Cause of death: cerebral ventriculitis, due to penetrating head injury. Toxicologist's report: negative.

Mr Frank was working at his son's farm, where he went to undertake a variety of tasks three times a week.

Following lunch one day, the son went to the farm building to do some welding on a trailer. The father decided to fetch the slurry tank across and clean the valve out. The tank was a 900 gallon variety which the son had possessed for 8–9 years.

The valve is situated on the back of the slurry tank and to clean the valve out one would have to unscrew six allen screws to remove the top housing. The father tried to loosen these screws but was having difficulty, so the son went across to help him. He managed to unscrew the six screws and lifted the housing off. He handed it to his father who then started to clean it out with a screwdriver. They decided between them to start the tractor up, which was attached to the tank with hydraulic system connectors in order to draw the ram rod in. The rod is positioned in the centre of the housing and it is difficult to clean it out due to lack of space. By drawing the ram rod in it leaves the 'D' shape top housing clear to clean out completely.

The son went and started the tractor up and engaged the hydraulic lever. As he was getting off the tractor he saw oil squirt into his father's face. The ramrod had, in fact, shot out at great force and penetrated the father's head.

*Verdict*: accidental death.

HSE prosecution: none.

## Case 26

COLNEFORD CORONER'S COURT
Before Mr Wentworth

*Inquest into the death of Mr Colin Williams (41) who died in a mine when he was crushed between two trucks on the underground railtrack.*

Cause of death: thoracic haemorrhage. Toxicologist's report: negative.

In this pit there are 40 miles of tunnels. The 'locos' (the small trains) are powered by batteries. At the critical time, a line of carriers was being shunted off the main track into a siding. The front and rear of each carrier is spring-loaded to avoid shocks when it jars with the one behind it or in front of it. So, a sort of large spring acts as a shock absorber. There came a time when two of the carriers needed uncoupling. Mr Williams went to do this. It had to be done manually but there were no safety chocks in the immediate vicinity to stop the carriages smashing together. Neither of the relevant vehicles – nos. 24 and 25 – was fitted with a lever to remove the coupling. Somehow Mr Williams managed to remove the dolly bar between the locos and was then instantly crushed with huge force between the two carriages.

*Verdict*: accidental death.

HSE prosecution: none.


**Case 27**

EASTSHIRE CORONER'S COURT
Before Dr Colborn

*Inquest into the death of Mr Vincent Tolley (58) who was killed when attempting to repair the roof on his industrial premises.*

Cause of death: multiple injuries. Toxicologist's report: negative.

It was the practice of Mr Tolley and his partner Mr Tony Carter to periodically clean the gutters of dirt and residue. Both of them went onto the roof at first on this occasion. It was 15–20 feet high. They could not be seen once they were on the roof. Carter came down to foot the ladder. Tolley reappeared at the top of the ladder, came down and requested a bucket, then returned up the ladder: two to three minutes passed. Then there was a crashing sound. Mr Masters, an employee who had been footing the ladder, went in to find Tolley flat on his back, arms out, on the concrete floor.

*Verdict*: accidental death.

HSE prosecution: none.

**Case 28**

EASTSHIRE CORONER'S COURT
Before Dr Colborn

*Inquest into the death of Mr Norton (68) who was killed when he fell from a ladder while working on an outside light at a garage.*

Cause of death: cerebral damage, due to skull fracture. Toxicologist's report: negative.

The deceased was employed as a part-time maintenance man by a car sales show room, Executive Cars Ltd, Benton. He was up a ladder, about 15 feet off the ground, checking a security light, when he fell off. He was taken to Benton Hospital but died later the same day.

*Verdict*: accidental death.

HSE prosecution: none.

**Case 29**

EASTSHIRE CORONER'S COURT
Before Dr Colborn

*Inquest into the death of Mr Donald Renshaw (65), a caretaker, who was killed when he was hit by an advertising board which had come off its frame in a car park in heavy winds and been projected through a 'wind-tunnel' made by the shape of the lower car park.*

Cause of death: secondary pneumonia, due to cerebral atrophy, due to earlier infarct, following devastating, severe head injury causing significant blood clots.

The deceased was the house manager at large offices in Port Lane. One day there were very strong winds and storms. An advertising hoarding broke loose in the car park and was flying about doing damage to vehicles. At one point, the board flew up suddenly, in a gust, and smashed into the face of the deceased who was out to try and capture the board so that it could not do any further damage to cars in the car park. He was taken, unconscious, to hospital and later to a nursing home. He died three years later.

*Verdict*: accidental death.

HSE prosecution: none.

## Case 30

DOWNTON CORONERS' COURT
Before Mr Purser

*Inquest into the death of Samuel Forbes (58) who died while working on an industrial tank containing chemicals including hydrocarbon solvents and alcohols.*

Cause of death: bronchopneumonia and septicaemia due to heptocellular necrosis due to hyperpyrexia (heatstroke). Toxicologist's report: negative.

Mr Forbes was the leader of a team of industrial tank cleaners. They went to a site to clean a large tank (10 feet high x 7 feet diameter). Access was through a hatch in the top, 1 metre across. The cleaners had to scrape thick varnish residue from the sides and bottom of the tank, fill buckets with the scrapings and wait for them to be hoisted up, emptied and sent down again. The workers were wearing thick rubberised suits (to protect from chemicals) without any ventilation and had no breathing apparatus. After several stints scraping in the tank, Mr Forbes spent longer on one session than he had previously and collapsed unconscious. In hospital his condition deteriorated with liver failure and collapse of the immune system and he died two weeks later.

*Verdict*: accidental death.

HSE prosecution: Factory Act 1961 s29(1),(2) pending; court: Magistrates; disposal: £2,000 and costs.

## Case 31

STONETOWN CORONER'S COURT
Before Mr Watts

*Inquest into the death of Mr Arthur Powis (59) who was killed when a grinding wheel he was operating exploded and a piece hit him in the head.*

Cause of death: severe head injuries – shattered skull, massive missile injury to right forehead. Toxicologist's report: negative.

Mr Powis had been a swing-grinder for 20 years. One morning, he loaded a new wheel which rotates at very high speed (2,980 rpm) to polish steel. These wheels need frequently replacing. He took the old worn one off, replaced it with a new one, closed the guard door, turned the wheel on and just as it had risen to the right speed, he placed it on the large steel rod (20 feet long) that he was going to grind. The wheel exploded, bursting through the guard door. Some pieces of the exploded wheel were projected 25 feet away. A large piece struck Mr Powis in the face and lodged in his head.

*Verdict*: accidental death.

HSE prosecution: Abrasive Wheels Regs (1970) Reg. 11(b); court: Magistrates; disposal: £3,250.

## Case 32

ROSSFORD CORONER'S COURT
Before Mr Donald

*Inquest into the death of Mr Reginald Morris (38), a decorator, who was killed by a fall from a ladder on top of scaffolding while painting a house exterior.*

Cause of death: diffuse cerebral trauma, due to fractures of the skull, due to impact injury to head. Toxicologist's report: negative.

The deceased and his workmate were painting the front elevation of a house.

To reach the central gable they had to use a scaffold. The one prepared for them was of the mobile type, with wheels that can be locked. The scaffold was still not high enough for the painters to be able to reach the top of the front gable so they used a ladder on the top platform. During a manoeuvre in which the two men were changing positions, lateral force was applied to the ladder (pushing it against the house) and the scaffold tower overturned. Both men were flung off. Mr Morris fell between the house and the collapsed tower and smashed his head on the concrete ground.

*Verdict*: accidental death.

HSE prosecution: HSWA 1974 s.3; court: Magistrates; disposal: £5,000 fine and costs.

**Case 33**

ROSSFORD CORONER'S COURT
Before Mr Duncan

*Inquest into the death of Mr David Appleton (26) on board a large freight vessel, a ship docked in Lowtide Port. He was crushed by a load of timber which he was helping to unload.*

Cause of death: rupture of aorta. Toxicologist's report: negative.

David was a dock worker. On the day in question, he was helping to unload a large commercial freight vessel (1,000 feet). With two workmates, he was in a hold of the vessel (60 x 60 x 30 feet) unloading large sets of mahogany using a crane. The hold had been tightly packed. The wood was stacked, in pre-slung and unslung packets, very high, to the brim of the hold. One wall of stacks was leaning forward into the hold. This was questioned by those in the hold. Because the hold was so full of wood, there would be nowhere to run to if the stacks collapsed. This is what occurred. The whole wall of stacks fell into the hold. All three workers dived for cover. Two were hurt and David was crushed.

*Verdict*: accidental death.

HSE prosecution: none.

## Case 34

CASTLEBRIDGE CORONER'S COURT
Before Mr Allen

*Inquest into the death of Mr Jonathon Wood (33) who was killed after he had been crushed by a large tank which fell from a forklift truck.*

Cause of death: bronchopneumonia from severe crush injuries. Toxicologist's report: negative.

Mr Wood, a forklift truck driver, had collected a large tank (22 x 11 feet diameter) on his truck for loading on to a lorry. He drove the truck so that it was a few metres from the lorry, with the tank facing the lorry. He got out of the truck cabin and stood between the truck and the lorry, discussing the loading with the lorry driver. The forks on the forklift truck then gave way and the tank rolled off, smashing into Mr Wood and crushing him against the side of the lorry.

*Verdict*: accidental death.

HSE prosecution: none.

## Case 35

STAR FIELDS CORONER'S COURT
Before Dr Austin

*Inquest into the death of Mr Stewart Trent (31) who fell from a ladder while working on an alarm installation in Greenslade hospital.*

Cause of death: multiple skull fractures; both frontal lobes were lacerated, there was haemorrhaging and cerebral bleeding. Toxicologist's report: negative.

Stewart was an alarm engineer who had been sent with two others by his firm to instal an alarm system in an office block of a large hospital. At one point, surveying the building to decide on positions of wiring, etc., Stewart was alone in a corridor. He took the ladder which was clasped to the wall near a loft hatch, hooked it to a bracket beside the hatch opening and then climbed up the ladder. Initially it took his weight, but when he was at the top, the bracket gave way and the ladder came crashing down with Stewart to the hard floor below.

*Verdict*: accidental death.

HSE prosecution: none.

## Case 36

BLUEPORT CORONER'S COURT
Before Dr Austin

*Inquest into the death of Mr Patrick Foster (33) who died when he fell, in his mechanical digger, through the roof of the building he was helping to demolish.*

Cause of death: brain haemorrhage from severe head injury. Toxicologist's report: negative.

Mr Foster was working on the seventh floor of a large city building which was being demolished. He was driving a mechanical digger with a pneumatic hammer on the end of a telescopic arm. At one point late on during the day, Mr Foster was seen manoeuvring the digger to clear up some of the rubble near the place he was working on when, suddenly, his machine just flipped backwards into a hole and fell through a disused lift shaft.

*Verdict*: accidental death.

HSE prosecution: none.

## Case 37

BLUEPORT CORONER'S COURT
Before Dr Austin

*Inquest into the death of Mr Philip Cousens (38) who fell 7– metres from a scaffold to his death while working on a city construction development.*

Cause of death: cerebral contusions due to fracture of skull. Toxicologist's report: negative.

Mr Cousens had climbed up scaffolding about 30 feet high on the face of a city building in order to adjust one of the long horizontal poles which had bowed out. He tied a rope around the pole and then loosened the grips on either end of that pole, preparatory to repositioning it. A crawling board behind that pole (i.e. between the pole and the building) then gave way and Mr Cousens fell to the ground.

*Verdict*: accidental death.

HSE prosecution: none.

## Case 38

VALETON CORONER'S COURT
Before Mr Garrett

*Inquest into the death of Mr Terrence Bretherton (20) when the tank of chemicals he was working on at a fertilizer plant exploded, throwing him 30 metres away.*

Cause of death: multiple injuries (every bone broken) and severe burns, due to blast from an explosion. Toxicologist's report: negative.

Terrence worked for a farm fertiliser company as a JCB operator. On the day in question there was a fault on the gauge of one of the tanks. The tank contained liquid chemicals and there was a highly flammable atmosphere at the top of the tank. At one point, Mr Bretherton lifted the top of the tank with a stick and then something ignited the vapours and there was a huge explosion which sent him flying. What ignited the vapours could have been the torch Paul was carrying or some static charge on his clothing or a spark from welding which was being done on another part of the tank by a workmate of Terrence's.

*Verdict*: accidental death.

HSE prosecution: none.

**Case 39**

COLNEFORD CORONER'S COURT
Before Mr Wentworth

*Inquest into the death of Mr John Holley (31) who died when the tipper truck he was driving crashed over the side of a quarry.*

Cause of death: haemorrhage, due to ruptured spleen and other injuries. Toxicologist's report: negative.

The accident occurred at the Borton Quarry where Mr Holley was working as a dumper truck driver. He was manoeuvring his truck into position down a slight incline prior to tipping the truck but was unable to stop prior to the truck going over the top of the quarry and crashing into the quarry floor. Mr Holley was thrown about in the vehicle in its descent and then thrown from the cabin as the forepart of the articulated vehicle was torn from the tipper section. He subsequently died from his injuries.

*Verdict*: accidental death.

HSE prosecution: HSWA s.3; court: Magistrates; disposal: £8,000.

**Case 40**

MARFIELD CORONER'S COURT
Before Mr Portland

*Inquest into the death of Mr Paul Morton (59) who was crushed to death when a long shaft full of lime broke through its makeshift sealed door.*

Cause of death: asphyxia, due to traumatic compression and crushing injury to chest. Toxicologist's report: negative.

Mr Morton worked as a chargehand at Construct Co., Lindup, in Boxshire. On the evening in question at about 5.30 pm he was found pinned under some old railway sleepers and a large limestone debris, having received an injury that proved fatal. The debris had accumulated over a period in a 70 foot chute in the wall which had been blocked off at the ground end by a makeshift blockade: a number of vertical railway sleepers pressed by a horizontal metal bar bolted to the wall at each side. This structure gave way when Mr Morton was close by and the chute's contents shot out and crushed him.

*Verdict*: accidental death.

HSE prosecution: none.